Challenges and Chances of a
Written State Report

BOCHUMER SCHRIFTEN
zur **FRIEDENSSICHERUNG** und
zum **HUMANITÄREN VÖLKERRECHT**

Herausgegeben von
Prof. Dr. Hans-Joachim Heintze
Prof. Dr. Pierre Thielbörger

Begründet von
Prof. Dr. Horst Fischer
Prof. Dr. Dr. h.c. mult. Knut Ipsen
Prof. Dr. Joachim Wolf

Jule Giegling
—
Challenges and Chances of a Written State Report

Analysis and Improvement of a Monitoring Instrument on the Implementation of Human Rights

Bibliografische Information der Deutschen Nationalbibliothek:
Die Deutsche Nationalbibliothek verzeichnet diese Publikation in der Deutschen
Nationalbibliografie; detaillierte bibliografische Daten sind im Internet über
http://dnb.d-nb.de abrufbar.

Dieses Werk einschließlich aller seiner Teile ist urheberrechtlich geschützt.
Jede Verwertung außerhalb der engen Grenzen des Urheberrechtes ist unzulässig
und strafbar.

© 2021 BWV | BERLINER WISSENSCHAFTS-VERLAG GmbH,
Behaimstraße 25, 10585 Berlin,
E-Mail: bwv@bwv-verlag.de, Internet: http://www.bwv-verlag.de

Layout und Herstellung durch den Verlag
Satz: DTP + TEXT Eva Burri, Stuttgart Druck: docupoint, Magdeburg
Gedruckt auf holzfreiem, chlor- und säurefreiem, alterungsbeständigem Papier.
Printed in Germany.

ISBN Print   978-3-8305-5051-8
ISBN E-Book   978-3-8305-4217-9

Contents

Acknowledgements 9

Preface 11

Abbreviations and Legal Citation Format 13

Part One: Introduction 17
I. Scope and Aim of the Thesis 20
II. Research Method and Application 21

Part Two: Unravelling a Confused System 25

Chapter 1: The State Reporting Obligation 27
I. Human Rights Monitoring through State Reporting 27
II. State Reporting Obligations and their Procedures 32
    1. United Nations Human Rights System 33
        a. Procedure of Reporting to the United Nations Treaty Bodies 34
            aa. Standard Reporting Procedure 35
                (1) Common Core Document 36
                (2) Treaty Specific Report 37
            bb. Simplified Reporting Procedure 37
    2. Regional Human Rights Systems and the State Reporting Obligation 39
        a. European Human Rights System 39
            aa. Provisions that Prescribe State Reporting 39
            bb. Procedure of State Reporting in Europe 40
        b. Inter-American Human Rights System 43
            aa. Provisions that Prescribe State Reporting 43
            bb. Procedure of State Reporting in the Americas 45
        c. African Human Rights System 47
            aa. Provisions that Prescribe State Reporting 47
            bb. Procedure of State Reporting in Africa 50
        d. Arabian Human Rights System 52
    3. Conclusion 53

Contents

III.	What is the Content, Purpose and Nature of the State Reporting Obligation?	53
	1. Content of the State Reporting Obligation in Relation to the Written Report	53
	2. Object and Purpose of the State Reporting Obligation	59
	3. Dogmatic Classification of the State Reporting Obligation	61
	a. The Legal Nature of the State Reporting Obligation	61
	b. The Obligee of the State Reporting Obligation	63
	4. Conclusion	65
IV.	Challenges of the State Reporting Procedure as Violations of International Law	65
	1. The Violation of the Principle *Pacta Sunt Servanda*	68
	2. Fragmentation of International Law and the State Reporting Obligation	69
	3. Conclusion	72

Chapter 2: Previous Reform Proposals — 73

I.	The Alston Proposals, 1988–1997	75
	1. The Initial Report, 1989	76
	2. The Interim Report, 1993	76
	3. The Final Report, 1997	78
II.	Single State Report, 2002–2006	79
	1. Coordination	80
	2. Global Approach	81
III.	Unified Standing Treaty Body, 2006	82
IV.	Harmonized Reporting Guidelines, 2006	84
V.	Treaty Body Strengthening Process, 2009–2014	85
	1. Report of the Secretary-General, 2011	86
	2. Consultations with Stakeholders, 2010–2012	87
	a. National Human Rights Institutions	87
	b. Treaty Bodies	87
	c. Non-Governmental Organizations	88
	d. State Parties	89
	e. Academia	91
	f. United Nations Entities	92
	g. Multi-Stakeholder Meetings	92
	3. Report of the High Commissioner for Human Rights, 2012	93

VI. Review 2020.. 96
    1. General Assembly Resolution 68/268, 2014 96
    2. Biennial Reports... 97
        a. First and Second Biennial Report 97
        b. Preparation for the Third Biennial Report. 98
        c. Third Biennial Report.. 102
VII. Conclusion.. 103

Chapter 3: Integrative Reporting 'Bottom-Up' and Sanctions under International Law for the Breach of the State Reporting Obligation.. 107

I.   Integrative Reporting.. 108
    1. The Concept of Integrative Reporting 109
    2. Rationale of Integrative Reporting 114
    3. Content Components of an Integrative Report...................... 116
        a. Baseline Report.. 117
        b. Bottom-Up Review 120
            aa. Identification of Relevant Legislation 122
            bb. Procedure of the Bottom-Up Review...................... 124
        c. Periodic Q&A.. 128
    4. Evaluation of the Integrative Reporting Procedure................ 130
II. Sanctions for the Breach of the State Reporting Obligation under
     International Law... 134
    1. International Treaties 136
        a. International and Regional Human Rights Treaties
            and their Supplements 136
        b. Vienna Convention on the Law of Treaties (1969) 139
        c. Conclusion... 141
    2. Draft Articles on Responsibility of States for Internationally
        Wrongful Acts 142
    3. Evaluation of Sanctioning According to the Rules
        of International Law.. 144
III. Résumé on the Considerations Made in this Chapter 146

Part Three: Conclusion – Call to Uphold and Advance the State Reporting Procedure... 149

Index of Authorities... 155

Acknowledgements

This thesis was submitted and accepted as a doctoral thesis by the University of Greifswald (Germany) in December 2019. The publication was revised and updated according to the recommendations of my supervisor and my second reviewer.

The initial idea for pursuing this project was sparked during my voluntary service in Lesotho. Mr. Booi Mohapi gave me space and his trust to develop my own project, which introduced me to state reporting in the first place. Professor Frans Viljoen from the Centre for Human Rights at the University of Pretoria (South Africa) indicated that my project could be interesting for a PhD thesis, a thought that I took up and followed through. I wish to thank both for their confidence in my work.

My sincerest gratitude goes to my first supervisor Professor Claus Dieter Classen, whom I approached with this project while working in Lesotho and who accepted me as his PhD student without having met me. His advice and excellent supervision were significant for the successful completion of this project. Furthermore, I want to thank Professor Pierre Thielbörger, my second reviewer, for his detailed review which was helpful and motivating for the finalization of this publication. I want to extend my thanks to Professor Stefan Harrendorf for being part of the committee and to Ms. Dietlind Behnke for her help with the formalities of the procedure.

I would also like to thank Professor Adelheid Puttler for her organizational support and interest in my development, Dr. Isabella Risini for always patiently answering my various questions and the Chair's student assistant Mr. Van Hoang for saving me from drowning in footnotes.

For organizing this publication, my thanks goes to Ms. Jessica Gutsche from the Berliner Wissenschaftsverlag for her kind way of guiding me from the first contact to the publication.

Last but not least I want to thank my dear friends Dr. Judit Beke-Martos and Ms. Ella Schönleben, my wonderful husband Marco and my beloved family for their tireless support which made this endeavor not only possible, but even delightful.

Jule Giegling

Preface

State Reporting is the oldest monitoring instrument and one of the truly universal procedures to monitor states' compliance with their treaty obligations. First introduced by the League of Nations and the International Labor Organization in 1918, the State Reporting Procedure today is enshrined in nine treaties and two optional protocols within the United Nations Treaty Body System as well as in several regional human rights treaties. Nevertheless, monitoring through state reports cannot be considered a success. Its sensitivity towards state sovereignty is at the same time the reason for its widespread positive acceptance and one of its biggest challenges. For decades, the lack of sanctions combined with a massive overburdening of States parties has significantly paralyzed the effectivity of the system. Full compliance with all reporting obligations is rare. The challenges of the instrument have been intensively assessed by interdisciplinary scholarship and multiple United Nation organs over the past 30 years. Despite all the difficulties the instrument has, it holds great potential for the protection of human rights. The importance of the procedure and the ambitions to continue its application can be seen in the recent review process of the UN General Assembly, which was initiated in 2014 and culminates in the General Assembly Review 2020. This thesis contributes to the reform debate with a detailed analysis of the state reporting obligation and, based on the findings, the proposal of integrative reporting as a new reporting procedure combined with sanctions. Simplification of the procedure and strengthening compliance by presenting the prospect of sanctions is expected to improve compliance as well as the efficiency of the procedure. Herewith, the state reporting procedure may finally be able to fulfill its object and purpose in the protection of human rights.

Abbreviations and Legal Citation Format

The legal citation format follows the *Australian Guide to Legal Citation*, 4th edn 2018, Melbourne University Law Review Association Inc., Melbourne Journal of International Law Inc.

Where considered necessary and if not indicated otherwise, the following abbreviations are used:

ACFC	Advisory Committee of the Framework Convention for the Protection of National Minorities
ACHR	American Convention on Human Rights
a. F.	alte Fassung (former edition)
ARS	Draft Articles on the Responsibility of States for Internationally Wrongful Acts
Art.	Article
BGBl.	Bundesgesetzblatt [Federal Law Gazette]
CAT	Convention against Torture and Other Cruel, Inhuman or Degrading Treatment or Punishment
CED	International Convention for the Protection of All Persons from Enforced Disappearance
CEDAW	Convention on the Elimination of All Forms of Discrimination against Women
CETS	Council of Europe Treaty Series
CM/Del/Dec	Decisions of the Committee of Ministers of the Council of Europe
CoE Doc.	Document of the Council of Europe
CRC	Convention on the Rights of the Child
CRC-OPAC	Optional Protocol to the Convention on the Rights of the Child on the involvement of children in armed conflict
CRC-OPSC	Optional Protocol to the Convention on the Rights of the Child on the sale of children, child prostitution and child pornography
CRPD	Convention on the Rights of Persons with Disabilities
ECHR	European Court of Human Rights
edn	edition
e. g.	exempli gratia (for example)
et al	et alii/aliae/alia
f	following page
f. e.	former edition

ff	following pages
fn	Footnote
Ger YIL	German Yearbook of International Law
GREVIO	Group of Experts on Action against Violence against Women and Domestic Violence
HRLR	Human Rights Law Review
HRQ	Human Rights Quarterly
ibid	ibidem
ICCPR	International Covenant on Civil and Political Rights
ICERD	International Convention on the Elimination of All Forms of Racial Discrimination
ICESCR	International Covenant on Economic, Social and Cultural Rights
ICJ Rep	ICJ Reports
ICJ Statute	Statute of the International Court of Justice
ICQL	International and Comparative Law Quarterly
ICRMW	International Convention on the Protection of the Rights of All Migrant Workers and Members of their Families
i. c. w.	in conjunction with
ILC Ybk	Yearbook of the International Law Commission
I. L. M.	International Legal Materials
ILO	International Labour Organization
ILO Constitution	Constitution of the International Labour Organization
IRRC	International Review of the Red Cross
JHR	Journal of Human Rights
lit	litera
MESCEVI	Follow-up Mechanism to the Belém do Pará Convention
NGO/NGOs	Non-governmental organization/Non-governmental organizations
NILR	Netherlands International Law Review
NJHR	Nordic Journal of Human Rights
NJIHR	Northwestern Journal of International Human Rights
no	Number
NQHR	Netherlands Quarterly of Human Rights
OAS	Organization of American States
OP CRPD	Optional Protocol to the Convention on the Rights of Persons with Disabilities
p.	page
para	paragraph
Penn St L Rev	Penn State Law review

Rev Int Organ	The Review of International Organizations
UN	United Nations
UN Doc.	Document of the United Nations
UNTS	United Nations Treaty Series
VCLT	Vienna Convention on the Law of Treaties

Part One:
Introduction

The state reporting procedure is one of the oldest monitoring instruments in international law. Used since 1919, it has been included in numerous multilateral treaties as a tool to evaluate the process of implementation by the states party to the respective treaty. At its core a self-evaluation procedure, it evolved into an increasingly sophisticated system with multiple stakeholders. In human rights treaty law, the stakeholders involved in the procedure are the state parties, oversight committees, civil society and even individuals. State reporting is the only monitoring instrument that becomes mandatory as soon as a state ratifies the treaty containing it. Furthermore, it is one of the few instruments that focuses on constant monitoring to prevent violations of the treaty framework – contrary to repressive measures such as court trials. Due to its sovereignty-sensitive nature, it is widely accepted by the States. Nevertheless, over the years of operation, it proved to be ineffective. Especially the large number of states which did and do not comply with the obligation by not submitting a report, submitting it late or submitting it in an inadequate quality has been hindering the effectivity of the procedure and prevented the achievement of its object and purpose. The challenges to the system derived on the one hand from the unwillingness of states to report. On the other hand, a fundamental systemic dysfunction has been challenging the procedure for decades: the increasing amount of reporting obligations on the international[1] and regional level made compliance increasingly difficult and burdensome for state parties.[2] Especially those states which neither have the institutional and structural nor the financial capacities struggle to comply with every reporting obligation they have. The difficulties the reporting procedure has been facing were recognized early in the system of the United Nations Treaty Bodies, and reform efforts were initiated.

In 1989, Mr. Philip Alston issued his initial report on the effectivity of the human rights Treaty Body System of the United Nations (UN).[3] Mandated by the General Assembly he undertook a detailed investigation towards the effectivity of the whole system. In

---

1 'International' in this thesis is used as a synonym to globally, specifically in the sphere of the United Nations Treaty System.
2 See already: Note by the Secretary-General, *Effective Implementation of International Instruments on Human Rights, Including Reporting Obligations under International Instruments on Human Rights*, UN Doc. A/44/668, 8 November 1989, p. 21 ff.
3 Note by the Secretary-General, *Effective Implementation of International Instruments on Human Rights, Including Reporting Obligations under International Instruments on Human Rights*, UN Doc. A/44/668, 8 November 1989.

his final report[4], he came to the conclusion that the system was indeed not successful and in need of reforms, for which he offered various proposals. However, those reforms were only partly implemented, wherefore the system in major parts stayed as it was until today. For the past 30 years, various experts published their own ideas on possible reforms of the system. Within the UN system the need for reform has been addressed by multiple officials of the UN: by the Secretary-General 2002 ('Strengthening of the United Nations: an agenda for further change')[5], 2005 ('In larger freedom: towards development, security and human rights for all')[6] and by the then High Commissioner for Human Rights in 2012 ('Strengthening the UN Treaty Body System')[7]. The last document introduced a well-founded study of the most pressing problems of the system including possible solutions and their expected costs. An unlimited working group was concerned with the topic and mandated with finding possible solutions following this report. In 2014, the General Assembly in Resolution 68/268 decided to request biennial reports on the progress of implementing said resolution (and thereby strengthen the treaty body system). The Secretary-General[8], according to Resolution 68/268, is obliged to submit biennially a status report as part of the reform process towards the strengthening of the Unites Nations Treaty Body System.[9] On 18 July 2016, the Secretary-General provided the General Assembly with the first biennial report on the status of the human rights Treaty Body System, on 6 August 2018 with the second.[10]

Even though the reform process has now been going on for thirty years, none of the reform proposals was able to solve those problems within the UN system so far.

Reporting compliance by the state parties remains low. In the Treaty Body System of the UN, by 19 January 2016, only 13 percent of the state parties were fully compliant with their reporting obligations.[11] Three committees informed the Secretary-General

---

4 Note by the Secretary-General, *Effective Functioning of Bodies Established Pursuant to United Nations Human Rights Instruments*, 27 March 1997, UN Doc. E/CN.4/1997/74.
5 Report of the Secretary-General, *Strengthening of the United Nations: an agenda for further change*, UN Doc. A/57/387, 9 September 2002.
6 Report of the Secretary-General, *In larger freedom: towards development, security and human rights for all*, UN Doc. A/59/2005, 21 March 2005.
7 Note by the Secretary-General, *United Nations reform: measures and proposals*, UN Doc. A/66/860, 26 June 2012.
8 The notation 'Secretary-General' refers to the Secretary General of the United Nations (as opposed to 'Secretary General').
9 UN General Assembly, *Strengthening and enhancing the effective functioning of the human rights treaty body system*, UN Doc. A/Res/68/268, 21 April 2014, operative clause 40.
10 Report of the Secretary-General, *Status of the human rights treaty body system*, UN Doc. A/73/309, 6 August 2018.
11 Report of the Secretary-General, *Status of the human rights treaty body system*, UN Doc. A/71/118, 18 July 2016, para 5.

that they had 15 state parties overdue with their initial report for more than ten years. Two treaty bodies had State parties with periodic reports overdue for more than ten years.[12] In 2019, only 35 state parties fully complied with their reporting obligations.[13] Of those, only 15 had reporting obligations for 10 or more human rights treaties or protocols.[14] In the second biennial report of the Secretary General, presented in 2018[15], an increased reporting rate was described, despite of the fact that every Treaty Body claimed to have a decrease in submitted reports.[16] In 2019, only 18.7 % of the State Parties were reporting. At least 66 % of the submitted reports were submitted in 'a timely manner'.[17] As the challenges remain, the General Assembly decided to review the overall progress and decide on the way forward in 2020.[18]

For some states, however, the difficulties with reporting, resulting in large parts from the amount of reports requested, do not end with the UN Treaty Body System. The three biggest regional human rights systems – Europe, Inter-America and Africa – also oblige States to report on the implementation of several of their regional treaties. Those reporting obligations are similar to, if not the same as those of the UN system. This leads to the difficulty that States are not only obliged to report on the implementation of the UN treaties – which, in many cases, already leads to double reporting – but also on various regional treaties, which for the most part regulate the same topics. The workload for those states is therefore immense.

The challenges of the reporting procedure have been subject to discussion in academia as well as in the sphere of the human rights treaty bodies. Reform proposals of a great variety have been discussed over decades. This thesis wants to contribute to the discourse on the topic by identifying the legal nature of the obligation and the challenges as well as the conclusions that can be drawn from the extensive discussions about this instrument. Based on those findings, the final contribution of this thesis will be a proposal encompassing the legal core, the legal challenges and the lowest common denominators to develop a procedure which caters to all needs and provides a feasible solution against persistent non-compliance based on public international law.

---

12 *Ibid*, para 6.
13 United Nations Treaty Body Database, <https://tbinternet.ohchr.org/_layouts/TreatyBodyExternal/LateReporting.aspx> [accessed 02 December 2019].
14 *Ibid*.
15 Report of the Secretary-General, *Status of the human rights treaty body system*, A/73/309, 6 August 2018.
16 *Ibid*, para 19, 21.
17 Chairs of the Human Rights Treaty Bodies, *Implementation of human rights instruments*, UN Doc. A/74/256, 30 July 2019, para 14.
18 UN General Assembly, *Strengthening and enhancing the effective functioning of the human rights treaty body system*, UN Doc. A/Res/68/268, 21 April 2014, operative clause 41.

I. Scope and Aim of the Thesis

Even though state reporting is just one of the human rights monitoring instruments, this thesis is restricted to an evaluation of the state reporting system for the reason that it is the only monitoring instrument which is binding on the state party immediately after it ratified the concrete treaty.[19] No additional declaration on the acceptance of this monitoring instrument is required. Reporting is compulsory for every state party. Therefore, this instrument holds a great potential for the protection of human rights through continuous and extensive monitoring. The aim of this thesis is to evaluate the content and problems of this instrument, to identify the legal issues of the challenges of this instrument and provide a proposal for its improvement.

The state reporting procedure consists of different steps which altogether create the reporting cycle under the relevant treaty. Each step requires a different action from the state party, be it written or oral, comprehensive or specific. However, as every process, the reporting cycle starts with the first act by the state: the initial report and/or the first periodic report. If a state does not initiate the process, the reporting procedure is stopped before it even begins. Strengthening the state reporting system must therefore begin with the first step of the reporting procedure.

Therefore, this thesis focuses on the written state report. It analyzes the act of written reporting, its object and purpose, its challenges, the previous reforms and perspectives. While it is acknowledged that the procedure functions as a whole and may not be artificially divided, it is important to have a closer look on the functioning and options of the first step of the procedure.

The state reporting system and the reform process have been of interest to a number of scholars[20] and United Nation organs[21] for years. Nevertheless, there are aspects which

---

19 See for further details Part Two, Chapter 1.
20 See for example O'Flaherty & O'Brien, 'Reform of UN Human Rights Treaty Monitoring Bodies: A Critique of the Concept Paper on the High Commissioner's Proposal for a Unified Standing Treaty Body' (2007) 7 HRLR 141, 141–172; Bowman, 'Towards a Unified Treaty Body for Monitoring Compliance with UN Human Rights Conventions – Legal Mechanisms for Treaty Reform' (2007) 7 HRLR 225; Kjaerum, 'State Reports', in Alfredsson, Grimheden, Ramcharan & Zayas (eds), *International Monitoring Mechanisms: Essays in Honour of Jacob Th. Möller* (2009), 17–24; O'Flaherty, 'Reform of the UN Human Rights Treaty Body System: Locating the Dublin Statement' (2010) 10 HRLR 319; Spenlé, *Die Staatenberichtsverfahren der UNO-Menschenrechtsverträge* (2011); Morijn, 'Reforming United Nations Human Rights Treaty Monitoring Reform' (2011) 58 NILR 295; Kälin, 'Examination of state reports' in: Keller & Ulfstein (eds), *UN human rights treaty bodies: law and legitimacy* (2012) 16 ff. [hereinafter Kälin, *'Examination of state reports'*]; Egan, 'Strengthening the United Nations Human Rights Treaty Body System' (2013) 13 HRLR 209, 209–243; de Schutter, *International Human Rights Law* (2nd edn, 2014) [hereinafter de Schutter], 923 ff.; Gaer, 'The Institutional Future of the Covenants: A World Court for Human Rights?' in Moeckli, Keller & Heri (eds), *The Human Rights Covenants at 50: Their Past,*

have not been sufficiently discussed even though they should be considered, such as the inclusion of the regional reporting obligations into the reform considerations. Also, the most recent developments such as the biennial reports of the Secretary-General and the General Assembly 2020 Review have not yet been analyzed and embedded in the framework of the previous proposals. This thesis addresses those gaps:

First, it clarifies the nature of the obligation, *second*, it integrates the recent developments, meaning the General Assembly Review 2020 process and the biennial reports issued in accordance with this process, into the comprehensive framework of the previous reform proposals within the UN and *third*, it takes into consideration the regional human rights systems, which are repeatedly mentioned, but not yet integrated into the discussion. Based on the findings, a comprehensive proposal for the 2020 Review is made.

II. Research Method and Application

The research follows an evaluative approach, meaning that it is conducted by assessing the current situation in comparison to the previous situation as well as from an external and objective perspective to identify its shortfalls and give suggestions on its improvement. It is partly based on the ideas described by *Wibren van der Burg*, who examines the value of an evaluative approach in the case of normative recommendation, meaning a change of legal norms.[22] Leading questions for this approach are 'Is the law 'good'? How can it be improved?'.[23] He makes it clear that normative recommendation is just one possible field of research and that the approach is not restricted to it.[24] *Van der Burg* holds that the evaluation of the effectivity of a norm has to be assessed in light of the realization of certain values and principles.[25] He considers that 'Effectiveness is only an instrumental value insofar as the goals served by the law are valuable.'[26]

Present and Future (2018) [hereinafter Gaer, 'The Institutional Future of the Covenants: A World Court for Human Rights?'], 334–356.

21 For an overview see Homepage of the Office of the High Commissioner for Human Rights, Human Rights Bodies, on Treaty Body Strengthening: <https://www.ohchr.org/EN/HRBodies/HRTD/Pages/TBStrengthening.aspx> [accessed 02 December 2019].

22 van der Burg, The Merits of Law: An Argumentative Framework for Evaluative Judgements and Normative Recommendations in Legal Research, Archiv für Rechts- und Sozialphilosophie, Forthcoming; Erasmus Working Paper Series on Jurisprudence and Socio-Legal Studies, No. 17–01, 22 February 2018, <http://dx.doi.org/10.2139/ssrn.3020624> [accessed 02 December 2019], 7.

23 Ibid, 3.
24 Ibid, 7.
25 Ibid, 21.
26 Ibid, 21.

II. Research Method and Application

Hence, in this thesis, the evaluative approach was applied to the practice emanating from the substantive norm of state reporting, including the rules of procedure as adopted by the individual committees, as the legal basis for the process and as the subject to change. The evaluative approach combined with norm interpretation was considered to be to most beneficial for the research on the complex topic of state reporting, not only situated in the international law sphere, but also touching upon political, sociological and ethical topics.[27] By applying the combination of evaluation and norm interpretation, the research could be focused on the legal dimension.

The essential abstract question of the thesis is 'How can the execution of the law on which the current system is based be improved?'. Hence, the first question raised by the evaluative approach ('Is the law good?') is, as a result of decades of attempting to reform, to be answered with a 'no'. Therefore, the research of this thesis is focusing on the second question ('How can it be improved?') with the aim to identify possibilities to enhance the effectivity of the protection of human rights by increasing compliance with the essential monitoring regulation enshrined in almost every human rights treaty. Compliance is assessed in light of the principle of *pacta sunt servanda* and against the valued goal of preservation of stability of multilateral treaties – as those are the leading principles in the legal framework governing the international law of treaties – and based on data provided by the UN Treaty Bodies as well as available numbers from the regional human rights oversight committees. Therefore, only the compliance of the states as ratifying parties to the treaties in question is examined. It would exceed the scope of this thesis to include the effectivity of the whole procedure as well as that of the oversight committees themselves.

The nature of the state reporting obligation in general as well as the specific topic of the written submission of the state report are of a complex nature and therefore require a multilayered examination. The course of the research went as follows:

To understand the concept of the state reporting obligation, the development and historical context was tracked by using former treaties encompassing the obligation as well as scholarship on the development of the obligation in the international context. The restriction to human rights treaties is due to the fact that the state reporting system is currently subject to review by academia as well as UN organs. Most prominently, the UN General Assembly announced that they will review the whole system in 2020.[28] The

---

[27] The complexity of research in International Law was also described by Peters in *Realizing Utopia as a Scholarly Endeavour* (2013) 24 EJIL 2, 533 ff., where she proposes 'Multidimensional International Legal Scholarship research' (*ibid*, 545 ff.).

[28] UN General Assembly, *Strengthening and enhancing the effective functioning of the human rights treaty body system*, UN Doc. A/Res/68/268, 21 April 2014, operative clause 41.

state reporting obligations were identified not only in the treaties of the UN, but also in the regional human rights treaties due to their comparable nature.

Following the clarification of the development, the content, object and purpose as well as the doctrinal classification of the state reporting obligation were identified by conducting an exemplary norm interpretation. The findings of this interpretation subsequently helped to examine the effectivity of the state reporting obligation in light of the identified object and purpose as well as the principle *pacta sunt servanda*, which underlies every treaty in international law. Resulting from this examination the legal challenges to the procedure were determined.

After identifying the content and nature as well as the challenges of the state reporting obligation, the previous reform process was examined. Documentation concerning the Treaty Body Reform (or Strengthening) Process conducted by several UN organs (most prominently the Secretary-General and the Office of the High Commissioner for Human Rights) was studied to identify those aims common to all stakeholders as well as those reform proposals rejected by the majority of them. As a result, the requirements for a procedure which could be acceptable to every stakeholder involved were identified.

Following those requirements, a proposal for an improved procedure was developed. Furthermore, as it became clear over the course of the research that a possibility to sanction states persistently in breach of their reporting obligation could be beneficial to the system, it was examined whether there would be an option to sanction such states within the existing legal framework.

Part Two:
Unravelling a Confused System
The State Reporting Obligation, its Challenges, Previous Reforms and a Possible Solution

The state reporting system is a system occupying several levels of international law. It is the most often used and most long-standing instrument to supervise compliance. However, (state reporting) obligations established in the sphere of the UN, the regional human rights systems and further spheres of international law often overlap or contravene each other.[29] Over the past decades this led to a confusing system of intertwined reports which became even worse through those reform efforts that were simply adding to the existing system without easing the burden.

To shed some light on and eventually organize the procedure, this part of the thesis contains information on the state reporting obligation as such, the previous reform proposals within the sphere of the UN and a proposal for a possible solution (or 'entanglement') of the system.

Chapter 1 is concerned with the development, sources, content and challenges of the state reporting obligation. *Chapter 2* examines in detail the reform process of the past decades within the sphere of the UN as the most prominent example of a strengthening process of the state reporting procedure. Finally, *Chapter 3* proposes a twofold solution to the challenges of the state reporting instrument, which are derived from the findings of Chapters 1 and 2.

---

29 A table of overlapping treaty obligations in the system of the United Nations Treaty Bodies was already produced in the 1990 s, covering the then existing human rights treaties, see Report of the Secretariat, *Guidelines on an expanded core document and treaty-specific targeted reports and harmonized guidelines on reporting under the international human rights treaties*, UN Doc. HRI/MC/2004/3, 9 June 2004, paras 9 f.

Chapter 1:
The State Reporting Obligation
Concretization and Analysis of the State Reporting Obligation

Even though state reporting is one of the oldest monitoring instruments in international law, it is generally not well known. This is due to the modest visibility of the whole treaty body system in the public sphere, as well as the various challenges the system faces. This difficulty has been addressed by multiple UN organs[30] as well as academia[31], but only in specialized fields. The state reporting procedure generally remains in the background and is not given much attention. Hence, there is a big knowledge-gap when it comes to this monitoring instrument. This Chapter aims at closing this gap.

For this reason, this Chapter (I) introduces the idea of monitoring human rights through the instrument of state reporting, (II) identifies the content, object and purpose as well as the nature of the state reporting obligation, (III) explains the exact sources in regional and international human rights law which establish reporting obligations with their respective procedures and (IV) presents the challenges of the state reporting obligation. Herewith, this Chapter contains the basic information to understand the subsequent discussion of challenges and reforms.

I. Human Rights Monitoring through State Reporting

The monitoring system of state reporting as an international procedure was first introduced by the Covenant of the League of Nations in 1919.[32] Before that time, the idea that States ought to justify themselves for their actions in the international sphere was rare, and the principle of sovereign states as the exclusive subjects of international law

---

30   For an overview see Homepage of the Office of the High Commissioner for Human Rights, Human Rights Bodies, on Treaty Body Strengthening: <https://www.ohchr.org/EN/HRBodies/HRTD/Pages/TBStrengthening.aspx> [accessed 02 December 2019].
31   See for example O'Flaherty, '*Reform of the UN Human Rights Treaty Body System: Locating the Dublin Statement*' (2010) 10 HRLR 319; Morijn, '*Reforming United Nations Human Rights Treaty Monitoring Reform*' (2011) 58 NILR 295; Egan, '*Strengthening the United Nations Human Rights Treaty Body System*' (2013) 13 HRLR 209; Kälin, '*Examination of state reports*', 16–72; Gaer, '*The Institutional Future of the Covenants: A World Court for Human Rights?*', 334–356; see also supra, fn 19; for a very comprehensive and detailed assessment Spenlé, *Die Staatenberichtsverfahren der UNO-Menschenrechtsverträge* (2011).
32   Art. 22 Covenant of the League of Nations, 28 April 1919, reprinted 13 American Journal of International Law 128 [hereinafter: Covenant of the League of Nations].

I. Human Rights Monitoring through State Reporting

had been prevailing.[33] Nevertheless, in 1919, the state parties agreed upon a reporting procedure which obliged those states with colonies, the Mandatories, to annually report to the Council about the territory under its power.[34] Although not yet applicable to every state, it created a first limitation to the concept of uninfringeable sovereignty of a state. In the same year, the International Labor Organization (ILO), introduced a similar procedure in its Constitution.[35] The reporting obligation under Art. 22 Constitution of the International Labour Organization (ILO Constitution) was binding on every state party to the treaty without restriction.[36] Reporting as a monitoring instrument for the ILO is still in operation.[37]

With the establishment of the UN and the consolidation of international human rights after the Second World War, states began to increasingly accept limitations to their sovereignty in the international sphere. With the adoption of the UN Charter in 1945 and the Universal Declaration of Human Rights in 1948, they agreed that individuals have rights which need to be protected.[38]

In 1956, the first monitoring mechanism concerned with human rights compliance was established by the UN Economic and Social Council.[39] In the requested reports states were supposed to inform the Council in a three-year regular cycle about the progress made within their sovereign territory in realizing human rights, especially those under the Universal Declaration of Human Rights.[40] Apart from a minor amendment, this procedure was upheld – parallel to the reporting under the ILO Constitution – until the first human rights treaty, the International Convention on the Elimination of All Forms of Racial Discrimination, was adopted in 1965.[41] This first human rights convention with a reporting procedure was soon followed by seven other treaties and two protocols containing a periodic reporting obligation within a short period of time.[42] These documents also oblige states to regularly submit reports to an oversight

---

33   Shaw, *International Law*, (8th edn, 2017) [hereinafter Shaw], 213.
34   Art. 22 Covenant of the League of Nations.
35   Art. 22 Constitution of the International Labour Organisation, 1 April 1919, 15 UNTS 40 [hereinafter ILO Constitution]; see also Kälin, *'Examination of state reports'*, 17; Tomuschat, *'Human Rights – Between Idealism and Realism'*, (3rd edn, 2014) [hereinafter Tomuschat], 214.
36   Kälin, *'Examination of state reports'*, 17.
37   Tomuschat, 215.
38   For detailed information on the emergence of international human rights at the universal level see de Schutter, 14 ff.
39   See UN General Assembly, *Draft International Covenants on Human Rights, Annotation by the Secretary-General*, UN Doc. A/2929, 1 July 1955, 12 (para 27).
40   Kälin, *'Examination of state reports'*, 17.
41   International Convention on the Elimination of All Forms of Racial Discrimination [hereinafter ICERD], 21 December 1965, 660 UNTS 195; Tomuschat, 215.
42   See for details *infra* Part Two, Chapter 1, II. 1. of this thesis.

committee to this day.⁴³ Outside of the human rights system, state reporting as a monitoring instrument on the international level today is *inter alia* used by the World Health Organization⁴⁴, the Food and Agriculture Organization⁴⁵, the UN Educational, Scientific and Cultural Organization⁴⁶, in areas such as arms control⁴⁷ and environmental

---

43   Art. 40 International Covenant on Civil and Political Rights [hereinafter ICCPR]: Initial report within one year, subsequent reports whenever the Committee to requests (today a periodicity of four years is now established); Art. 16, 17 International Covenant on Economic, Social and Cultural Rights [hereinafter ICESCR]: program for submission; Art. 9 ICERD: Initial report within one year, Periodic Report every two years; Art. 19 Convention against Torture and Other Cruel, Inhuman or Degrading Treatment or Punishment [hereinafter CAT]: Initial report within one year, Periodic Report every four years; Art. 44 Convention on the Rights of the Child [hereinafter CRC]: Initial report within two years, Periodic Report every five years; Art. 18 Convention on the Elimination of All Forms of Discrimination against Women [hereinafter CEDAW]: Initial report within one year, Periodic Report every four years and upon request; Art. 73 International Convention on the Protection of the Rights of All Migrant Workers and Members of their Families [hereinafter ICRMW]: Initial report within one year, Periodic Report every five years and upon request; Art. 35 Convention on the Rights of Persons with Disabilities [hereinafter CRPD]: Initial report within two years, Periodic Report every four years; Art. 12 Optional Protocol to the Convention on the Rights of the Child on the sale of children, child prostitution and child pornography [hereinafter CRC-OPSC]: Initial report within 2 years, Periodic Report either included in CRC Report or every five years; Art. 8 Optional Protocol to the Convention on the Rights of the Child on the involvement of children in armed conflict [hereinafter CRC-OPAC]: Initial report within 2 years, Periodic Report either included in CRC Report or every five years; for an overview see also Tomuschat, 215; Art. 29 International Convention for the Protection of All Persons from Enforced Disappearance [hereinafter CED] is not considered in this thesis as it only establishes the obligation to submit an Initial report to the Committee, no periodic reports are required under the CED.
44   Article 54 International Health Regulations (2005), accessible <http://www.who.int/ihr/publications/9789241596664/en/> [accessed 02 December 2019]; see also Resolution A61/7, Implementation of the International Health Regulations (2005), Sixty-First World Health Assembly, 3 April 2008, <http://apps.who.int/gb/archive/e/e_wha61.html> [accessed: 02 December 2019]; for further details see Homepage of the World Health Organization, Strengthening health security by implementing the International Health Regulations (2005), <https://www.who.int/ihr/procedures/annual-reporting/en/> [accessed 2 December 2019].
45   Article XI of the Constitution of the Food and Agriculture Organization, 16 October 1945, reprinted in Basic texts of the Food and Agriculture Organization of the United Nations, Volumes I and II, 2017 edn, p. 3 ff., accessible <http://www.fao.org/3/a-mp046e.pdf> [accessed 02 December 2019], p. 10.
46   Art. 29 Convention Concerning the Protection of the World Cultural and Natural Heritage, 16 November 1972, 1037 UNTS 151; see also Operational Guidelines for the Implementation of the World Heritage Convention, WHC.17/01, 12 July 2017, paras 199 ff.; further information: Homepage of the United Nations Educational, Scientific and Cultural Organization, accessible: <https://whc.unesco.org/en/periodicreporting/> [accessed 02 December 2019].
47   See for example Part IV(A) para 36 of the Annex on Implementation and Verification to the United Nations Convention on the Prohibition of the Development, Production, Stockpiling and Use of Chemical Weapons and on Their Destruction, Annex on Implementation and Verification ('Verification Annex'), 13 January 1993, 1974 UNTS 361; plans for state reporting in International Humanitar-

protection[48], as well as by regional human rights systems[49]. In recent treaty drafts, such as the Revised Draft on Business and Human Rights, state reporting is included as the one obligatory monitoring instrument.[50]

The initial idea underlying the reporting procedure was to develop and increase cooperation between states during the Cold War period.[51] Even though reporting in effect created a limitation on their sovereignty, most states did not consider it a monitoring mechanism, but rather a tool for cooperation.[52] This idea of cooperation was maintained by the Human Rights Committee in the first reporting guidelines in 1977, the first report to the General Assembly, as well as the (by then not yet established) procedure of Concluding Observations.[53] In light of the Post-Cold-War developments, especially in the field of human rights, state reporting slowly evolved into the monitoring instrument it represents today. The limitation on a state's sovereignty reached its (so far) maximum with introducing the practice of examining state parties in the absence of a report.[54]

Parallel to state reporting, various other monitoring instruments have been and continue to be used for the protection of human rights. The most successful and renowned compliance mechanism is the court system. In the international law sphere human

---

ian Law were already made in the 1980s, see Kornblum, 'A comparison of self-evaluating state reporting systems' (1995) 304 IRRC 39, 42 ff.

48   See for example Article VIII (7) Convention on the International Trade in Endangered Species of Wild Fauna and Flora, 3 March 1973, 993 UNTS 243; Article 7 of the Montreal Protocol on Substances that Deplete the Ozone Layer (with annex), 16 September 1987, 1522 UNTS 3; Article 7 of the Kyoto Protocol to the United Nations Framework Convention on Climate Change (United Nations Framework Convention on Climate Change), 11 December 1997, 2303 UNTS 162.

49   See Chapter 1, II, 2. of this thesis.

50   Section III, Article 13, subsection 2 Open-ended intergovernmental working group on transnational corporations and other business enterprises with respect to human rights, *Revised draft legally Binding Instrument to regulate, in International Human Rights Law, the Activities of Transnational Corporations and other Business Enterprises*, 16 July 2019, accessible: <ohchr.org/en/hrbodies/hrc/wgtranscorp/pages/igwgontnc.aspx> [accessed 02 December 2019].

51   Tomuschat, 215.

52   Kälin, 'Examination of state reports', 35; see also Spenlé, *Die Staatenberichtsverfahren der UNO-Menschenrechtsverträge* (2011), 31 f.; cf O'Flaherty, 'The Concluding Observations of United Nations Human Rights Treaty Bodies' (2006) 6 HRLR 27, 28 ff.

53   Kälin, 'Examination of state reports', 35 f.

54   See for example the practice of the Human Rights Committee, *General Comment No. 30*, UN Doc. CCPR/C/21/Rev.2/Add.12, 18 September 2002, para 4; Rule 17 (7) Committee of Experts of the European Charter for Regional or Minority languages, *Rules of Procedure of the Committee of Experts of the European Charter for Regional or Minority languages*, 2001 (most recently modified 18 March 2019), MIN-LANG (2019) 7, <https://rm.coe.int/minlang-2019–07-comex-rules-of-procedure-final/1680954878> [accessed 02 December 2019]; Kälin, 'Examination of state reports', 36.

rights courts are used in every established regional human rights system.[55] Amongst them the European Court of Human Rights is considered to be the most successful. A 'World Court of Human Rights', which is also frequently discussed,[56] does not exist. Apart from courts, there are procedures such as inquiries[57] and individual communications[58] to enforce state compliance with the relevant regulations. From all measures mentioned above, state reporting seems to be the least powerful tool to enforce compliance; it is considered to be primarily a tool of self-evaluation and dialogue[59] and, if not conducted properly, or even done at all, is not followed by sanctions. The oversight committees have very limited possibilities to convince a State reluctant to submit a report to actually comply with this obligation.[60]

Nevertheless, the reporting procedure, though not the most powerful instrument to enforce compliance, is of great value to the protection of human rights. The state reporting procedure has been used for over a century to monitor compliance with relevant provisions in international treaties. State reporting becomes a binding obligation the moment a state ratifies a treaty which contains this procedure;[61] this makes state reporting an immediate universal instrument for monitoring.[62] Every other monitoring mechanism has to be explicitly accepted by the respective state. Reporting is the lowest

---

55 The Inter-American System with the Inter-American Court of Human Rights, the European System with the European Court of Human Rights and the African Human Rights System with the African Court on Human and Peoples' Rights.
56 See for example Gaer, 'The Institutional Future of the Covenants: A World Court for Human Rights?', 334–356; Nowak, 'The Need for a World Court of Human Rights' (2013), 13 HRLR 209; Scheinin, *Towards a World Court of Human Rights*, 2009 Swiss Initiative to Commemorate the 60th Anniversary of the Universal Declaration of Human Rights, accessible <https://www.eui.eu/Documents/Departments Centres/AcademyofEuropeanLaw/CourseMaterialsHR/HR2009/Scheinin/ScheininClassReading1.pdf> [accessed 02 December 2019], at 63; Trechsel, 'A World Court for Human Rights?' (2004) 1 NJIHR 1; Kirkpatrick, 'A Modest Proposal: A Global Court of Human Rights' (2014), 13 JHR 230; repudiating Alston, 'Against a World Court for Human Rights' (2014), 28 Ethics&International Affairs 197, 197–212.
57 See for example Art. 20 CAT; Art. 8 CEDAW; Art. 6 Optional Protocol to the Convention on the Rights of Persons with Disabilities; Art. 22 CED; for further information see Homepage of the United Nations Human Rights Office of the High Commissioner, Committee on the Elimination of Discrimination Against Women, Inquiry Procedure, accessible: <https://www.ohchr.org/EN/HRBodies/CEDAW/Pages/InquiryProcedure.aspx> [accessed 02 December 2019].
58 See for details de Schutter, 882 ff.
59 Kälin, 'Examination of state reports', 35, 39.
60 Kälin, 'Examination of state reports', 32; see already Kornblum, 'A comparison of self-evaluating state reporting systems' (1995) 304 IRRC 39, 49; for more information on sanctions see Part Two, Chapter 3, II.
61 See also Kälin, 'Examination of state reports', 16.
62 Gaer, 'First Fruits: Reporting by States under the African Charter on Human and Peoples' Rights' (1992) 10 NQHR 29, 32; Kälin, 'Examination of state reports', 17.

common denominator on which every state party could agree,[63] and the least intrusive to a state's sovereignty,[64] which is why it is accepted so widely despite being the only immediately compulsory procedure in human rights law. Furthermore, it is the only instrument which constantly reviews the general situation in a country and thereby detects systemic failures.[65] The more forcible mechanisms, as regressive measures, are applied in cases when a violation of an individuals' rights has already occurred. The individual complaint procedure as well as the protection granted by established courts or tribunals may only be invoked to provide the harmed individual with a remedy for the violation suffered. Hence, those procedures enforce compliance only in individual cases and only after a violation occurred. In contrast, state reporting establishes a general and preventive rather than an individual and remedial control.[66]

II. State Reporting Obligations and their Procedures

The state reporting procedure can be found in various treaties covering different topics of international and regional law. The most prominent state reporting obligations, however, can be found in human rights systems, especially in the system of the UN Treaty Bodies. Eight treaties and two Optional Protocols of the UN human rights system contain the obligation to periodically report on the progress of implementation of the respective human rights treaty.[67] The core function of most of the Treaty Bodies is the consideration of state reports.[68]

In addition to the reporting obligations under international human rights treaties, a great number of states is obliged to report in a comparable manner to regional human rights bodies, specifically in Africa, Inter-America and Europe. This remains one of the biggest challenges to this monitoring instrument, as cross-cutting issues do not only occur in the international sphere but also between the international and regional treaties. Many treaties regulate the same or similar content, and while cross-referencing is

---

63 See Spenlé, *Die Staatenberichtsverfahren der UNO-Menschenrechtsverträge* (2011), 34.
64 *Ibid*, 21, 27.
65 cf Kälin, *'Examination of state reports'*, 40.
66 *Ibid.*
67 Art. 40 ICCPR; Art. 16, 17 (1) ICESCR; Art. 9 ICERD; Art. 19 CAT; Art. 44 CRC; Art. 18 CEDAW; Art. 73 ICRMW; Art. 35 CRPD; Art. 12 CRC-OPSC; Art. 8 CRC-OPAC; Art. 29 CED is not considered in this thesis as it only establishes the obligation to submit an Initial report to the Committee. No periodic reports are required under the CED.
68 Oette, *'The UN Human Rights Treaty Bodies: Impact and Future'*, in Oberleitner, *International Human Rights Institutions, Tribunals and Courts* (2018) 95 [hereinafter Oette, *'The UN Human Rights Treaty Bodies: Impact and Future'*], 100.

increasingly recommended in the sphere of the international Treaty Bodies[69], cross-referencing between international and regional bodies is not yet (widely) practiced.

The state reporting obligation is enshrined in the respective treaties, always as an obligation which is binding upon the state parties automatically after the ratification of the relevant document.

1. United Nations Human Rights System

The obligation for states to submit reports on the progress of implementation of human rights treaties can most prominently be found in international human rights law, specifically in the UN human rights treaties that establish the human rights Treaty Bodies. Those Treaty Bodies are expert committees mandated to oversee the state parties' progress in implementing the respective covenants.[70] The relevant norms establishing periodic reporting obligations are Art. 40 International Covenant on Civil and Political Rights (ICCPR)[71], Art. 16, 17 International Covenant on Economic, Social and Cultural Rights (ICESCR)[72], Art. 9 International Convention on the Elimination of All Forms of Racial Discrimination (ICERD)[73], Art. 19 Convention against Torture and Other Cruel, Inhuman or Degrading Treatment or Punishment (CAT)[74], Art. 44 Convention on the Rights of the Child (CRC)[75], Art. 18 Convention on the Elimination of All Forms of Discrimination against Women (CEDAW)[76], Art. 73 International Convention on the Protection of the Rights of All Migrant Workers and Members of their Families (ICRMW)[77], Art. 35 Convention on the Rights of Persons with Disabilities (CRPD)[78], Art. 12 Optional Protocol to the Convention on the Rights of the Child on the sale of children, child prostitution and child pornography (CRC-OPSC)[79] and Art. 8 Optional Protocol

---

69 Advisory Council on Human Rights of Morocco, *Marrakesh Statement on strengthening the relationship between NHRIs and the human rights treaty bodies system*, 10 June 2010, accessible: <https://www.ohchr.org/en/hrbodies/hrtd/pages/documents.aspx> [accessed 02 December 2012], reprinted in Netherlands Quarterly of Human Rights 28 (2010), 121–27, para 16 c); Dublin II Meeting, *Strengthening the United Nations Human Rights Treaty Body System*, Outcome Document, 10–11 November 2011, <https://www.ohchr.org/EN/HRBodies/HRTD/Pages/Documents.aspx> [accessed 02 December 2019], para 72.
70 Kälin, *'Examination of state reports'*, 16.
71 ICCPR, 16 December 1966, 999 UNTS 171.
72 ICESCR, 16 December 1966, 993 UNTS 3.
73 ICERD, 21 December 1965, 660 UNTS 195.
74 CAT, 10 December 1984, 1465 UNTS 85.
75 CRC, 20 November 1989, 1577 UNTS 3.
76 CEDAW, 18 December 1979, 1249 UNTS 13.
77 ICRMW, 18 December 1990, 2220 UNTS 3.
78 CRPD, 13 December 2006, 2515 UNTS 3.
79 CRC-OPSC, 25 May 2000, 2171 UNTS 227.

II. State Reporting Obligations and their Procedures

to the Convention on the Rights of the Child on the involvement of children in armed conflict (CRC-OPAC)[80]. All of them establish the same monitoring system with only slight differences in their wording.[81]

Generally, those norms prescribe the obligation to submit to the relevant committee a report on the progress made with the implementation of the respective treaty. The scope and content of the report is not explicitly prescribed. Only the regulation of the Convention on the Rights of the Child may be understood to contain a reference to the quality of the report by requesting 'sufficient information.'[82] The aforementioned articles regulate the periodicity of the reporting cycle.[83] None of the articles prescribes a specific form of reporting. The procedure of reporting is determined by each Treaty Body in its rules of procedure.

a. Procedure of Reporting to the United Nations Treaty Bodies

The reporting procedure to the UN Treaty Bodies is the most commonly known. The 'reporting cycle' which states are supposed to undergo consists traditionally of six steps (State Report, List of Issues, Reply to List of Issues, Constructive Dialogue, Concluding Observations, Follow-Up Procedure).[84] However, recently a simplified version of said cycle is increasingly used (simplified reporting procedure). It consists of five steps (List of Issues Prior to Reporting, Reply to the List of Issues, Constructive Dialogue, Concluding Observations, Follow-Up Procedure).[85]

---

80 CRC-OPAC, 25 May 2000, 2173 UNTS 222.
81 Tomuschat, 215; already Kornblum, '*A comparison of self-evaluating state reporting systems*' (1995) 304 IRRC 39, 46.
82 Art. 44 (2) CRC.
83 Art. 40 ICCPR: Initial report within one year, subsequent reports whenever the Committee to requests (today a periodicity of four years is now established); Art. 16, 17 ICESCR: programme for submission; Art. 9 ICERD: Initial report within one year, Periodic Report every two years; Art. 19 CAT: Initial report within one year, Periodic Report every four years; Art. 44 CRC: Initial report within two years, Periodic Report every five years; Art. 18 CEDAW: Initial report within one year, Periodic Report every four years and upon request; Art. 73 ICRMW: Initial report within one year, Periodic Report every five years and upon request; Art. 12 CRC-OPSC: Initial report within 2 years, Periodic Report either included in CRC Report or every five years; Art. 8 CRC-OPAC: Initial report within 2 years, Periodic Report either included in CRC Report or every five years.
84 Broecker/O'Flaherty, '*The Outcome of the General Assembly's Treaty Body Strengthening Process: An Important Milestone on a Longer Journey*', Policy Brief Universal Rights Group, June 2014, <https://www.universal-rights.org/urg-policy-reports/the-outcome-of-the-general-assemblys-treaty-body-strengthening-process-an-important-milestone-on-a-longer-journey/> [accessed 02 December 2019], 9.
85 *Ibid*, 9.

aa. Standard Reporting Procedure

After ratification or accession to a human rights treaty, the state party is required to submit an initial report within a specific timeframe, generally one or two years.[86] Its content presents general information about the new state party with detailed information about the factual situation and the practical availability of the rights guaranteed in the treaty.[87] This report is supposed to give the relevant committee an overview over the measures in place or planned that will implement the treaty provisions in a certain period of time.[88] Subsequently, the state party is requested to submit reports periodically, the periodicity depending on the specific treaty. Formally, the state party is requested to submit any information which the Treaty Body needs to fully understand the status of implementation of the treaty and the situation in the country.[89] It must not be of excessive length, though. Under the international human rights treaties, initial reports are limited to 60, periodic reports to 40 pages.[90]

After the periodic report was considered by the responsible committee, the committee would send a list of issues, to which the state party is supposed to answer. Subsequently, the state party is invited for a constructive dialogue with the oversight committee. Such dialogue is based on the report and the answer to the list of issues sent prior to the discussion. After the dialogue, the oversight committee draws its conclusions, writes its Concluding Observations and initiates the Follow-Up Mechanism. Herewith, the reporting cycle is finished and starts all over again.[91]

In 2006, following years of reform efforts, draft harmonized guidelines were presented by an Inter-Committee Technical Working Group[92], which the Secretary-General published as harmonized guidelines to further streamline the process in 2009[93]. Those guidelines proposed the compilation of a common core document to tackle the issue of overlapping information. According to those so called 'harmonized reporting guidelines',

---

86 Report of the Secretary-General, *Status of the human rights treaty body system*, UN Doc. A/73/309, 6 August 2018, para 7.
87 Human Rights Committee, *Consolidated Guidelines for State Reports under the International Covenant on Civil and Political Rights*, UN Doc. CCPR/C/66/GUI/Rev.2, 26 February 2001.
88 Report of the Secretary-General, *Compilation on the form and content of reports to be submitted by States parties to the international human rights treaties*, UN Doc. HRI/GEN/2/Rev.6, 3 June 2009, para 16.
89 *Ibid*, para 19.
90 *Ibid*, para 19.
91 For a detailed description see Kälin, *'Examination of state reports'*, 20 ff.
92 Report of the Inter-Committee Technical Working Group, *Harmonized guidelines on reporting under the international human rights treaties, including guidelines on a common core document and treaty-specific documents*, UN Doc. HRI/MC/2006/3, 10 May 2006.
93 Report of the Secretary-General, *Compilation on the form and content of reports to be submitted by States parties to the international human rights treaties*, UN Doc. HRI/GEN/2/Rev.6, 3 June 2009.

each State report shall consist of two parts: first, a general common core document, which may be relevant for several oversight committees, and second, a report on the specifics of the relevant treaty.[94]

(1) Common Core Document

The content of a common core document should cover general and factual information of relevance to all or at least several treaty bodies. Any change in the information provided shall be updated, either by annex or by submitting a new revised version.[95] In the 2009 Report 'Compilation of Guidelines on the Form and Content of Reports to be Submitted by States Parties to the International Human Rights Treaties' by the Secretary-General an exact guideline is provided on how to prepare the common core document.[96] Accordingly, it should be structured in three sections:

Section 1 should provide the reader with general political, legal, social, economic and cultural information, which is needed for a deeper understanding of the structure of the state itself. The demographic, social, economic and cultural characteristics should be explained, but not too detailed – only key elements should be highlighted. Information about the political and legal system should be described in general, but in the necessary depth, covering the main characteristics of the state (such as type of government, electoral system, and main organs), its recognition of NGOs and its administration of justice.[97]

Section 2 should contain information on the general framework for the protection and promotion of human rights. The status of the main international human rights treaties, especially on ratification, reservations and declarations, are of interest. Further information should be provided on specifics concerning the implementation of the treaties (such as restrictions or derogations) and the ratification of other international or regional treaties and covenants covering human rights and related areas. In the same section, more in depth-information is required on the specific legal framework protecting human rights as well as the framework within which human rights are promoted within the state. The information on the legal framework should elaborate on incorporation, jurisdiction, court cases and remedies. Information on the promotion of human rights requires information on, inter alia, the roles of the various actors, such as parliament, national institutions, NGOs, and on awareness raising, educational programs, and budgets.

---

94 *Ibid*, para 17.
95 *Ibid*, paras 18, 27; this procedure was already used before the relevant guidelines were adopted, see Kornblum, 'A comparison of self-evaluating state reporting systems' (, [1995]) 304 IRRC 39, 47.
96 Report of the Secretary-General, *Compilation on the form and content of reports to be submitted by States parties to the international human rights treaties*, UN Doc. HRI/GEN/2/Rev.6, 3 June 2009, paras 31 ff.
97 *Ibid*, paras 32 ff.

Furthermore, states should describe the preparation of their reports, common core document as well as treaty-specific report, the publicity of the reports and the involvement of other stakeholders, as well as measures for effective follow-ups to Concluding Observations. Any further human rights information may be included if appropriate.[98]

Section 3 should contain information on non-discrimination, equality and effective remedies against violations of human rights. General information is required on the overall elimination of discrimination and inequality on the theoretical (legal) and practical level, the measures to assist people from vulnerable groups, educational programs to reduce prejudices and measures to improve equality. Specific information is required concerning measures towards the reduction of economic, social and geographical disparities.[99]

The common core document should not be of excessive length, 60 to 80 pages are recommended.[100]

(2) Treaty Specific Report

The treaty specific report contains information relevant for the respective oversight committee. In this document, the state provides information on the specific regulations enshrined in the treaty. It is guided by recent guidelines issued by the respective committee as well as the Concluding Observations the committee delivered in the previous reporting cycle. Especially relevant is information on the implementation and the effects such implementation had on the ground. This report is supposed to provide a more focused and detailed insight into the status of the relevant rights in the particular state.[101] The treaty specific document should not exceed 40 pages.[102]

bb. Simplified Reporting Procedure

The reporting procedure within the Treaty Body System of the UN was subject to further change in the last decade. Especially due to the amount of treaties that were concluded since the first treaty in 1965, the Treaty Bodies became increasingly aware of the difficulties the practiced reporting cycle presented. Following a long period of efforts to reform the system,[103] they eventually adopted a simplified procedure which can be used by states instead of subjecting themselves to the previously described standard

---

98   *Ibid*, paras 40 ff.
99   *Ibid*, paras 50 ff.
100 *Ibid*, para 19.
101 *Ibid*, para 60.
102 *Ibid*, para 19.
103 The whole reform process is explained in greater detail in Part Two, Chapter 2 of this thesis.

II. State Reporting Obligations and their Procedures

procedure.[104] The Committee Against Torture first introduced a procedure in which the periodic report shall be replaced by a reply to a list of issues sent by the committee.[105] The Human Rights Committee adopted the same procedure including revised reporting guidelines in 2010.[106] In 2019, it decided to adopt the procedure based on the list of issues prior to reporting, also referred to as 'simplified reporting procedure', as the standard procedure with the option for states to opt-out until 31 December 2019.[107]

The idea was to have states submit focused reports consisting of replies to a list of issues which would be compiled by the respective committee prior to reporting.[108] This procedure gives state parties the option to submit an answer to a list of issues instead of a comprehensive periodic report. It consists of two sections: one containing general information on the human rights situation and a second with answers to specific clustered questions based on information gained through previous engagements.[109] This shortens the reporting cycle by one step, eradicating the first comprehensive report to be submitted and starting the cycle with the actual 'second step'. The intention hereby was to facilitate the drafting process and better focus the result.[110] Today, the simplified reporting procedure is increasingly used and generally accepted as a positive change.[111]

---

104 Human Rights Committee, *Focused reports based on replies to lists of issues prior to reporting (LOIPR): Implementation of the new optional reporting procedure (LOIPR procedure)*, UN Doc. CCPR/C/99/4, 29 September 2010.
105 UN General Assembly, *Report of the Committee against Torture*, UN Doc. A/64/44, Supp. (No. 44), 28 September 2009, para 20.
106 Human Rights Committee, *Focused reports based on replies to lists of issues prior to reporting (LOIPR): Implementation of the new optional reporting procedure (LOIPR procedure)*, UN Doc. CCPR/C/99/4, 29 September 2010.
107 Human Rights Committee, *Decision on additional measures to simplify the reporting procedure and increase predictability*, 1–26 July 2019 (will be reflected in the Committee's annual report (UN Doc. A/75/40, to be issued in 2020), accessible: <https://www.ohchr.org/EN/HRBodies/CCPR/Pages/PredictableReviewCycle.aspx> [accessed 02 December 2019].
108 Human Rights Committee, *Focused reports based on replies to lists of issues prior to reporting (LOIPR): Implementation of the new optional reporting procedure (LOIPR procedure)*, UN Doc. CCPR/C/99/4, 29 September 2010, para 1.
109 *Ibid*, paras 11 f.
110 *Ibid*, paras 2 f.; also in Human Rights Committee, *Simplified reporting procedure*, Report of the Working Group, UN Doc. CCPR/C/123/3, 6 December 2018, Summary; UN General Assembly, *Strengthening and enhancing the effective functioning of the human rights treaty body system*, UN Doc. A/Res/68/268, 21 April 2014, operative clause 4
111 For a comprehensive assessment of the simplified reporting procedure see Human Rights Committee, *Simplified reporting procedure*, Report of the Working Group, UN Doc. CCPR/C/123/3, 6 December 2018, Summary; UN General Assembly, *Strengthening and enhancing the effective functioning of the human rights treaty body system*, UN Doc. A/Res/68/268, 21 April 2014, operative clause 1.

Chapter 1: The State Reporting Obligation

2. Regional Human Rights Systems and the State Reporting Obligation

In addition to the reporting obligations of the UN Treaty Bodies, there are a number of regional human rights instruments which contain a similar reporting obligation. Reports submitted in compliance with those instruments are considered by regional oversight committees. The cooperation between international and regional committees is increasingly described as desirable;[112] however, true cooperative relationships are not yet visible.

a. European Human Rights System

The main institution of human rights protection in Europe is the European Court of Human Rights.[113] The individual complaints procedure as provided under the Convention for the Protection of Human Rights and Fundamental Freedoms[114] is a widely used and accepted way to protect the rights of the individual within the scope of its application. Nevertheless, some treaties take recourse to the preventive rather than regressive measure of monitoring through State Reporting.

aa. Provisions that Prescribe State Reporting

Compliance with the European human rights system today is for the most part enshrined in the Convention for the Protection of Human Rights and Fundamental Freedoms[115] and monitored by the European Court of Human Rights.[116] Neither the Convention nor one of its Protocols today contain a reporting obligation for state parties. However, the human rights system evolved under the Council of Europe and established a few treaties that contain reporting obligations. Those are Art. 21, 22 European Social

---

112 Dublin II Meeting, *Strengthening the United Nations Human Rights Treaty Body System*, Outcome Document, 10–11 November 2011, <https://www.ohchr.org/EN/HRBodies/HRTD/Pages/Documents.aspx> [accessed 02 December 2019], para 31.
113 This thesis excludes the laws and regulations of the European Union and focuses on Europe in the sense of the regulations by the Council of Europe due to its comparability to the other human rights systems examined in this thesis. The inclusion of the Law of the European Union would exceed the scope of this thesis.
114 Art. 34 Convention for the Protection of Human Rights and Fundamental Freedoms (as amended by Protocols No. 11 and No. 14, 1 June 2010), 4 November 1950, CETS No. 005
115 Convention for the Protection of Human Rights and Fundamental Freedoms, 4 November 1950, CETS No. 005.
116 For an overview, see de Schutter, 983 ff.

II. State Reporting Obligations and their Procedures

Charter[117], Art. 79 European Code of Social Security[118], and Art. 74 of its Protocol[119], Art. 15 European Charter for Regional or Minority Languages[120], Art. 25 Framework Convention for the Protection of National Minorities[121] and Art. 68 Convention on Preventing and Combating Violence against Women and Domestic Violence[122].

The **European Social Charter** requires state parties to report annually (before 2007 biennial) to the European Committee of Social Rights to monitor the implementation of the rights in the Charter. Reporting is split in core provisions (to be reported on in even years) and half of the remaining provisions in uneven years, respectively.[123]

States party to the **European Code of Social Security** are required to submit annually a report to the Secretary General (of the Council of Europe, Art. 1 (1) (c)) on the laws and regulations covering the implementation as well as evidence concerning specific regulations.[124]

Under the **Charter for Regional or Minority Languages**, state parties submit periodic reports to the Committee of Ministers on the implementation of and hereby compliance with the Charter.[125]

The **Framework Convention for the Protection of National Minorities** obliges States to submit an initial report on the measures taken to implement the Convention within one year of the entry into force for the respective state and hereinafter periodical reports or reports upon request to the Secretary General of the Council of Europe (Art. 25 (1), (2)), who then transfers the reports to the Committee of Ministers for consideration (Art. 25 (3)). The Committee is assisted by an Advisory Committee, Art. 26.

The implementation of the **Convention on Preventing and Combating Violence against Women and Domestic Violence** is monitored by a Group of Experts on Action against Violence against Women and Domestic Violence (GREVIO) established

---

117 European Social Charta, 18 October 1961, CETS No. 035; the supervision by reporting remained unchanged by the Charters' revision in 1996, see Part. IV Art. C European Social Charter (Revised), 3 May 1996, CETS No. 163.
118 European Code of Social Security, 16 April 1964, CETS No.048; the Revised European Code of Social Security (European Code of Social Security (revised), 6 November 1990, CETS No. 139)] still needs two ratifications to enter into force.
119 Protocol to the European Code of Social Security, 16 April 1964, CETS No. 48A.
120 European Charter for Regional or Minority Languages, 5 November 1998, CETS No.148.
121 Framework Convention for the Protection of National Minorities, 1 February 1995, CETS No. 157.
122 Council of Europe Convention on preventing and combating violence against women and domestic violence, 11 May 2011, CETS No.210.
123 Shelton, *Regional Protection of Human Rights* (2008), 96.
124 Article 74 European Code of Social Security.
125 Shelton, *Regional Protection of Human Rights* (2008), 99 f.

under Art. 66 (1). GREVIO prepares a questionnaire the answer to which is considered a report by the state parties (Article 68). The periodicity and length of this monitoring ('evaluation') procedure is determined by GREVIO (Art. 68 (2)).

bb. Procedure of State Reporting in Europe

Reporting in the European human rights system is more focused on the written submissions of the state parties.

Under the **European Social Charter**, the procedure was changed in 2006 from a comprehensive biennial reporting to annual reports on a specific thematic group.[126] The change in the procedure did not follow a change of treaty, but rather a decision taken by the Committee of Ministers.[127] Procedural steps after the submission of the report by the state are: (1) the report is reviewed by the European Committee of Social Rights[128]. (2) Following review, the Committee of Social Rights will draft conclusions on the status of the state party and the progress of implementation. (3) The reports and the conclusions are transferred to a Governmental Committee. (4) The Committee of Ministers closes the review with a resolution in which it may recommend further action to be taken by the state party.[129] Unlike with reporting to the UN Treaty Bodies, there is no constructive dialogue with the reporting state party.

The supervisory procedure under the **Code of Social Security** and its Protocol (as well as under the Revised Code, as soon as it enters into force[130]) requires a report by the respective state party which is examined by the Governmental Committee of the European Social Charter and the European Code of Social Security. This Governmental

---

126 Committee of Ministers of the Council of Europe, Decision of the Committee of Ministers, European Social Charter, Governmental Committee of the European Social Charter, *New system for the presentation of reports on the application of the European Social Charter, Proposal of the Governmental Committee*, CoE Doc. CM/Del/Dec(2006)963/4.2, 3 May 2006.
127 Tomuschat, 216.
128 15 independent experts elected by the Council of Europe's Committee of Ministers. For more information visit European Committee of Social Rights, Homepage of the European Committee of Social Rights, <https://www.coe.int/en/web/european-social-charter/european-committee-of-social-rights> [accessed 02 December 2019].
129 For more information visit the Homepage of the Council of Europe, Homepage, European Social Charter, Reporting system of the European Social Charter, <https://www.coe.int/en/web/european-social-charter/national-reports> [accessed 02 December 2019].
130 European Code of Social Security (revised), 6 November 1990, CETS No. 139; two ratifications are missing until it will enter into force (Homepage Council of Europe, Details of Treaty No. 139, European Code of Social Security (Revised), <https://www.coe.int/en/web/conventions/full-list/-/conventions/treaty/139> [accessed 02 December 2019]).

II. State Reporting Obligations and their Procedures

Committee reports to the Committee of Ministers, which then decides whether the state party is in compliance with the rights and standards of the respective treaties.[131]

Under the **Charter for Regional or Minority Languages** a new procedure is in place since 1 July 2019.[132] State parties shall submit to the Secretary General of the Council of Europe every five years a comprehensive and every two and a half years a mid-cycle report on the measures taken to implement the Charter. This report then is examined by the Committee of Ministers, which, if necessary, asks follow-up questions. The Committee will visit the state party, talk to members of the civil society for additional information and will then draft an evaluation report including recommendations for that state. The evaluation report may be made public.[133]

Under the **Framework Convention for the Protection of National Minorities**, reporting is conducted in four different cycles. In the first cycle, the state is obliged to submit an initial report, consisting of a general part (as a basis) and a specific part following the individual provisions of the Convention.[134] The second[135], third[136] and fourth[137] cycle request information on the further implementation in greater detail.

The **Council of Europe Convention on Preventing and Combating Violence against Women and Domestic Violence** has a short procedure consisting of questionnaires

---

131 See Homepage Council of Europe, European Social Charter, Reporting procedure of the European Code of Social Security, <https://www.coe.int/en/web/european-social-charter/reporting-procedure> [accessed 02 December 2019].

132 Committee of Ministers of the Council of Europe, Decision of the Committee of Ministers, *10.4 European Charter for Regional or Minority Languages, e. Strengthening the monitoring mechanism of the European Charter for Regional or Minority Language*, 28 November 2018, CoE Doc. CM/Del/Dec(2018)1330/10.4e.

133 Rule 17, 18 Committee of Experts of the European Charter for Regional or Minority languages, *Rules of Procedure of the Committee of Experts of the European Charter for Regional or Minority languages*, 2001 (most recently modified 18 March 2019), MIN-LANG (2019) 7, <https://rm.coe.int/minlang-2019-07-comex-rules-of-procedure-final/1680954878> [accessed 02 December 2019].

134 Committee of Ministers of the Council of Europe, *Outline for Reports to be submitted pursuant to Article 25 Paragraph 1 of the Framework Convention for the Protection of National Minorities*, 30 September 1998, CoE Doc. ACFC/INF(98)1, paras 1 ff.

135 Advisory Committee on the Framework Convention for the Protection of National Minorities, *Outline for State Reports to be submitted under the second monitoring Cycle, in conformity with Article 25 Paragraph 1 of the Framework Convention for the Protection of National Minorities*, 15 January 2003, CoE Doc. ACFC/INF(2003)001.

136 Committee of Ministers of the Council of Europe, *Outline for the State Reports to be submitted under the third monitoring Cycle, in conformity with Article 25 Paragraph 1 of the Framework Convention for the Protection of National Minorities*, 11 June 2008, CoE Doc. ACFC/III(2008)001.

137 Committee of Ministers of the Council of Europe, *Outline for the State Reports to be submitted under the fourth monitoring Cycle, in conformity with Article 25 Paragraph 1 of the Framework Convention for the Protection of National Minorities*, 30 April 2013, CoE Doc. ACFC/III(2013)001.

sent to the state parties by the Group of Experts on Action against Violence against Women and Domestic Violence (GREVIO), the reply to which is the report of the state party.[138] After the initial report, the procedure is split into rounds which are determined by GREVIO. Each round is only concerned with specific provisions. Additional information can be collected from civil society and country visits. Finally, GREVIO drafts a report and conclusions, which are sent to the state party and made public.[139]

b. Inter-American Human Rights System

The Inter-American human rights system monitors compliance mainly through the Inter-American Court of Human Rights, the judicial institution of the Inter-American human rights system, mandated to give advisory opinions (Art. 64 American Convention on Human Rights[140] [ACHR]) as well as to hear and decide on violations of individual human rights by states (Art. 61, 63 ACHR), and the Inter-American Commission on Human Rights, which is mandated to entertain individual petitions (Art. 44 ACHR) and generally monitor the human rights situation in the member states (Art. 41 ACHR). Hence, monitoring the implementation and compliance with the rights enshrined in the relevant documents for the most part is done by the commission and the court.

aa. Provisions that Prescribe State Reporting

Despite relying mainly on the work of the Inter-American Commission on Human Rights and the Inter-American Court of Human Rights, some treaties in this regional system additionally use the state reporting procedure to monitor compliance. Specifically, those are Art. 19 Additional Protocol to the American Convention on Human Rights in the Area of Economic, Social and Cultural Rights ('Protocol of San Salvador')[141], Art. 10 Convention on the Prevention, Punishment and Eradication of Violence

---

138   Art. 68 (1) of the Council of Europe Convention on Preventing and Combating Violence against Women and Domestic Violence; Group of Experts on Action against Violence against Women and Domestic Violence (GREVIO), *Questionnaire on legislative and other measures giving effect to the provisions of the Council of Europe Convention on Preventing and Combating Violence against Women and Domestic Violence (Istanbul Convention)*, 11 March 2016, GREVIO/Inf(2016), 4 f.
139   The whole procedure is prescribed in Article 68 of the Council of Europe Convention on preventing and combating violence against women and domestic violence.
140   American Convention on Human Rights ('Pact of San Jose, Costa Rica'), 22 November 1969, OAS Treaty Series, No. 36.
141   Additional Protocol to the American Convention on Human Rights in the Area of Economic, Social and Cultural Rights ('Protocol of San Salvador'), 17 November 1988, OAS Treaty Series No. 69.

against Women ('Convention Belem do Para')[142], Art. 15 (v) Convention against Racism, Racial Discrimination and Related Forms of Intolerance[143], Art. 35 Convention on Protecting the Human Rights of Older Persons[144] and Art. VI Convention on the Elimination of All Forms of Discrimination against Persons with Disabilities[145].

The **Additional Protocol to the American Convention on Human Rights in the Area of Economic, Social and Cultural Rights** establishes in its Art. 19 (1)-(5) the obligation to periodically report on the measures taken to ensure due respect for the provisions in the protocol. State parties shall submit the report to the Secretary General of the Organization of American States (OAS) who then shall distribute it not only to the Inter-American Economic and Social Council and the Inter-American Council for Education, Science and Culture but also (as copies) to further specialized entities the state party in question is a member to. The information so received shall be summarized by the Inter-American Economic and Social Council and the Inter-American Council for Education, Science and Culture and included in their annual report to the General Assembly of the OAS.[146]

The **Convention on the Prevention, Punishment and Eradication of Violence against Women** obliges the state parties in its Article 10 to submit national reports on the measures taken to implement the Convention as well as on the difficulties the state was facing while applying those measures. The national reports requested shall be interconnected with the national reports a state shall submit to the Inter-American Commission of Women. The Convention remains silent on the periodicity of such reports.[147]

The **Convention against Racism, Racial Discrimination and Related Forms of Intolerance** requests the state parties to submit an initial report to the Inter-American Committee for the Prevention and Elimination of Racism, Racial Discrimination, and All Forms of Discrimination and Intolerance, established under Art. 15 (iv) of the Convention, within one year of the Committee's first meeting. Subsequently, a periodic report must be submitted every four years. Those reports shall serve the purpose of the

---

142 Inter-American Convention on the Prevention, Punishment and Eradication of Violence against Women ('Convention of Belem do Para'), 9 June 1994, OAS Treaty No. A-61, 33 I. L. M. 1534 (1994).
143 Inter-American Convention against Racism, Racial Discrimination and related forms of Intolerance, 5 June 2013, OAS Treaty No. A-68.
144 Inter-American Convention on Protecting the Human Rights of Older Persons, 15 June 2015, OAS Treaty No. A-70.
145 Convention on the Elimination of All Forms of Discrimination against Persons with Disabilities, 8 June 1999, OAS Doc. A-65.
146 Article 19 (1)-(5) Additional Protocol to the American Convention on Human Rights in the Area of Economic, Social and Cultural Rights ('Protocol of San Salvador').
147 Art. 10 Convention on the Prevention, Punishment and Eradication of Violence against Women.

Committee so established, namely, to exchange ideas and experiences, examine the progress of implementation and recommend measures to increase compliance.[148]

In its Article 35 the **Convention on Protecting the Human Rights of Older Persons** established the Committee of Experts as the oversight committee to the Convention. One of the Committee's functions is the monitoring of the implementation of the Convention through a technical review of state reports to be submitted by the state parties. An initial report is required within one year of the first meeting of the Committee, followed by reports of a periodicity of four years.[149]

The **Convention on the Elimination of All Forms of Discrimination against Persons with Disabilities** establishes in its Article VI the Committee for the Elimination of All Forms of Discrimination against Persons with Disabilities. Said Committee is mandated with the monitoring of the implementation of the rights enshrined in the Convention by the states. According to its Art. VI. (3), states are required to submit an initial report to the Secretary General of the OAS for the first meeting of the oversight committee. Hereinafter, there are obligatory reports in a periodicity of four years. The reports shall contain information on the measures taken pursuant to the Convention and generally to eradicate discrimination based on disability as well as difficulties with the fulfillment of the rights enshrined in the Convention.[150]

bb. Procedure of State Reporting in the Americas

The **Protocol of San Salvador** requires state parties to submit an initial report one year after the Protocol's entry into force. Subsequently, a report shall be submitted every three years to the Secretary General of the OAS, who will forward them to the Inter-American Council for Integral Development for examination and a copy to the Inter-American Commission on Human Rights.[151] Within the framework of the Inter-American Council for Integral Development a Working Group for the examination of state reports is established.[152] It is prescribed that the reports submitted shall be examined by said Working Group.[153] Examination shall start within 60 days of receipt. The

---

148 Art. 15(v) Convention against Racism, Racial Discrimination and Related Forms of Intolerance.
149 Art. 35 Convention on Protecting the Human Rights of Older Persons.
150 Article VI (4) Convention on the Elimination of All Forms of Discrimination against Persons with Disabilities.
151 Article 19 (1)-(5) Additional Protocol to the American Convention on Human Rights in the Area of Economic, Social and Cultural Rights ('Protocol of San Salvador').
152 Organization of American States [OAS] General Assembly, *Protocol of San Salvador: Composition and Functioning of the Working Group to examine the Periodic Reports of States Parties*, OAS Doc. AG/RES. 2262 (XXXVII-O/07), 5 June 2007.
153 OAS General Assembly, *Protocol of San Salvador: Composition and Functioning of the Working Group to examine the Periodic Reports of the States Parties*, OAS Doc. AG/Res. 2506, (XXXIX-O/09), 4 June 2009.

II. State Reporting Obligations and their Procedures

Working Group may take into account any other information deemed relevant. After examination, preliminary conclusions shall be presented to the state party, which then has 60 days to comment on those conclusions for further analysis. Subsequently, the Working Group adopts final conclusions, of which the state party is notified.[154] With Resolution 2506 (XXXIX-O/09), the General Assembly of the OAS initiated the activities of the Working Group.[155]

Under the **Convention on the Prevention, Punishment and Eradication of Violence against Women** the reports are reviewed by the Committee of Experts who prepare and circulate the relevant questionnaire for the state parties, evaluate the responses in working groups, produce recommendations for the state parties and take care of the follow-up mechanism (Follow-up Mechanism to the Belém do Pará Convention [MESCEVI]).[156] The Committee is supported by a Technical Secretariat.[157] The MESCEVI procedure was established in 2004[158] as a specific procedure for this Convention. Contrary to the wording of Art. 10 there is no information on a reporting mechanism to the Inter-American Commission of Women[159], which is why it is considered as an independent procedure.[160]

No information on the procedure under the **Convention against Racism, Racial Discrimination and Related Forms of Intolerance**, the **Convention on Protecting the Human Rights of Older Persons** and the **Convention on the Elimination of**

---

154 OAS General Assembly, *Standards for the Preparation of the Periodic Reports Pursuant to Article 19 of the Protocol of San Salvador*, 7 June 2005, approved by OAS Doc. AG/RES. 2074 (XXXV-O/05), paras 9 ff.
155 OAS General Assembly, *Protocol of San Salvador: Composition and Functioning of the Working Group to examine the Periodic Reports of the States Parties*, OAS Doc. AG/Res. 2506, (XXXIX-O/09), 4 June 2009, para 2.
156 See Homepage of the OAS, Committee of Experts, <http://www.oas.org/en/mesecvi/experts.asp> [accessed 02 December 2019].
157 See Homepage of the OAS, MESECVI Secretariat, <http://www.oas.org/en/mesecvi/secretariat.asp> [accessed 02 December 2019].
158 See OAS, *Mechanism to Follow Up on Implementation of the Inter-American Convention on the Prevention, Punishment, and Eradication of Violence Against Women*, 'Convention of Belém do Pará', OAS Doc. AG/Res. 2162 (XXXVI-O/06), 6 June 2006.
159 See Homepage of the Inter-American Commission of Women, CIM Mission and Mandate: <https://www.oas.org/en/cim/about.asp> [accessed 02 December 2019].
160 It is also described as an independent procedure in OAS (Conference of States Parties), *Mechanism to Follow Up on the Implementation of the Inter-American Convention on the Prevention, Punishment and Eradication of Violence against Women 'Convention of Belém do Pará'-MESECVI (First Hemispheric Report)*, First Multilateral Evaluation Round: Second Conference of States Parties, Caracas, Venezuela 9–10 July 2008, accessible: <http://www.oas.org/en/mesecvi/library.asp> [accessed 02 December 2019], 5.

All Forms of Discrimination against Persons with Disabilities but for what is prescribed in the respective articles[161] was accessible while writing this thesis.

c. African Human Rights System

The African human rights system consists of the African Commission on Human and Peoples' Rights as well as the African Court on Human and Peoples' Rights as institutions and a growing number of human rights treaties that are monitored by these institutions. Contrary to the previous systems, the African system relies for the most part on monitoring through state reporting.[162]

aa. Provisions that Prescribe State Reporting

The African Charter on Human and People's Rights, adopted in 1981 and entered into force in 1986, is the basis and the main document of the African human rights system. Various human rights treaties followed its adoption, which further concretized the protection framework of human rights. The reporting system is the main method of supervision under the African Charter of Human Rights.[163] The majority of human rights treaties rely on reporting to monitor the compliance with the rights enshrined in their respective texts. Periodic state reporting is obligatory under Art. 62 African Charter on Human and People's Rights[164], Art. 26 of the Protocol to the African Charter on Human and People's Rights on the Rights of Women in Africa[165], Article 22 Protocol to the African Charter on Human and Peoples' Rights on the Rights of Older Persons in Africa[166], Art. 34 (1) of the Protocol to the African Charter on Human and Peoples' Rights on the Rights of Persons with Disabilities in Africa[167], Art. 43 of the African Charta on the Rights and Welfare of the Child[168], Art. 49 African Charter on Democracy, Elections

---

161 See *supra* Part Two, Chapter 1, II. 2. b. aa.
162 For a thorough assessment of the state reporting obligations of the Banjul-Charta, the Maputo Protocol and the African Charta on the Rights and Welfare of the Child see Lauer, *Die Implementierung menschenrechtlicher Verträge in Afrika* (2018), 127–169.
163 Smith, *Textbook on International Human Rights* (7th edn, 2003) [hereinafter Smith], 146.
164 African Charter on Human and People's Rights, 27 June 1981, OAU Doc. CAB/LEG/67/3 rev. 5, 21 I.L.M. 58 (1982).
165 Protocol to the African Charter on Human and Peoples' Rights on the Rights of Women in Africa, 13 September 2000, CAB/LEG/66.6; reprinted in 1 African Human Rights Law Journal 40.
166 Protocol to the African Charter on Human and Peoples' Rights on the Rights of older Persons in Africa, 31 January 2016, reprinted in 22 African Yearbook of International Law Online 269.
167 Protocol to the African Charter on Human and Peoples' Rights on the Rights of Persons with Disabilities in Africa, 29 January 2018, <https://au.int/en/treaties/protocol-african-charter-human-and-peoples-rights-rights-persons-disabilities-africa> [accessed 02 December 2019].
168 African Charter on the Rights and Welfare of the Child, 1 July 1990, OAU Doc. CAB/LEG/24.9/49 (1990).

II. State Reporting Obligations and their Procedures

and Governance[169], Art. 14 of the African Union Convention for the Protection and Assistance of Internally Displaced Persons in Africa (Kampala Convention)[170], Art. 19 of the African Charter on the Values and Principles of Decentralisation, Local Governance and Local Development[171]. Art. 22 (7) of the African Union Convention on Preventing and Combating Corruption[172] is based on the idea of state reporting but prescribes a slightly different procedure[173]. For this reason it is not included in the following paragraphs.

Every state party to the **African Charter on Human and Peoples' Rights** is obliged under its Art. 62 to submit reports to the African Commission on Human and People's Rights.[174] The content of the report is substantiated by Rule 73 of the Rules of Procedure of the African Commission on Human and People's Rights.[175] The states are supposed to follow the Guidelines for National Periodic Reports.[176] Their reports shall contain information on the measures taken to give effect to the rights enshrined in the Charter as well as any difficulty arising from its implementation. If the African Commission considers a report to not contain adequate information, it can request additional information until a deadline specified by the Commission.[177] The reports under the African Charter on Human and Peoples' Rights are complemented by three Protocols. Depending on whether the respective state party is also party to the relevant Protocol, the reporting obligation is extended according to that Protocols' provision.

---

169 African Charter on Democracy, Elections and Governance, 30 January 2007, <https://au.int/en/treaties/african-charter-democracy-elections-and-governance> [accessed 02 December 2019].
170 African Union Convention for the Protection and Assistance of Internally Displaced Persons in Africa (Kampala Convention), 23 October 2009, UN Registration No. 52375.
171 African Charter on the Values and Principles of Decentralisation, Local Governance and Local Development, 27 June 2014, < https://au.int/en/treaties/african-charter-values-and-principles-decentralisation-local-governance-and-local> [accessed 02 December 2019].
172 African Union Convention on Preventing and Combating Corruption, 1 July 2003, <https://au.int/en/treaties/african-union-convention-preventing-and-combating-corruption> [accessed 02 December 2019].
173 States Parties shall communicate – without a prescribed form – to the board the progress of implementation. Hereinafter, the national authorities or agencies mandated with the execution of the Charter are obliged to report minimum once a year, see Article 22 (7) African Union Convention on Preventing and Combating Corruption.
174 For a comprehensive review of the state reporting procedure under the African Charter on Human and People's Rights see Gaer, 'First Fruits: Reporting by States under the African Charter on Human and Peoples' Rights' (1992) 10 NQHR 29.
175 African Commission on Human and People's Rights, *Rules of Procedure*, adopted 2–13 February 1988, revised 2–11 October 1995, approved 12–26 May 2010, <https://www.achpr.org/legalinstruments/detail?id=34> [accessed 02 December 2019].
176 Cf Lauer, *Die Implementierung menschenrechtlicher Verträge in Afrika* (2018), 131 ff. (with further information on the Guidelines for national periodic reports).
177 Shelton, *Regional Protection of Human Rights* (2008), 543 f.

Under the **Protocol to the African Charter on Human and People's Rights on the Rights of Women in Africa**, also called Women's Protocol or Maputo Protocol, reporting is obligatory according to its Art. 26. The reporting procedure under this Protocol is interconnected with the state reports to be submitted under the African Charter on Human and Peoples' Rights. The progress of the implementation of the rights enshrined in the Protocol shall be integrated in the state report to the African Commission. Therefore, the periodicity as well as the procedure is coupled with the state report under the African Charter on Human and People's Rights (*supra*).

Art. 22 **Protocol to the African Charter on Human and Peoples' Rights on the Rights of Older Persons in Africa** requires state parties to submit information on measures taken for the full realization of the rights enshrined in the Protocol. Such information shall be included in the report delivered on the African Charter on Human and Peoples' Rights. The same information and form are required under Art. 34 (1) of the **Protocol to the African Charter on Human and Peoples' Rights on the Rights of Persons with Disabilities** in Africa. Again, periodicity is the same as for the state report under the African Charter on Human and People's Rights (*supra*).

Furthermore, the report to the African Charter on Human and Peoples' Rights can be complemented by Art. 14 of the **African Union Convention for the Protection and Assistance of Internally Displaced Persons in Africa (Kampala Convention)**. Art. 14 prescribes that a state party shall include information on the relevant measures that give effect to the rights and obligations enshrined in this Convention.

Apart from the African Charter on Human and Peoples' Rights, other independent human rights treaties developed since its adoption. Despite their independence, those treaties also rely on the state reporting procedure as the main instrument of monitoring.

> The African Committee of Experts on the Rights and Welfare of the Child is the oversight committee to the **African Charter on the Rights and Welfare of the Child**. It was established under Art. 32 of the Charter and held the first meeting in 2002.[178] Under Art. 43 of the Charter of the Rights and Welfare of the Child, state parties are obliged to submit an initial report to the African Committee of Experts on the Rights and Welfare of the Child two years after the treaty entered into force for the respective state party and thereafter every three years. Basic information on the state given in the initial report does not have to be repeated in the periodic reports (Art. 43 (3)). The state report shall contain information on the implementation of the Charter within the country of such quality and quantity that the Committee can understand the

---

178 Heyns & Killander, 'Africa', in: Moeckli, Shah, Sivakumaran & Harri (eds), *International Human Rights Law*, (2ⁿᵈ edn, 2014), 441, 447.

progress of implementation as well as the difficulties with the fulfillment of such implementation (Art. 43 (2)).

The **African Charter on Democracy, Elections and Governance** obliges its state parties under Art. 49 to submit periodic reports on the measures taken to give effect to the Charter every two years after the Charter entered into force. Those reports shall be submitted to the African Commission (Art. 49 (1)). A copy of the report shall be forwarded to other relevant organs of the African Union concerned with the matters enshrined in the Charter (Art. 49 (2)).

Under Art. 19 of the **African Charter on the Values and Principles of Decentralisation, Local Governance and Local Development** a report on the measures supporting the implementation of the Charter is required every three years. The report shall be submitted to the African Union Commission (Art. 19 (1)).

bb. Procedure of State Reporting in Africa

Reporting in the African human rights system does not differ greatly from the general reporting procedure to the UN Treaty Bodies. State reports consist of an initial report containing basic information on the state party and subsequent periodic reports consisting of two parts: part one containing general information on the state and part two information on the individual provisions of the treaty.[179] But for the reports to be submitted under the African Charter on the Rights and Welfare of the Child[180], every report must be submitted to the African Commission. The procedural steps following submission of the report to the African Commission by the state party are as follows: (1) pursuant to receiving the report, the Secretariat (to the African Commission on Human and Peoples' Rights) publishes the document together with the date of examination following Rule 78 of the 2010 African Commissions' Rules of Procedure.[181] With this publication, members of civil society are invited to send their contributions for the examination.[182] The Secretariat of the African Commission then informs the respective

---

179 See for example General Guidelines on the African Charter and General Guidelines on the Maputo Protocol, both accessible at Homepage of the African Commission on Human and Peoples' Rights, State Reporting Procedures and Guidelines, <https://www.achpr.org/statereportingproceduresandguidelines> [accessed 02 December 2019].
180 The African Charter on the Rights and Welfare of the Child is monitored by the African Committee of Experts on the Rights and Welfare of the Child, Art. 32 African Charter on the Rights and Welfare of the Child.
181 African Commission on Human and People's Rights, *Rules of Procedure*, adopted 2–13 February 1988, revised 2–11 October 1995, approved 12–26 May 2010, <https://www.achpr.org/legalinstruments/detail?id=34> [accessed 02 December 2019].
182 'Rule 74: Transmission of State Reports: 1. Upon receipt of a State Report, the Secretary shall upload the Report on the Commission's website and indicate when the Report will be examined by

Chapter 1: The State Reporting Obligation

state party of the date and venue of its review. With this information the state receives the questions to be asked in the session. The state is supposed to send a capable representative who is prepared to answer the questions of the African Commission. Such questions are not restricted to the report but may also include content from, inter alia, shadow reports submitted by NGOs. The report is then examined in open session. The state party presents the report, subsequently the Commission will ask their questions. After this discussion, the rapporteur of the session (generally the Commissioner responsible for promotional activities in the country concerned[183]) wraps up and the session is closed by the Chairperson of the African Commission.[184] The examination of a report without a state representative is conducted after two unsuccessful notifications.[185] According the Rules of Procedure of the African Commission on Human and People's Rights, the Commission shall then draft Concluding Observations which shall be sent to the state party and be made publicly available (Rule 77). After the examination of a report, the African Commission on Human and Peoples' Rights decides whether it sends a follow-up letter to the relevant state party to request information on questions that were left unanswered or not to the satisfaction of the Commission.[186]

Under the **African Charter on the Rights and Welfare of the Child**, the procedure differs in two points from the procedure of the African Commission[187]: first, the reports are not published; rather, the relevant stakeholders are notified and invited to

---

the Commission. 2. Institutions, organizations or any interested party wishing to contribute to the examination of the Report and the human rights situation in the country concerned, shall send their contributions, including shadow reports, to the Secretary at least 60 days prior to the examination of the Report. 3. The Secretary may also invite specific institutions to submit information relating to the state report within a time limit that he/she may specify' (African Commission on Human and People's Rights, *Rules of Procedure*, adopted 2–13 February 1988, revised 2–11 October 1995, approved 12–26 May 2010, <https://www.achpr.org/legalinstruments/detail?id=34> [accessed 02 December 2019]).

183 Homepage of the African Commission on Human and Peoples' Rights, State Reporting Procedures and Guidelines, State Reporting Procedure, IV. Procedures adopted when examining State Reports, 1. Procedure at the Secretariat, <https://www.achpr.org/statereportingproceduresandguidelines> [accessed 26 November 2019].

184 *Ibid.*

185 Rule 74 (4) African Commission on Human and People's Rights, *Rules of Procedure*, adopted 2–13 February 1988, revised 2–11 October 1995, approved 12–26 May 2010, <https://www.achpr.org/legalinstruments/detail?id=34> [accessed 02 December 2019].

186 Homepage of the African Commission on Human and Peoples' Rights, State Reporting Procedures and Guidelines, State Reporting Procedure, IV. Procedures adopted when examining State Reports, 1. Follow-up, <https://www.achpr.org/statereportingproceduresandguidelines> [accessed 02 December 2019].

187 The procedure is prescribed in Chapter XIII, Rule 69–75 of the Revised Rules of Procedure of the African Committee of Experts on the Rights and Welfare of the Child, <https://www.acerwc.africa/working-documents/revised-rules-of-procedures-final/> [accessed 02 December 2019].

contribute.[188] Second, the follow-up on the implementation of Concluding Observations is considered as a core activity of the Committee and must be ensured within the framework of its promotional activities.[189]

d. Arabian Human Rights System

While the previously depicted regional human rights systems are rather well established, a slow evolution of comparable systems can similarly be observed in other parts of the world as well.[190] The League of Arab States is to be mentioned here as the most recently developed regional human rights system. The Council of the Arab League passed a first attempt on the Arab Charter on Human Rights in 1994. However, an insufficient number of states ratified this Charter, which is why it never entered into force.[191] After almost a decade of debates, a new version was drafted. It was signed and ratified by seven states and thereby entered into force in March 2008.[192]

In its Art. 48, the Charter prescribes the reporting obligation for its state parties. It requires a report on the measures taken to give effect to the rights and freedoms recognized in the Charter and the progress made in the enjoyment thereof (Art. 48 (1)). The initial report is due within one year of ratification, subsequent periodic reports every three years. Until June 2019, the Arab Human Rights Committee reviewed the reports of ten states.[193]

---

188 Rule 70 Revised Rules of Procedure of the African Committee of Experts on the Rights and Welfare of the Child, <https://www.acerwc.africa/working-documents/revised-rules-of-procedures-final/> [accessed 02 December 2019].
189 Rule 74 Revised Rules of Procedure of the African Committee of Experts on the Rights and Welfare of the Child, <https://www.acerwc.africa/working-documents/revised-rules-of-procedures-final/> [accessed 26 November 2019].
190 Most recent and prominent is the development of the Arabian Human Rights System. Neither in Asia nor in Oceania exists an established regional human rights system. The main difficulty hindering the development of such a system seems to be the lack of a common human rights understanding (Tomuschat, 39). The societies in those regions seem to be too diverse. However, the first step on the way for the establishment of an Asian regional human rights system seems to be done as on 18 November 2012 the ASEAN States adopted a (non-binding) Declaration on Human Rights (ASEAN Human Rights Declaration, 18 November 2012, <https://asean.org/asean-human-rights-declaration/> [accessed 02 December 2019]). The International Commission of Jurists condemned the Declaration as being fatally flawed and published a detailed booklet on why it fails to comply with international standards: International Commission of Jurists, *The Asean Human Rights Declaration: Questions and Answers*, 30 July 2013, <https://www.icj.org/all-what-you-need-to-know-about-the-asean-human-rights-declaration/> [accessed 27 November 2019].
191 Tomuschat, 39.
192 League of Arab States, *Arab Charter on Human Rights*, 22 May 2004, reprinted in 12 International Human Rights Report 893 (2005).
193 Homepage of the League of Arab States, <http://www.lasportal.org/ar/humanrights/Committee/Pages/Reports.aspx> [accessed 12.06.2020].

Furthermore, a reporting obligation is established by Art. 50 of the Charter of the Rights of the Arab Child. There are no further specifications and the reports are not publicly available.

3. Conclusion

Multiple treaties in the sphere of the UN as well as in the individual regional human rights systems use the state reporting obligation to monitor the implementation of the rights enshrined in the respective charters. The procedures of the individual treaties differ slightly from each other; yet, they are based on the same idea of self-evaluation and dialogue. While some treaties request comprehensive reports (such as those under the UN and the African system) an increasing number of treaties take recourse to questionnaires and replies as well as clustered reviews to simplify the procedure and thereby increase effectiveness. Some systems, especially the Inter-American human rights treaties, refer to the treaties and reporting obligation in the UN sphere with the aim to establish a harmonized procedure for coherence in reporting, implementation and protection of human rights.[194] Such coherence can be achieved by a complementary and integrative application of the different provisions.[195]

III. What is the Content, Purpose and Nature of the State Reporting Obligation?

To fully understand the system of state reporting and its extensive usage as a monitoring instrument, the obligation itself needs to be evaluated. In order to uncover those parts which might be relevant for the constant challenges the system is facing, a closer look into the content, the object and purpose as well as the legal nature of the state reporting obligation is necessary.

1. Content of the State Reporting Obligation in Relation to the Written Report

The state reporting obligation in its wording is not entirely explicit on its actual content.[196] Without the content, however, the scope of the obligation and possible violations of international law cannot be ascertained. Although the Treaty Bodies provided

---

194 See for example Inter-American Commission on Human Rights, *Guidelines for Preparation of Progress Indicators in the Area of Economic, Social and Cultural Rights*, OAS Doc. OEA/Ser.L/V/II.132, Doc. 14, 19 July 2008, para 13.
195 An integrative approach is examined in greater detail in Part Two, Chapter 3, I. of this thesis.
196 See also Oette, 'The UN Human Rights Treaty Bodies: Impact and Future', 101.

III. What is the Content, Purpose and Nature of the State Reporting Obligation?

some clarification on the content of their respective obligation,[197] the exact common content of the state reporting obligation as an international monitoring instrument is yet to be determined. This interpretation is conducted in the following.

The reporting obligation needs to be interpreted in view of the question whether the recognized challenges to the system are actually encompassed by the scope of the provision and whether those challenges are of a legal nature. The content and legal nature of the state reporting obligation then can be used to create an appropriate proposal for improvement.

Rules of treaty interpretation in public international law can be found in Art. 31 of the Vienna Convention on the Law of Treaties[198] (VCLT) which largely reflects customary international law.[199] Therefore, the rules of interpretation which reflect the underlying custom can be used even if a state is not party to the VCLT and even if a treaty was concluded and entered into force before the VCLT.[200] According to Art. 31 (1), a treaty shall be interpreted in good faith in accordance with the ordinary meaning of the terms in the treaty text, the context and its object and purpose.

To identify the content of the state reporting obligation, every norm establishing it would have to be interpreted individually. However, the interpretation of every individual norm containing the state reporting obligation would exceed the scope of this thesis. Therefore, one norm shall be interpreted exemplarily.

As can be seen from the different texts of the norm, generally, all relevant treaties use very comparable language for the norm establishing the reporting obligation. What is common to the wording of every norm establishing the reporting obligation is the vague content of the report, the oversight committee to whom the report must be submitted as well as the periodicity of the submission, be it with an exact timeframe or without. Those common denominators can clearly be seen in for example the wording

---

197 For example Human Rights Committee, *Consolidated Guidelines for State Reports under the International Covenant on Civil and Political Rights*, UN Doc. CCPR/C/66/GUI/Rev.2, 26 February 2001.
198 Vienna Convention on the Law of Treaties [VCLT], adopted 22 May 1969, 115 UNTS 331.
199 ICJ, *Arbitral Award of 31 July 1989*, Judgment, 1991, ICJ Rep 53, para 48; ICJ, *Kasikili/Sedudu Island (Botswana/Namibia)*, Judgment, ICJ Rep 1999, 1045, para 18; Dörr, in Dörr & Schmalenbach (eds), *Vienna Convention on the Law of Treaties – A Commentary* (2nd edn, 2018)[hereinafter *VCLT Commentary*], Art. 31, para 6.
200 Dörr, in Dörr & Schmalenbach (eds), *VCLT Commentary*, Art. 31, para 7; generally, according to Art. 26 VCLT, the rules of the VCLT '[…] do not bind a party in relation to any act or fact which took place or any situation which ceased to exist before the date of the entry into force of the treaty with respect to that party.' (Art. 26 VCLT).

of Art. 18 of the Convention on the Elimination of All Forms of Discrimination against Women (CEDAW).[201]

Art. 18 CEDAW reads as follows:

> '1. States Parties undertake to submit to the Secretary-General of the United Nations, for consideration by the Committee, a report on the legislative, judicial, administrative or other measures which they have adopted to give effect to the provisions of the present Convention and on the progress made in this respect:
>
> (a) Within one year after the entry into force for the State concerned;
>
> (b) Thereafter at least every four years and further whenever the Committee so requests.
>
> 2. Reports may indicate factors and difficulties affecting the degree of fulfilment of obligations under the present Convention.'[202]

The wording of Art. 18 CEDAW can be found in a more or less detailed manner in every norm establishing a state reporting obligation. CEDAW is almost universally accepted with 189 parties to it and one of its authentic languages is English. It is broad enough to include the more specific regulations and is on a comparable level with the other norms using a broad wording. Hence, Art. 18 CEDAW shall be interpreted as an example for the state reporting obligations. Consequently, findings from the interpretation of Art. 18 CEDAW are transferable to every state reporting obligation.

Art. 18 CEDAW obliges state parties in its subsection (1) to submit a report to the Secretary-General of the UN *first*, within one year after the entry into force for the respective State, *second*, following the initial report, in a four year periodicity and *third*, upon request of the Committee on the Elimination of Discrimination against Women. The periodic report has to contain information on legislative measures, judicial measures, administrative measures and other, not further specified measures which were implemented in relation to the Convention with the aim to give effect to its provisions. Furthermore, the reports have to contain information on the progress of implementation, indicating that information has to be given on improvements since the previous report. Subsection (2) further specifies that the reports may provide information on problems hindering the progress of implementation of the obligations under the Convention. The inclusion of such problems is not obligatory, as the word 'may' indicates. The wording

---

201 CEDAW, 18 December 1979, 1249 UNTS 13.
202 Art. 18 CEDAW.

III. What is the Content, Purpose and Nature of the State Reporting Obligation?

therefore indicates that the provision entails the obligation to submit a report and to submit it within a not further specified time frame.[203]

Context-wise, Art. 18 CEDAW is embedded in Part V of the Convention (Art. 17 ff.) which contains provisions on the establishment, mandate and functioning of the Committee on the Elimination of Discrimination against Women. Art. 17 CEDAW describes the process of the election of the Committee members and the overall composition of the Committee. Art. 19 CEDAW deals with rules of procedure, Art. 20 CEDAW with time and place of the Committee meetings. None of those provisions contains further information on the content of the reporting obligation. According to Art. 31 (2) and (3) VCLT the context further comprises the preamble, annexes, agreements (either relating to the treaty or the interpretation and application), subsequent practice in application of the treaty and any relevant rule of international law applicable in the relations between the parties. The preamble emphasizes the importance of the eradication of discrimination against women by recurring to the historical development, the rights being violated by such discrimination and the great contributions by women to the society. While those are important aspects and fundamental to the treaty, they do not provide further information on the content of the reporting obligation. Further information on the reports of state parties under Art. 18 CEDAW can be found in Rule 48 ff. of the Rules of Procedure of the Committee on Elimination of Discrimination against Women.[204] Even though the wording of Art. 31 (2) and (3) VCLT would not include those Rules because they were not adopted by the state parties,[205] they have to be taken into account as practice of the relevant organization.[206] Yet, interpreting Art. 18 CEDAW in light of the Rules of Procedure, the quality of the report is still not addressed. The Rules of Procedure regulate the processing of the reports submitted and, in Rule 49, the procedure if a state did not submit or did submit late. There is no further detail on the relevance of the quality of a report.

Finally, a norm must be interpreted according to its object and purpose. This element of interpretation must not be seen independently of the context and wording of the

---

203 In comparison: the Committee of Experts of the European Charter for Regional and Minority Languages accepts a delay of twelve months, see Rule 17 (7) Committee of Experts of the European Charter for Regional or Minority languages, *Rules of Procedure of the Committee of Experts of the European Charter for Regional or Minority languages*, 2001 (most recently modified 18 March 2019), MIN-LANG (2019) 7, <https://rm.coe.int/minlang-2019-07-comex-rules-of-procedure-final/1680954878> [accessed 02 December 2019].
204 UN Secretariat, *International Human Rights Documents, Compilation of rules of procedure adopted by Human Rights treaty bodies*, UN Doc. HRI/GEN/3/Rev.3, 28 May 2008, 93–126, 110 ff.
205 For a detailed explanation on which subsequent agreement may be regarded during interpretation see Dörr, in Dörr & Schmalenbach (eds), *VCLT Commentary*, Art. 31, paras 72 ff.
206 On the importance of subsequent practice see Dörr, in Dörr & Schmalenbach (eds), *VCLT Commentary*, Art. 31, paras 77 ff.

treaty or norm, but rather as intrinsic to the text. It can only be used to clarify the meaning of the norm.[207] The object and purpose of CEDAW is the elimination of all forms of discrimination against women and the recognition and achievement of equality of women and men.[208] To effectively protect women, a minimum degree of oversight is needed. This oversight is conducted by the Committee, which uses the instrument of state reporting. Therefore, the object and purpose of Art. 18 CEDAW is to establish said minimum oversight possibility. To monitor the effective protection of the rights of women within a country the Committee must have access to information that reflect the actual situation within the relevant country. If the information is missing, late or insufficient, the Committee cannot fulfill its mandate. If the Committee is unable to effectively monitor the situation within a country, the object and purpose of the state reporting procedure cannot be fulfilled. This interpretation is neither in contrast to the context nor the wording. The wording is not exhaustive in the sense that only submission is relevant. Concerning the context, especially considering the preamble, which strives for the eradication of discrimination against women, the quality of a report falls well within the scope of the interpretative possibilities. This conclusion can be backed up with a view to the Convention on the Rights of the Child, established to protect another vulnerable group, following a comparable object and purpose, which in its Article 44(2) requests reports that contain 'sufficient information to provide the Committee with a comprehensive understanding of the implementation of the Convention in the Country concerned'[209].

In conclusion, according to the object and purpose, a report, which does not contain sufficient information for the Committee to make an informed decision on the situation in the country contravenes Art. 18 CEDAW.[210]

Based on the foregoing, the obligation enshrined in Art. 18 CEDAW is fulfilled when a state party submits a report on the implementation of the rights enshrined in the respective treaty on time and with such quality, that the oversight committee can make an informed decision on the situation.

---

207 Dörr, in Dörr & Schmalenbach (eds), *VCLT Commentary*, Art. 31, para 57.
208 Šimonović, *Convention on the Elimination of all Forms of Discrimination Against Women*, United Nations Audiovisual Library of International Law, United Nations 2009, <http://legal.un.org/avl/ha/cedaw/cedaw.html> [accessed 02 December 2019].
209 Art. 44(2) CRC.
210 This conclusion is in accordance with the Harmonized Reporting Guidelines, which state that 'Reports should contain information sufficient to provide each respective treaty body with a comprehensive understanding of the implementation of the relevant treaty by the State.' (Report of the Inter-Committee Technical Working Group, *Harmonized guidelines on reporting under the international human rights treaties, including guidelines on a common core document and treaty-specific documents*, UN Doc. HRI/MC/2006/3, 10 May 2006, para 24).

III. What is the Content, Purpose and Nature of the State Reporting Obligation?

As the exemplary treaty interpretation shows, the state reporting obligation contains (1) the obligation to submit a report, (2) the obligation to submit said report on time and (3) to submit a report of a minimum quality, so the committees can make an informed decision on the situation within the reporting state.[211] The example of Art. 18 CEDAW is figurative for each state reporting obligation, especially those being more general. If a state party does not fulfill those requirements, it is in breach of the respective treaty and thereby violates international law.

Of course, the violation of non-submission and inadequate submission ceases as soon as the state party properly performs its obligation.[212] Questionable is, whether and how the violation of late-submission ceases. Generally, late-submission is the cessation of non-submission, whereby it would actually be a treaty abiding act. Nevertheless, the conducted treaty interpretation shows that submission on time is an obligation enshrined in the state reporting obligation. As a result, one has to conclude, that by submitting late, the state ceases its breach of non-submission, however, simultaneously breaches the treaty by late-submission and cannot cease this violation through another act. Hence, the breaching behavior of the state cannot and will never cease.

This dilemma can be resolved by taking into account the interplay of the individual obligations included in the state reporting obligation. When combining the three individual obligations within the state reporting obligations, the following scenarios can occur: (1) the state submits a report in adequate quality in time and hereby complies with all of its obligations. (2) The state submits a report in time in inadequate quality and hereby is in breach with its obligation to submit a report in adequate quality. (3) The state is late with submission and hereby is in breach with the obligation to submit on time, which can be remedied by a timely submission of a report of adequate quality. (4) The state is late with submission and hereby is in breach with the obligation to submit on time, but eventually the state submits a report, however in inadequate quality, whereby the state breaches the obligation to submit on time and in adequate quality. (5) The state does not submit a report at all, whereby the state is in breach of the obligation to submit a report in general.

To further clarify those scenarios, the breach of non-submission and late submission need further consideration. In this thesis, non-reporting is defined as persistent

---

211 See also Gaer, *'First Fruits: Reporting by States under the African Charter on Human and Peoples' Rights'* (1992) 10 NQHR 29, 36; cf Rule 71(2) [Examination of reports] Revised Rules of Procedure of the African Committee of Experts on the Rights and Welfare of the Child, <https://www.acerwc.africa/working-documents/revised-rules-of-procedures-final/>[accessed 02 December 2019].
212 Cf Art. 14 *Draft Articles on Responsibility of States for Internationally Wrongful Acts*, ILC Ybk 2001, / II(2), 26 (also available as Report on the work of the fifty-third session (2001), UN Doc. A/56/10 + Corr. 1, IV. E., 32 ff.).

resistance to submit a report at all. It is considered to be the most aggravated form of breaching the reporting obligation. Late-reporting, on the contrary, encompasses the act not to submit the report on time and relates to such states which have submitted reports before but not within the given timeframe. The line between these two obligations cannot be drawn sharply and there is a grey zone in which both apply. Hence, in situations in which the reports are so long overdue that one has to take into consideration the possibility that the respective state will not submit any report despite being previously compliant, it shall be permissible to consider this a non-submission for this reporting cycle. Whether the obligation to submit or to submit on time was breached in a specific situation may be determined on a case-by-case basis depending on the individual circumstances.

From the aforementioned scenarios, scenario (2)-(3) may be remedied, even though they are violating the reporting obligation. As many states consider themselves overburdened with the amount of reports they are obliged to submit, they should be given the benefit of the doubt that those breaches are anticipatory, meaning albeit the state is breach of its obligation it is interested in and striving for cessation of said breach. Hence, in those scenarios, especially if the state notifies the responsible oversight committee, the breach can be made good by remedial submission[213]. In scenarios (4) and (5), however, the breach is considered a grave violation of the reporting obligation. In scenario (4), the remedial submission leads into the next breach, whereby the good faith of the submitting state may be doubted. In scenario (5), the state is unwilling to submit at all. Those scenarios may give rise to sanctions as described in part two, chapter 3, III. of this thesis.

2. Object and Purpose of the State Reporting Obligation

The object and purpose of the state reporting obligation as an abstract obligation (meaning unrelated to a specific treaty) under international law was subject to development over time.[214] The first to elaborate on the purpose of reporting was the UN Committee on Economic, Social and Cultural Rights in its General Comment No. 1 in 1989.[215] It attributed seven objectives to state reporting, namely to undertake a comprehensive review, monitoring of the situation (in the sense of a detailed overview) by

---

213   The term 'remedial submission' in this thesis means that the breach can be remedied by submitting the proper report.
214   See Kälin, *'Examination of state reports'*, 35 ff.
215   Committee on Economic, Social and Cultural Rights, *General Comment No. 1: Reporting by States Parties*, UN Doc. E/1989/22, 24 February 1989, 87 f. (Annex III), reprinted in *Compilation of General Comments and General Recommendations*, adopted by Human Rights Treaty Bodies, UN Doc. HRI/GEN/1/Rev.6 at 8, 12 May 2003.

III. What is the Content, Purpose and Nature of the State Reporting Obligation?

the States, demonstration of principles policy-making, facilitation of public scrutiny, effective evaluation, identification of problems and shortcomings and facilitation of communication between state parties concerning common problems.[216] Today, the objectives have slightly changed, but in essence are still following the initial ideas.[217] Two main aims of the procedure are introspection by the state and inspection by the committees.[218] The consolidation of the reports is considered to assist the reporting state in self-evaluating its progress in implementing the provisions of the relevant treaties into its national framework. During the preparation of the report the state can engage in a constructive dialogue on national level with the relevant stakeholders. Resulting from the report the government and the different stakeholders are enabled to adapt suitable policies in accordance with the findings in the report. The reports can raise awareness amongst members of the civil society and individuals on human rights issues within the relevant state party, whereby public scrutiny is facilitated. International supervision is equally facilitated, which serves the fulfillment of the objectives of the UN. Through the report the committees are enabled to oversee the main contemporary challenges to human rights and act accordingly. Last but not least, states have the possibility to exchange views and best practices with one another or with the independent experts comprising the respective committee to improve their compliance with human rights law.[219]

From the list of identified goals, it can be seen that the reporting obligation is not mainly aimed at identifying state parties' human rights violations. Violations of human rights are dealt with by judicial and quasi-judicial bodies to remedy the victim.[220] The reporting mechanism is rather aimed at the constant evaluation of the actions of the responsible

---

216 *Ibid*, paras 2–9.
217 See for example Centre of Human Rights Education (PHZ Lucerne), *Lucerne Academic Consultation on Strengthening the United Nations Treaty Body System*, 24–25 October 2011, <https://www.ohchr.org/EN/HRBodies/HRTD/Pages/Documents.aspx> [accessed 02 December 2019], 4.
218 Human Rights Committee, *Simplified reporting procedure*, Report of the Working Group, UN Doc. CCPR/C/123/3, 6 December 2018, Summary; Viljoen, *International human rights law in Africa* (2nd edn, 2012), 37.
219 As expressed in the Harmonized guidelines on reporting under the international human rights treaties, including guidelines on a common core document and treaty-specific documents (Report of the Inter-Committee Technical Working Group, *Harmonized guidelines on reporting under the international human rights treaties, including guidelines on a common core document and treaty-specific documents*, UN Doc. HRI/MC/2006/3, 10 May 2006, paras 7 ff. and Report by the Secretariat, *Concept Paper on the High Commissioner's Proposal for a Unified Standing Treaty Body*, UN Doc. HRI/MC/2006/2, 22 March 2006, para 8; see also Inter-American Commission on Human Rights, *Guidelines for Preparation of Progress Indicators in the Area of Economic, Social and Cultural Rights*, OAS Doc. OEA/Ser.L/V/II.132, Doc. 14, 19 July 2008, para 7; and Oette, 'The UN Human Rights Treaty Bodies: Impact and Future', 100.
220 For information on supervision by International Tribunals see Tomuschat, 276 ff.

authorities to determine whether they respect, protect and fulfill their obligations under the respective treaties.[221]

3. Dogmatic Classification of the State Reporting Obligation

The state reporting obligation discussed in this thesis belongs in the sphere of public international law. It is enshrined in treaties concluded by states; it is hence a treaty obligation in the sense of Art. 38 (1) (a) of the Statute of the International Court of Justice.[222] Such treaty obligations create legal relations between subjects of international law. Traditionally, those subjects of international law are exclusively states.[223] However, the scope of actors in international law and thereby potential subjects thereof extended over time[224] and does increasingly include International Organizations[225] and sometimes even individuals.[226] As the state reporting obligation examined in this thesis is enshrined in human rights treaties, the dogmatic classification, in this case meaning the legal nature and the obligee of this obligation, appears unclear. Therefore, it has to be evaluated, to whom the state reporting obligation is owed and what kind of obligation (primary or secondary) it is. A dogmatic classification of this obligation has not yet been conducted. This is inevitable and absolutely necessary for the proposal for improvement made in this thesis. Hence, in the following, the state reporting obligation is classified accordingly.

a. The Legal Nature of the State Reporting Obligation

The first step for a dogmatic classification of a norm is to evaluate whether it represents a primary or secondary obligation. Primary obligation, as defined in Black's law dictionary, is 'a fundamental contractual term imposing a requirement on a contracting party from which other obligations may arise'[227]. In contrast, a secondary obligation is 'a duty, promise or undertaking that is incident to a primary obligation'[228].

Applying those definitions to the obligations arising from human rights treaties, the following distinction can be drawn: Those rights which are clear in their wording and expressively give a certain right to an individual or contain a specific call for a certain

---

221 See also Kälin, *'Examination of state reports'*, 36 f.
222 Statute of the International Court of Justice, adopted 26 June 1945, 15 U. N. C. I. O. 355, Blackstone's International Law Documents (14th edn 2019), 30 ff. [hereinafter ICJ Statute].
223 See eg Shaw, 157.
224 *Ibid*, 156.
225 *Ibid*, 205 f., 989 ff.
226 *Ibid*, 204 f. (with further references).
227 Garner, *Black's Law Dictionary* (9th edn, 2009) [hereinafter Black's Law Dictionary], 925.
228 *Ibid*.

III. What is the Content, Purpose and Nature of the State Reporting Obligation?

action are such obligations which impose a specific requirement on the state party and – upon its violation – may give rise to (international) liability. An example would be Article 7 ICCPR: 'No one shall be subjected to torture or to cruel, inhuman or degrading treatment or punishment. In particular, no one shall be subjected without his free consent to medical or scientific experimentation.' Therefore, it is a primary obligation of a state party to respect and protect this right and act accordingly. In contrast, such obligations relating to the breach of those primary norms are to be considered secondary obligations.[229] An example would be the obligation to cease the wrongdoing and make reparations. Secondary obligations are not always enshrined in the treaty text. They can also be deducted from the customary international law rules as laid down in the Draft Articles on Responsibility of States for Internationally Wrongful Acts.[230]

The classification of the state reporting obligation according to those definitions is difficult. On the one hand, the obligation establishes a clear obligation towards the state which, if violated, might give rise to further liabilities. This indicates that it is a primary obligation. On the other hand, it does not enshrine a right which could be claimed by the actual beneficiary of the contract, the individual. It is rather supportive of the individual rights by monitoring their effective implementation towards the international society. This could indicate that it is a secondary obligation. As those categories do not lead to a clear result, the differentiation has to be altered to the question whether the state reporting obligation carries a substantive or a procedural right. A substantive right is 'a right that can be protected or enforced by law'[231] while a procedural right is 'a right that derives from legal or administrative procedure; a right that helps in the protection or enforcement of a substantive right'[232].

The state reporting obligation entails the duty of a state to submit reports to the respective oversight committees. This obligation exists independently of any violation of another norm in the treaty. It does not contain any pre-requisite for its application. Even though it does not contain a right claimable by an individual, it does impose a specific obligation which, if violated, constitutes a breach of international law. Hence, compliance could be enforced by law. In conclusion, the state reporting obligation is classified as a primary obligation.

---

229 International Law Commission, *Draft articles on Responsibility of States for Internationally Wrongful Acts (with commentaries), 2001,* submitted to the General Assembly as a part of the Commission's report covering the work of that session (UN Doc. A/56/10), Art. 31 para (1).
230 *Draft articles on Responsibility of States for Internationally Wrongful Acts,* ILC Ybk 2001, /II(2), 26 (also available as Report on the work of the fifty-third session (2001), UN Doc. A/56/10 + Corr. 1, IV. E., 32 ff.
231 Black's Law Dictionary, 1127.
232 *Ibid.*

b. The Obligee of the State Reporting Obligation

The state reporting obligation as enshrined in inter-state-treaties is a treaty obligation governed by the international law of treaties. Within the regime of international law only subjects of international law are able to contract with each other. Therefore, treaty obligations can only be established between the subjects contracting with each other[233] – be it in bilateral or multilateral agreements. Subjects of international law are entities that are subject to or have the possibility to possess international rights and obligations and have the capacity to bring international claims and to be held responsible for violations of their own international obligations.[234] Traditionally, such entities are states.[235] This would lead to the conclusion that the state reporting obligation is owed to the other states being party to the relevant (multilateral) treaty.

However, more and more exceptions to this doctrine have been established. International Organizations can be subjects of international law,[236] and also individuals are partially considered as such[237]. Especially in human rights law, it has been questioned, whether it is the individual, who has to be considered the subject of international law, since it is they, who are the beneficiaries of the substantive rights enshrined in the multilateral human rights conventions.[238] In light of those developments, it has to be clarified who is the obligee[239] of the state reporting obligation.

Obligee is the one 'to whom an obligation is owed'.[240] Hence, the obligee is the subject entitled to benefit from a certain behavior of the party who must perform the obligation (obligor[241]). To actually benefit from the required behavior of the obligor, the obligee must be entitled to enforce the obligors' performance in the case of non-compliance. It can be inferred from this, that the obligee must be able to initiate proceedings if the obligation is not adhered to. Hence, to be the obligee of an international obligation, the

---

233 Shaw, 685.
234 Crawford, *Brownlie's Principles of Public International Law* (9th edn, 2019) [hereinafter Crawford], 109.
235 See e.g. Shaw, 157; Crawford, 105.
236 Cf ICJ, *Reparation for Injuries Suffered in the Service of the United Nation*, Advisory Opinion of 11 April 1949, ICJ Reports 1949, 174, 179; Shaw, 156; Crawford, 110.
237 Shaw, 204 f. (with further references).
238 Tomuschat, 112 ff.
239 In this thesis 'obligee' is used for the party of a treaty to whom another is legally obligated (see 'Obligee.' The Merriam-Webster.com Dictionary, Merriam-Webster Inc., <https://www.merriam-webster.com/dictionary/obligee> [accessed 02 December 2019]; Black's Law Dictionary, 926).
240 Black's Law Dictionary, 926.
241 In this thesis 'obligor' is used for the party of a treaty who is bound by a legal obligation (see 'Obligor.' The Merriam-Webster.com Dictionary, Merriam-Webster Inc., <https://www.merriam-webster.com/dictionary/obligor> [accessed 02 December 2019]; Black's Law Dictionary, 926).

III. What is the Content, Purpose and Nature of the State Reporting Obligation?

subject to whom the obligation is owed must be a subject of international law and be able to initiate proceedings against the obligor.[242]

The report is not owed to the Treaty Bodies themselves. Even though they are the addressees of the reports and the ones being mandated with overseeing the implementation of the rights enshrined in the relevant treaty, they are not considered subjects of international law.[243] However, obligee of an obligation under international law can only be a subject of international law. Also, the Treaty Bodies are not empowered to initiate proceedings against a state in breach, neither in front of the International Court of Justice[244], nor in front of themselves as the oversight committee[245]. Hence, the obligation is not owed to the Treaty Bodies.

Obligee could be individuals as the beneficiaries of the treaty. Generally, an individual has no or little capacities in international law.[246] However, some human rights treaties grant individuals standing to bring their claims, either through ratification of a treaty or subject to the consent of the respective state parties.[247] This indicates that claims against the state, even on the basis of a violation of the substantive rights of an individual, are reduced to a minimum and depend largely on the consensus of the states. Furthermore, even if one considers individuals as subjects of international law with regards to human rights, the state reporting obligation does not entail a specific individual right a person would be able to claim.[248] It serves as a monitoring instrument and therefore cannot be subject to the individual complaint mechanisms offered by some of the committees.[249]

In conclusion, obligees of the state reporting obligation must be the other state parties. Those are without doubt subjects of international law, are able to initiate proceedings in front of the International Court of Justice and are the other contracting parties. Therefore, the state reporting obligation is owed by one state to the other contracting states of the relevant treaty which makes it an obligation *erga omnes partes*[250].

---

242 Cf ICJ, *Reparation for Injuries Suffered in the Service of the United Nation*, Advisory Opinion of 11 April 1949, ICJ Reports 1949, 174, 179.
243 Cf Keller & Ulfstein, 'Introduction', in: Keller & Ulfstein, *UN Human Rights Treaty Bodies: Law and Legitimacy* (2012) 1, 3.
244 Only States may initiate proceedings in front of the International Court of Justice, Art. 35 (1) ICJ Statute.
245 Cf de Schutter, 882; cf Tomuschat, 238; cf Johnstone, 'Cynical Savings or Reasonable Reform – Reflections on a Single Unified UN Human Rights Treaty Body' (2007) 7 HRLR 173, 189.
246 Crawford, 111.
247 Cf Tomuschat, 240 ff., 245 ff.
248 See *supra*, Part Two, Chapter 1, III. 3. b.
249 The individual complaint mechanism may only vindicate the violation of individual rights, cf Tomuschat, 239.
250 Obligations *erga omnes partes* were *inter alia* recognized by the International Law Commission, see *Draft articles on Responsibility of States for Internationally Wrongful Acts (with commentaries)*, 2001,

4. Conclusion

The state reporting procedure has been used for more than a century to evaluate and monitor the implementation of treaty obligations. Since the 1960s, it is the major monitoring procedure in human rights law. Starting with the International Convention on the Elimination of All Racial Discrimination in 1965, it was and is enshrined in most human rights treaties. Under international law, treaties are concluded by states. The state reporting obligation is owed to the other state parties to a treaty as a primary obligation. The respective state parties were able to agree on monitoring through reporting as the instrument least intrusive to a state's sovereignty. It is the only instrument that becomes binding with ratification.

The state reporting procedure is an instrument that allows oversight committees to monitor and evaluate the implementation of human rights enshrined in certain inter-state, multilateral treaties. Due to its nature it is an obligation within the sphere of international law. The idea of a monitoring procedure sensitive towards the sovereignty of states is reflected in the object and purpose attributed to state reporting. It is supposed to foster a constructive dialogue between the different stakeholders – committees, states, nationals – and to provide the state with a permanent possibility of self-evaluation and, following from this, constant improvement in protecting human rights.

The procedure of most reporting obligations mirrors this object and purpose through a constant exchange of documents between the oversight committee and the state under review. However, this extensive procedure, which requires detailed documents, which again require a vast amount of resources, led to many challenges instead of a good monitoring. Those challenges to the system are subject of the following.

IV. Challenges of the State Reporting Procedure as Violations of International Law

The state reporting procedure at its core follows a simple idea: the state evaluates itself and combines the findings in a written report, which is then provided to the respective committee for consideration.[251] The preparation of the report ideally is conducted through a constructive dialogue between the state and members of civil society, which

---

submitted to the General Assembly as a part of the Commission's report covering the work of that session (UN Doc. A/56/10), Art. 48 para (6).

251 Report by the Secretariat, *Concept Paper on the High Commissioner's Proposal for a Unified Standing Treaty Body*, UN Doc. HRI/MC/2006/2, 22 March 2006, para 3; see already Kornblum, 'A comparison of self-evaluating state reporting systems' (1995) 304 IRRC 39, 50 f.

IV. Challenges of the State Reporting Procedure as Violations of International Law

further fosters a dialogue between the state and the oversight committee.[252] After finishing one reporting cycle, and before the next reporting cycle starts, the state ideally obtains guidance from the oversight committee on the way forward.[253] However, it quickly became clear that the system does not function as intended. The two major parties involved in the process, the states and the oversight committees, soon became inefficient in fulfilling their obligations.[254]

From the various difficulties the system has faced,[255] two were especially pressing in relation to reporting: (1) the issue of non-submission and late submission[256] and (2) the low or inadequate quality of the documents provided.[257] While those 'symptoms'

---

252 See for example the African Commission for Human and Peoples' Rights, II. Purpose, <https://www.achpr.org/reportingprocedure> [accessed: 27 November 2019].
253 Oette, '*The UN Human Rights Treaty Bodies: Impact and Future*', 100; cf Kälin, '*Examination of state reports*', 26 ff.
254 This thesis focusses on the challenges of the procedure in relation to States; for a thorough assessment on the performance of the United Nations Treaty Bodies, especially the Human Rights Committee, see Kälin, '*Examination of state reports*', 41 ff.; the main challenge of the Treaty Bodies themselves are backlogs concerning the review of submitted reports, see Report of the Secretary-General, *Status of the human rights treaty body system*, UN Doc. A/73/309, 6 August 2018, para 46; for an empirical evaluation of the effectiveness of international monitoring mechanisms in the field of human rights see Krommendijk, *The domestic effectiveness of international human rights monitoring in established democracies. The case of the UN human rights treaty bodies* (2015), 10 Rev Int Organ 489, 489 ff.
255 For an overview see Report by the Secretariat, *Concept Paper on the High Commissioner's Proposal for a Unified Standing Treaty Body*, UN Doc. HRI/MC/2006/2, 22 March 2006, paras 16–26.
256 Report of the Secretary-General, *Status of the human rights treaty body system*, UN Doc. A/73/309, 6 August 2018, para 10; Note by the Secretary-General, *United Nations reform: measures and proposals*, UN Doc. A/66/860, 26 June 2012, 20 ff.; Report of the Secretary-General, *In larger freedom: towards development, security and human rights for all*, UN Doc. A/59/2005, 21 March 2005, para 96; Note by the Secretary-General, *Effective Implementation of International Instruments on Human Rights, Including Reporting Obligations under International Instruments on Human Rights*, UN Doc. A/44/668, 8 November 1989, para 34; Gaer, '*First Fruits: Reporting by States under the African Charter on Human and Peoples' Rights*' (1992) 10 NQHR 29, 35; Bayefsky, *The UN Human Rights Treaty System: Universality at the Crossroads* (2001), 8 ff.; cf Tomuschat, 231 f.
257 Note by the Secretary-General, *Effective Implementation of International Instruments on Human Rights, Including Reporting Obligations under International Instruments on Human Rights*, UN Doc. A/44/668, 8 November 1989, para 34; Broecker/O'Flaherty, '*The Outcome of the General Assembly's Treaty Body Strengthening Process: An Important Milestone on a Longer Journey*', Policy Brief Universal Rights Group, June 2014, <https://www.universal-rights.org/urg-policy-reports/the-outcome-of-the-general-assemblys-treaty-body-strengthening-process-an-important-milestone-on-a-longer-journey/> [accessed 02 December 2019], 7; Report by the Secretariat, *Concept Paper on the High Commissioner's Proposal for a Unified Standing Treaty Body*, UN Doc. HRI/MC/2006/2, 22 March 2006, para 24 f.; Smith, 156; Gaer, '*First Fruits: Reporting by States under the African Charter on Human and Peoples' Rights*' (1992) 10 NQHR 29, 36 f.; Bayefsky, *The UN Human Rights Treaty System: Universality at the Crossroads* (2001), 22 f.; cf Steiner, Alston & Goodman, *International Human Rights in Context* (3rd edn, 2007), 850 (on reports to the ICCPR Committee).

surfaced early, their nature and origin needed examination.[258] It was not quite clear, whether these challenges were of a political, social or legal nature – or a mixture of all of them. Concerning the origin of these challenges, many experts agreed on the two main root causes, namely the unwillingness and/or the inability of states to comply with their reporting obligations.[259] The unwillingness to report does not need further explanation; the inability to report, however, may have different root causes. The main causes are the lack of human or financial resources, structural deficiencies or the overburdening of the state due to the quantity of reporting obligations.[260] The overburdening of the states is increased by the great amount of overlapping obligations which are added with every new treaty the state ratifies.[261]

The challenges of the State reporting system exist in the sphere of the UN Treaty Bodies[262] as well as in the regional human rights systems[263], especially in the African human rights system[264]. In the following, *first*, the legal consequence of the challenges under international law are clarified and *second*, the causes and challenges are embedded in the current discourse of fragmentation in international law.

---

258 Some indices were identified by Bayefsky, *The UN Human Rights Treaty System: Universality at the Crossroads* (2001), 9.
259 Report by the Secretariat, *Concept Paper on the High Commissioner's Proposal for a Unified Standing Treaty Body*, UN Doc. HRI/MC/2006/2, 22 March 2006, para 16; Smith, 157; Heyns & Viljoen, 'The Impact of the United Nations Human Rights Treaties on the Domestic Level', 23 HRQ 3, 483, 508 ff.
260 Smith, 157; Schöpp-Schilling, 'Treaty Body Reform: The Case of the Committee on the Elimination of Discrimination against Women' (2007) 7 HRLR 201, 203.
261 Report of the Secretariat, *Guidelines on an expanded core document and treaty-specific targeted reports and harmonized guidelines on reporting under the international human rights treaties*, UN Doc. HRI/MC/2004/3, 9 June 2004, 9 f.; cf Johnstone, 'Cynical Savings or Reasonable Reform – Reflections on a Single Unified UN Human Rights Treaty Body' (2007) 7 HRLR 173, 181 f.
262 In 2019, only 18.7 % of the State Parties were reporting. However, 66 % of the submitted reports were submitted in 'a timely manner', see Chairs of the Human Rights Treaty Bodies, *Implementation of human rights instruments*, UN Doc. A/74/256, 30 July 2019, para 14.
263 Additional Remark: The European System has a comparatively high compliance rate. In 2017, out of 43 States only three submitted too late to be examined (Report Concerning Conclusions of 2017 of the European Social Charter (revised), Governmental Committee, GC(2018)24, paras 5, 6 in conjunction with Report Concerning Conclusions XXI-2 (2017) of the 1961 European Social Charter, Governmental Committee, GC(2018)23, 31 January 2019, paras 5, 6); nevertheless, there is a minority of States which recurrently do not submit or submit late. Concerning quality, 15–25 % of the reports are considered insufficient due to lack of information (information provided upon personal inquiry by Mr. Henrik Kristensen, Deputy Executive Secretary of the European Committee of Social Rights).
264 List of States of the African Union late with reporting: <https://www.achpr.org/statereportsandconcludingobservations> [accessed 02 December 2019]; see also Lauer, *Die Implementierung menschenrechtlicher Verträge in Afrika* (2018), 141 f., 165 f.; Olowu, *An integrative rights-based approach to human development in Africa* (2009), 60 f.

IV. Challenges of the State Reporting Procedure as Violations of International Law

1. The Violation of the Principle *Pacta Sunt Servanda*

While the challenges of late submission, non-submission and poor quality of state reports are problematic in a political dimension, there are also legal problems attached to those challenges. The legal challenges, such as the explicit violation of legal principles as well as the difficulty of overlapping obligations in relation to the collision norms in international law have not yet been examined. Since from a legal perspective these considerations are important to evaluate the scope of responsibility of states as well as the need to tackle the challenge of the overlaps, the following provides insight into the legal perspective on the challenges in the sphere of public international law. Every reporting obligation is enshrined in a treaty to which the respective states are party. If a state ratifies a treaty in the legal sphere of public international law, the subsequent performance of the obligations so accepted are governed by several rules of which one rule of international treaty law is fundamental: the general principle of *pacta sunt servanda*, also reflected in Art. 26 of the VCLT.[265] The principle of *pacta sunt servanda* is binding on every state, irrespective of this state's ratification of the VCLT, because it is acknowledged as a general principle of international law[266], or at least part of international customary law[267]. *Pacta sunt servanda* prescribes, that a state is bound to perform the obligations governed by the treaty it is party to in good faith as long as said treaty is in force.[268]

Pacta sunt servanda applies to treaties governed by international law.[269] Treaties are international agreements concluded between (primarily) states governed by international law.[270] Art. 1 (a) VCLT further requests that such treaties be concluded in a written form; however, this requirement is only relevant for states party to the VCLT. The agreements which contain a state reporting obligation are without doubt treaties according to this definition. Therefore, the principle of *pacta sunt servanda* can be applied. The major challenges of the state reporting obligation, as identified *supra*, being the non-submission, late submission and inadequate quality, are at the same time the respective opposite to the obligations identified earlier.[271] A violation of any of those obligations, which contributes to the challenges of the state reporting procedure, amounts to a violation of international law. As those obligations are treaty obligations which are governed by the principle of *pacta sunt servanda*, the challenges of the state reporting procedure display the breach of the relevant treaty and a violation of the principle *pacta*

---

265 VCLT, adopted 22 May 1969, 115 UNTS 331
266 Schmalenbach, in Dörr & Schmalenbach (eds), *VCLT Commentary*, Art. 26, para 22; Shaw, 685.
267 Schmalenbach, in Dörr & Schmalenbach (eds), *VCLT Commentary*, Art. 26, para 20.
268 *Ibid*, paras 2, 4; Shaw, 685.
269 Schmalenbach, in Dörr & Schmalenbach (eds), *VCLT Commentary*, Art. 26, para 26 f.; Shaw, 685.
270 Schmalenbach, in Dörr & Schmalenbach (eds), *VCLT Commentary*, Art. 2, paras 3, 23; Shaw, 685.
271 See *supra* Part Two, Chapter 1, III. 1.

sunt servanda. Therefore, the challenges to the human rights Treaty Body system are violations of international law.

2. Fragmentation of International Law and the State Reporting Obligation

The intensively discussed phenomenon of fragmentation of international law[272] also affects the state reporting obligation. While in the beginning of modern human rights monitoring only a maximum number of three reporting obligations were established,[273] the number of reporting obligations increased with the awareness and protection of human rights. Concerns were raised that the specific nature of each treaty, including the specific protection of vulnerable groups, could not be upheld if the system were to be unified.[274] Hence, almost every treaty concluded since the 1960s established its own reporting procedure. Consequently, the reporting obligations quickly increased in number and thereby created a complex and scattered system. Such systems are the subjects of the fragmentation debate, which defines fragmentation as '[...] the rise of specialized rules and rule-systems that have no clear relationship to each other.'[275] The difficulty arising from those scattered systems is that '[a]nswers to legal questions become dependent on whom you ask, what rule-system is your focus on.'[276]

The coexistence of a large number of reporting obligations imposed on each state party to more than one human rights treaty was and is considered highly burdensome.[277] Numerous rights protected under different conventions are of a similar nature, which forces the state party to report on similar rights to different committees. If a state is party to more than one human rights treaty, be it international or regional, it may be required to

---

272 See for a discussion Report of the Study Group of the International Law Commission, Finalized by Martti Koskenniemi, *Fragmentation of International Law: Difficulties Arising from the Diversification and Expansion of International Law*, UN Doc. A/CN.4/L.682, 13 April 2006.
273 Under Art. 40 ICCPR (1966), Art. 16, 17 ICESCR (1966) and Art. 9 ICERD (1965).
274 See for example Report by the Secretariat, *Concept Paper on the High Commissioner's Proposal for a Unified Standing Treaty Body*, UN Doc. HRI/MC/2006/2, 22 March 2006, para 59; Permanent Representative of Liechtenstein to the United Nations, *Letter dated 14 September 2006 from the Permanent Representative of Liechtenstein to the United Nations addressed to the Secretary General*, Annex (Chairperson's summary of a brainstorming meeting on reform of the human rights treaty body system ('Malbun II'), 18 September 2006, UN Doc. A/61/351, para 12.
275 Report of the Study Group of the International Law Commission, Finalized by Martti Koskenniemi, *Fragmentation of International Law: Difficulties Arising from the Diversification and Expansion of International Law*, UN Doc. A/CN.4/L.682, 13 April 2006, para 483.
276 Ibid.
277 See already Note by the Secretary-General, *Effective Implementation of International Instruments on Human Rights, Including Reporting Obligations under International Instruments on Human Rights*, UN Doc. A/44/668, 8 November 1989, paras 36 ff.; Kälin, *'Examination of state reports'*, 17.

IV. Challenges of the State Reporting Procedure as Violations of International Law

report to different committees about the implementation of a similar right, enshrined in various treaties.[278] States parties to all relevant international human rights instruments oblige themselves to periodically report to the committees of eight international treaties and two optional protocols in the UN system.[279] On average, the treaties require a comprehensive report every four to five years. Therefore, a state party to every one of the eleven international human rights instruments is obliged to submit circa two periodic treaty reports per year only to the UN Treaty Bodies (20 reports in 10 years).[280] Not included in this calculation are the Universal Periodic Review, the common core documents or reports required under regional human rights instruments. Unfortunately, many of the reporting obligations in the international and regional sphere significantly overlap. States parties to such overlapping obligations face not only the difficulties arising out of the cross-cutting in the international law sphere, but also those arising from the overlapping regional and international regulations. One major difficulty arising from those overlaps is that they are not exactly the same; there are slight discrepancies between the norms of the different instruments,[281] because every treaty contains its own specific requirements for the various rights.[282]

A result of those overlapping obligations is for example the challenges of non-submission, late-submission and inadequate quality of the submitted reports. Due to uncertainties to whom a report about which specificities is supposed to be submitted and the difficulties arising from the not yet widely accepted possibility of cross-referencing

---

278 UN Secretary-General, *In larger freedom: towards development, security and human rights for all*, Report of the Secretary-General, Addendum, UN Doc. A/59/2005/Add. 3, 26 May 2005, para 96.
279 Those are: International Convention on Civil and Political Rights (ICCPR); International Convention on Economic, Social and Cultural Rights (ICESCR); International Convention on the Elimination of Racial Discrimination (ICERD); Convention on the Elimination of Discrimination against Women (CEDAW); Convention against Torture (CAT); Convention on the Rights of the Child (CRC); Optional Protocol on the Convention on the Rights of the Child on the Sale of Children, Child Prostitution and Child Pornography (CRC-OPSC); Optional Protocol to the Convention on the Rights of the Child on the involvement of children in armed conflict (CRC-OPAC); International Convention on Migrant Workers (ICRMW); Convention on the Rights of Persons with Disabilities (CRPD); the International Convention on Enforced Disappearance (CED) is not considered in this thesis because the reporting obligation is not periodic.
280 See already Note by the Secretary-General, *United Nations reform: measures and proposals*, UN Doc. A/66/860, 26 June 2012, 21.
281 Note by the Secretariat, *Status of Preparation of Publications, Studies and Documents for the World Conference*, Interim report on updated study by Mr. Philip Alston, Addendum, UN Doc. A/CONF.157/PC/62/Add.11/Rev.1, 22 April 1993, paras 238 ff.; Smith, 158.
282 Note by the Secretary-General, *Effective Implementation of International Instruments on Human Rights, Including Reporting Obligations under International Instruments on Human Rights*, UN Doc. A/44/668, 8 November 1989, para 47.

there is a reluctance of states to report (apart from those cases in which the states do not have the resources to report) on relevant content.

If the treaties in question do not contain a derogation clause[283], this phenomenon may be solved with the traditional collision rules *lex specialis derogat legi generali*[284] and *lex posterior derogat legi priori*[285]. The validity of those rules under international law is undisputed.[286] In relation to human rights law, the following can be concluded: the human rights treaties in force, both international and regional, naturally followed each other over a certain amount of time. Regional treaties often contain more specific regulations than the international treaties because they refer to a specific part of the world and not the international sphere in general (territorial limitation). Therefore, the collision rules could be of relevance if a state is party to more than one human rights treaty. Exemplarily (and simplified), the rules could apply to a state being party to the International Convention on the Elimination of Discrimination against Women as well as to the Protocol to the African Charter on Human and People's Rights on the Rights of Women in Africa. Following the *lex specialis* rule, the Protocol to the African Charter on Human and People's Rights on the Rights of Women in Africa – as a regional treaty – would be more specific due to its focus on the region and hereby could suspend the operation of the International Convention on the Elimination of Discrimination against Women, including the reporting obligation, in case of a collision. In the same example, the *lex posterior* rule would have the same effect as the *lex specialis* rule because the Maputo Protocol was adopted in 2003, while the International Convention on the Elimination of Discrimination against Women was adopted in 1979.

However, such a derogation would be incompatible with the object and purpose of the treaties as well as the object and purpose of human rights protection in general. Human rights treaties, even if they contain similar or even the same rights, each establish a protective system for individuals. The implementation of this system has to be monitored, which can be and largely is conducted through state reporting. Consequently, the derogation of a treaty due to a normative collision cannot be accepted in human rights law.

---

283   Which does not automatically solve the problem of the overlap as the responsibility for a breach might not be affected (cf Kadelbach, *'International Law and the Incorporation of Treaties into Domestic Law*, (1999), 42 Ger YIL 66, 73).
284   For details see Report of the Study Group of the International Law Commission, Finalized by Martti Koskenniemi, *Fragmentation of International Law: Difficulties Arising from the Diversification and Expansion of International Law*, UN Doc. A/CN.4/L.682, 13 April 2006, para 46 ff.
285   For details see *Ibid*, para 223 ff.
286   *Ibid*, para 56 (*lex specialis*), para 225 (*lex posterior*) (with further references); Shaw, 92 (with further references).

IV. Challenges of the State Reporting Procedure as Violations of International Law

The difficulties arising from the fragmentation of international human rights law, especially concerning the state reporting obligation, cannot be solved by applying the collision rules of international law. Hence, the parallelism of the various reporting obligations must be accepted as part of the human rights system.

3. Conclusion

The major challenges of non-submission, late submission and inadequate quality of the reports are not only problematic in a political dimension. Legally, they amount to violations of international law as breaches of international treaty law as well as a violation of the principle of *pacta sunt servanda*. Those violations are not necessarily intentional. They result, inter alia, from the fragmentation of international law, which also affects human rights treaties and thereby the reporting obligations. Overlapping reporting obligations as well as the overwhelming amount of reports which the states are obliged to present are the result of the increasing specification and amount of human rights treaties. Those overlaps cannot be solved by applying the general collision rules of *lex specialis* and *lex posterior*, as this would contravene the object and purpose of human rights protection in general as well as the state reporting obligation in particular. The challenges to the system remain unsolved until this day, despite intensive efforts to reform the system to increase its efficiency and resolve the challenges. The most renowned ideas were proposed by UN organs, partly in collaboration with independent experts.[287] Those proposals are presented in the following Chapter.

---

287 For an overview over the most important developments see Homepage of the Office of the High Commissioner for Human Rights, Human Rights Bodies, on Treaty Body Strengthening: <https://www.ohchr.org/EN/HRBodies/HRTD/Pages/TBStrengthening.aspx> [accessed 02 December 2019].

Chapter 2:
Previous Reform Proposals
The Most Important Proposals from UN Organs for Improvement of the System

Even though the Treaty Body System, and especially the reporting procedure, is considered to be one of the greatest achievements in human rights protection, its inefficiency became clear already few years after the first treaty had been adopted in 1965. With the increasing amount of new human rights treaties, and with them the increasing amount of obligations, more and more stakeholders called for reforms to keep the system sustainable and effective. In 1988, the General Assembly decided to respond to those calls and initiated a process, which – with some variations – continues until today. Starting from the Alston Proposals, a great variety of ideas for the improvement of the system has been and continues to be exchanged between the stakeholders for over 30 years now. The most important stages of the process were the Alston Proposals in the 1980s and 1990s, the proposal of a 'single state report' which was debated from 2002 until 2006, the idea of a Unified Standing Treaty Body introduced in 2006, the beginning of streamlining the processes through adoption of the harmonized reporting guidelines in 2006, the proposed partial unification in 2007, the Treaty Body strengthening process initiated by the High Commissioner for Human Rights in 2009 which lasted until 2014, and from 2014 until present the Review 2020 initiated by the General Assembly.

In this Chapter, the previous reform proposals under the UN Treaty Body System are examined with specific focus on the problems of the state reporting procedure, more specifically on the written state reports and the ideas proposed to improve this process. The examination of the previous proposals within this specific area is necessary to understand the process which led to the proposal presented in the subsequent chapter. It is important to consider the whole picture instead of highlighting singled out proposals. The comprehensive review of the relevant documents provides an in-depth introduction to the relevant proposals and their context in the overall development. The proposals which are reviewed in this Chapter are those put forward by the UN organs or taken up by them during consultations with stakeholders. Due to the vast amount of proposals made over the course of time, the amount of proposals considered in this thesis had to be restricted. As the proposals of the UN organs largely take up ideas from scholars outside the UN, the proposals of the UN were chosen to examine the reform process. Therefore, proposals outside the UN system which did not receive attention in the relevant documents are not included here.[288]

Contrary to the numerous (short) summaries of the process[289], the following review covers the development holistically in order to create a broad context as basis for a proposal which entails as many requests from all stakeholders as possible.

The reform process in this Chapter is displaying the process in the UN Treaty Body System only. It is acknowledged that in the regional systems there have also been strengthening processes over the past decades.[290] Due to the accessibility and comprehensiveness of the information available on the reform process on the international level, and the upcoming 2020 review of the UN Treaty Body System by the General Assembly, the reform process of the UN is presented exemplarily to provide insight into the complexity of the challenges this monitoring instrument faces.

---

288 Proposals not made by UN organs were for example made by Bayefsky, *The UN Human Rights Treaty System: Universality at the Crossroads* (2001), 148 ff.; Morijn, *'Reforming United Nations Human Rights Treaty Monitoring Reform'* (2011) 58 NILR 295, 328–329; University of Nottingham, *Report of the Expert Workshop on Reform of United Nations Human Rights, Treaty Monitoring Bodies, Human Rights Law Centre*, 11–12 February 2006, <https://www.nottingham.ac.uk/hrlc/documents/publications/treatymonitoringbodies2006workshopreport.pdf> [accessed 02 December 2019]; Gaer, *'The Institutional Future of the Covenants: A World Court for Human Rights?'*, 334.

289 See for example Note by the Secretary-General, *United Nations reform: measures and proposals*, UN Doc. A/66/860, 26 June 2012, 28; Oette, *'The UN Human Rights Treaty Bodies: Impact and Future'*, 102; Gaer, *'The Institutional Future of the Covenants: A World Court for Human Rights?'*, 338 ff.; Broecker & O'Flaherty, *'The Outcome of the General Assembly's Treaty Body Strengthening Process: An Important Milestone on a Longer Journey'*, Policy Brief Universal Rights Group, June 2014, <https://www.universal-rights.org/urg-policy-reports/the-outcome-of-the-general-assemblys-treaty-body-strengthening-process-an-important-milestone-on-a-longer-journey/> [accessed 02 December 2019], 7 ff.; O'Flaherty & O'Brien, *'Reform of UN Human Rights Treaty Monitoring Bodies: A Critique of the Concept Paper on the High Commissioner's Proposal for a Unified Standing Treaty Body'* (2007) 7 HRLR 141, 145 ff.; Egan, *'Strengthening the United Nations Human Rights Treaty Body System'* (2013) 13 HRLR 209; de Schutter, 923 ff.; Morijn, *'Reforming United Nations Human Rights Treaty Monitoring Reform'* (2011) 58 NILR 295, 300 ff. (including a systematization of previous proposals, 314 ff.); from a personal perspective O'Flaherty, *'The High Commissioner and the Treaty Bodies'*, in Broecker et al (eds), *'The United Nations High Commissioner for Human Rights: Conscience for the World'* (2013) 101, 101–119; Scheinin, *'The Proposed Optional Protocol to the Covenant on Economic, Social and Cultural Rights: A Blueprint for UN Human Rights Treaty Body Reform without Amending the Existing Treaties'* (2006) 6 HRLR 131.

290 See for example Governmental Committee of the European Social Charter and the European Code of Social Security, *Abridged report concerning Conclusions 2012 of the European Social Charter (revised)*, Appendix II, 13 December 2013, CM Documents CM(2013)168; Lauer, *Die Implementierung menschenrechtlicher Verträge in Afrika* (2018), 145 ff.; cf Gaer, *'First Fruits: Reporting by States under the African Charter on Human and Peoples' Rights'* (1992) 10 NQHR 29, 37.

Chapter 2: Previous Reform Proposals

I. The Alston Proposals, 1988–1997

Shortly after the first Treaty Bodies took up their work by the end of 1960, it became clear that the monitoring system provided for in the treaties was not sustainable. In the second meeting of chairpersons of the then existing committees[291] especially the reporting procedure was identified as ineffective.[292] Pursuant to that finding, the UN General Assembly instructed the Secretary-General[293] to entrust an independent expert with preparing a report on new approaches to improve the operation of present and future oversight committees.[294] This request was repeated by the Commission on Human Rights in 1989[295] whereupon the Secretary-General tasked Mr. Philip Alston, then professor of international law, director of the Centre for Advanced Legal Studies at the Australian National University and special rapporteur of the Committee on Economic, Social and Cultural Rights, with conducting the requested study.[296]

---

291 Those were: Commission on Human Rights, the Human Rights Committee, the Sessional Working Group of Governmental Experts on the Implementation of the International Covenant on Economic, Social and Cultural Rights, the Committee on the Elimination of Racial Discrimination, see: Reporting obligations of States parties to the International Covenants on Human Rights and the International Convention on the Elimination of All Forms of Racial Discrimination, see UN Secretary-General, *Reporting obligations of States parties to the International Covenants on Human Rights and the International Convention on the Elimination of All Forms of Racial Discrimination*, UN Doc. A/39/484, 20 September 1984; Background document prepared by the UN Secretariat, *Methods of Work relating to the State Reporting Process*, UN Doc. HRI/ICM/2003/3, 11 April 2003, para 16.

292 UN Secretary-General, *Reporting obligations of States parties to the International Covenants on Human Rights and the International Convention on the Elimination of All Forms of Racial Discrimination*, UN Doc. A/39/484, 20 September 1984, para 10; Background document prepared by the UN Secretariat, *Methods of Work relating to the State Reporting Process*, UN Doc. HRI/ICM/2003/3, 11 April 2003, paras 16, 20.

293 By this time Mr. Javier Perez de Cuellar, see <https://www.un.org/sg/en/content/former-secretaries-general> [accessed 02 December 2019].

294 UN General Assembly, *Reporting obligations of States parties to international instruments on human rights and effective functioning of bodies established pursuant to such instruments*, UN Doc. A/RES/43/115, 8 December 1988, para 15(a); Note by the Secretary-General, *Effective Implementation of International Instruments on Human Rights, Including Reporting Obligations under International Instruments on Human Rights*, UN Doc. A/44/668, 8 November 1989, para 1; Background document prepared by the UN Secretariat, *Methods of Work relating to the State Reporting Process*, UN Doc. HRI/ICM/2003/3, 11 April 2003, para 24.

295 Note by the Secretary-General, *Effective Implementation of International Instruments on Human Rights, Including Reporting Obligations under International Instruments on Human Rights*, UN Doc. A/44/668, 8 November 1989, para 2.

296 *Ibid*, para 1.

I. The Alston Proposals, 1988-1997

1. The Initial Report, 1989

On 8 November 1989, Mr. Alston's initial report was presented to the General Assembly at its 44th session.[297] In part III. of his report, Mr. Alston described comprehensively the reporting obligations of state parties. He stressed the great value and importance of the reporting procedure to the international human rights regime due to its multi-faceted nature.[298] As the principal manifestation of the system's problems he identified non-submission of reports and their 'inadequate quality'.[299] He considered the overall reporting obligations as greatly burdensome for the States,[300] especially in light of the extensive double-reporting resulting from various overlapping competences of different treaty bodies.[301] To improve the situation, he proposed the extension of the reporting periodicity,[302] the consolidation of reporting guidelines,[303] and the reduction of overlapping reporting requirements,[304] for example by creating the option of cross-referencing[305].

2. The Interim Report, 1993

Four years after the initial report, on 22 April 1993, the UN Secretariat issued an interim report on the updated study by Mr. Alston.[306] The General Assembly had requested an updated version of Mr. Alston's initial report for the 50th session of the Commission on Human Rights, its own 48th session and the World Conference on Human Rights in June 1993.[307] The interim report was also prepared by Mr. Alston, by this time visiting professor of law at Harvard Law School and chairman of the Committee on Economic, Social and Cultural Rights.[308] The interim report reiterated the great importance of the reporting procedure.[309] It examined the challenges of the procedure in even greater

---

297 See Note by the Secretary-General, *Effective Implementation of International Instruments on Human Rights, Including Reporting Obligations under International Instruments on Human Rights*, UN Doc. A/44/668, 8 November 1989, Annex.
298 *Ibid*, 4 (para 2), 18 (paras 31-33, 35).
299 *Ibid*, 20 (para 34).
300 *Ibid*, 4 (para 3), 21 f. (paras 37, 38).
301 *Ibid*, 5 (para 6), 22 (paras 37, 38), 23 ff. (paras 44 ff.).
302 *Ibid*, 4 (para 4), 22 (paras 39, 40).
303 *Ibid*, 4 (para 5), 23 (para 43).
304 *Ibid*, 23 ff. (paras 43 ff.).
305 *Ibid*, 5 (para 6), para 48.
306 Note by the Secretariat, *Status of Preparation of Publications, Studies and Documents for the World Conference, Interim report on updated study by Mr. Philip Alston*, Addendum, UN Doc. A/CONF.157/PC/62/Add.11/Rev.1, 22 April 1993.
307 *Ibid*, para 4.
308 *Ibid*, para 5.
309 *Ibid*, paras 91 ff.

detail.³¹⁰ In addition to the initial report, Mr. Alston addressed the problems of disseminating the relevant texts of the international instruments of human rights protection, the modalities of preparation of the reports, the dialogue at the national level and between the reporting state and the committees. Furthermore, apart from the principal manifestations of the problems he had already addressed in his initial report (namely non-submission and inadequate quality), the issue of inadequate processing of the reports by the committees was included as well.³¹¹

The proposals made in the interim report were more extensive than those listed in the initial report. Concerning the non-submission of reports, Alston proposed the creation of advisory services to non-reporting states, especially those with inadequate resources,³¹² the review of states in absence of a report as a measure of last resort,³¹³ the creation of a list of non-reporting states,³¹⁴ and the provision of a positive incentive to report³¹⁵. Responding to the burden of coexisting reporting obligations, he referred back to his proposal of extending the periodicity of the submissions, which he considered to be implemented in an appropriate manner.³¹⁶ The other previous proposals, namely the extended stagger of submission dates and the reduction of overlapping requirements, however, were not implemented, wherefore he re-emphasized their importance and especially elaborated on the reduction of overlapping reporting obligations.³¹⁷ To achieve a satisfactory reduction, he proposed a single 'core document' as a basis for the consolidation of the various reporting guidelines,³¹⁸ re-emphasized the introduction of cross-referencing,³¹⁹ the centralization of the preparation of the reports on the national level,³²⁰ and the increased cooperation between the different Treaty Bodies³²¹. While these proposals were mainly in line with those made in the initial report, Mr. Alston added new options to improve the system in the long-term. First, he recommended the reduction of the number of Treaty Bodies by consolidating the treaty regime, either to a lesser number of committees or to a single committee requiring a single report.³²² Second, alternatively, he introduced the idea of a single 'global' report while keeping

---

310   *Ibid*, paras 97–182.
311   *Ibid*, para 103.
312   *Ibid*, paras 114 ff.
313   *Ibid*, paras 119 ff.
314   *Ibid*, para 121.
315   *Ibid*, para 122.
316   *Ibid*, para 136.
317   *Ibid*, paras 139 ff.
318   *Ibid*, para 114.
319   *Ibid*, paras 144 ff.
320   *Ibid*, para 153.
321   *Ibid*, para 154 and paras 156 ff.
322   *Ibid*, para 166.

the committees as they were. The report would then be submitted to each of the committees for consideration.[323] As a third alternative, Mr. Alston explored the possibility to replace the comprehensive reports by documents limited to a specific issue to be identified by the relevant committee prior to reporting.[324]

3. The Final Report, 1997

In 1997, Mr. Alston concluded his work by issuing his final report on the long-term effectiveness of the UN human rights treaty system.[325] Before elaborating on the then present situation, Mr. Alston acknowledged the progress achieved since he had been tasked with conducting the study in 1988. Concerning the reporting system, the recommendations implemented were the production of a study on overlapping provision to assist in the implementation of cross-referencing,[326] the use of the recommended list of issues by the committees prior to the dialogue with the respective state party (although not exactly as he proposed),[327] and the further survey for a solution of non-submissions, especially focusing on a review in absence of a report[328] as well as for two committees the publication of a list of non-reporting states[329]. Even though in the meantime there were radical calls from commentators, requesting inter alia that the whole reporting procedure be eradicated,[330] Mr. Alston emphasized again the great importance and value of this procedure, adding that reforms to enhance its effectivity needed time but were desirable to uphold the constructive dialogue and the continuous evaluation of the contemporary state of human rights protection.[331]

Taking into account the findings of his previous reports, the situation in 1997 and the prospective development, the final recommendations of the expert were (1) to introduce an advisory system for assistance with the reporting burden,[332] (2) to create a procedure for examining non-submitting states in absence of a report,[333] (3) to create a sustainable system through far reaching reforms, including, inter alia, the consolidation

---

323 *Ibid*, paras 167 ff.
324 *Ibid*, paras 174 ff.
325 Presented in Note by the Secretary-General, *Effective Functioning of Bodies Established Pursuant to United Nations Human Rights Instruments*, 27 March 1997, UN Doc. E/CN.4/1997/74.
326 *Ibid*, para 4.
327 *Ibid*, para 4.
328 *Ibid*, para 5.
329 *Ibid*, paras 38, 39.
330 *Ibid*, para 8.
331 *Ibid*, para 9.
332 *Ibid*, para 112.
333 *Ibid*, para 112.

of reports and/or Treaty Bodies and the elimination of comprehensive periodic reports by replacement through tailored guidelines for each state party[334].

II. Single State Report, 2002–2006

In September 2002, the Secretary-General[335] submitted to the General Assembly in its 57th session a report themed 'Strengthening of the United Nations: an agenda for further change'.[336] The report reviewed comprehensively the whole organization, including the human rights Treaty Bodies.[337] The Secretary-General did not elaborate extensively on the Treaty Body reform; rather, he referenced the 1997 final report of the independent expert Mr. Alston and pointed to the growing number of committees and the increasing difficulty for the state parties to fulfill their reporting obligations.[338] His proposal followed the more radical ideas introduced by Mr. Alston: the committees should standardize their reporting requirements, and they should allow the state parties to produce a single report for submission to every committee. Such report should summarize the adherence to every treaty to which the respective state is a party.[339]

His proposal was supported by a background document prepared by the UN Secretariat in 2003 for the second inter-committee meeting of the human rights Treaty Bodies.[340] The meeting was held to discuss the reform process of the state reporting procedure with special regard to his proposals.[341] The background documents entail initial reactions to the proposals of the Secretary-General, which are, for the most part,

---

334 *Ibid,* paras 112, 120.
335 By this time Mr. Kofi Atta Annan (1997–2006), see < https://www.un.org/sg/en/content/former-secretaries-general> [accessed 02 December 2019].
336 Report of the Secretary-General, *Strengthening of the United Nations: an agenda for further change,* UN Doc. A/57/387, 9 September 2002.
337 *Ibid,* paras 52 ff.
338 *Ibid,* para 53.
339 *Ibid,* para 54.
340 Background document prepared by the UN Secretariat, *Methods of Work relating to the State Reporting Process,* UN Doc. HRI/ICM/2003/3, 11 April 2003; the Background document also presented the basis for a report of international experts on the matter, see Permanent Representative of Liechtenstein to the United Nations, *Annex to the letter dated 13 June 2003 from the Permanent Representative of Liechtenstein to the United Nations addressed to the Secretary-General,* Report of a meeting on reform of the human rights treaty body system, Malbun, Liechtenstein, 4–7 May 2003, UN Doc. A/58/123, para 6.
341 Background document prepared by the UN Secretariat, *Methods of Work relating to the State Reporting Process,* UN Doc. HRI/ICM/2003/3, 11 April 2003, para 1.

disapprobative.[342] The main concerns were the prospective unspecific nature of such a report (and thereby incomplete monitoring)[343] and the risk of superficial reports.[344]

Following the acknowledgement of those concerns, the Secretary-General elaborated on his proposed ideas for reform in the background paper.[345]

1. Coordination

To achieve a more coordinated approach amongst the various reporting obligations, the Secretary-General first proposed harmonized reporting guidelines.[346] By that time, every Treaty Body had adopted individual guidelines for reporting, which resulted in an inconsistent system.[347] Although there were efforts to harmonize the procedure (which resulted in a harmonized guideline to the 'core document' on basic information about the country), the process was discontinued, leaving the system with still largely disparate reporting requirements.[348] The second proposal in this report was the encompassing introduction of a list of issues. Following the example of the Human Rights Commission, the Commission on Economic, Social and Cultural Rights, the Commission on the Rights of the Child and the Commission on the Elimination of Discrimination against Women, such list should be prepared pursuant to the submission but ahead of the consideration of the report. The written answers could guide the Treaty Body members in their dialogue with the state party[349] under review.[350] Third, the reports should be scheduled covering a long time period to leave the state parties as well as the committees more time to prepare.[351] Fourth, he recommended the standardization and harmonization of the Concluding Observations. As the basis for the subsequent

---

342   *Ibid*, paras 9 ff.
343   *Ibid*, para 9 lit(c), (e).
344   Note by the Office of the United Nations High Commissioner for Human Rights, *Effective Functioning of Human Rights Mechanisms, Treaty Bodies*, UN Doc. E/CN.4/2003/126, 26 February 2003, para 5 ff.; Background document prepared by the UN Secretariat, *Methods of Work relating to the State Reporting Process*, UN Doc. HRI/ICM/2003/3, 11 April 2003, para 9 lit(b).
345   Background document prepared by the UN Secretariat, *Methods of Work relating to the State Reporting Process*, UN Doc. HRI/ICM/2003/3, 11 April 2003, paras 27 ff.
346   *Ibid*, paras 30 ff.
347   *Ibid*, paras 28 f., 30 f.
348   *Ibid*, para 31.
349   The dialogue between State party under review and the respective Treaty Body is part of the reporting cycle in the system of the United Nations Treaty Bodies (see *supra* Part Two, Chapter 1, II, 1.).
350   Background document prepared by the UN Secretariat, *Methods of Work relating to the State Reporting Process*, UN Doc. HRI/ICM/2003/3, 11 April 2003, para 37.
351   *Ibid*, para 37.

periodic reports, they should be 'clear, specific and concrete'.[352] His last point under the coordination-approach was the review of state parties in absence of a report. While Mr. Alston introduced this idea as a last resort,[353] the Secretary-General reported that several Treaty Bodies were already engaging in this practice[354].

2. Global Approach

The other proposal favored by the Secretary-General was the submission of a single state report on the implementation of the provisions under all human rights instruments the relevant state is party to.[355] In the opinion of the Secretary-General, this could be combined with the creation of specific units within the state governments responsible for the preparation of such report.[356] The idea of a single state report was amongst the more radical proposals of the interim report of Mr. Alston.[357]

Alternatively, he recommended the harmonization of the core document,[358] the introduction of focused reports only requiring information on specific issues to be determined by the respective committee,[359] and/or the flexible handling of the periodicity of reports, especially in cases when a state party had to report to several committees at the same time[360]. However, the idea of a single state report was largely rejected.[361]

---

352 Ibid, para 38.
353 Note by the Secretariat, *Status of Preparation of Publications, Studies and Documents for the World Conference, Interim report on updated study by Mr. Philip Alston*, Addendum, UN Doc. A/CONF.157/PC/62/Add.11/Rev.1, 22 April 1993, para 119.
354 Background document prepared by the UN Secretariat, *Methods of Work relating to the State Reporting Process*, UN Doc. HRI/ICM/2003/3, 11 April 2003, para 40 ff.
355 Ibid, para 43.
356 Ibid, para 44.
357 UN Secretary-General, *Status of implementation of actions described in the report of the Secretary-General entitled 'Strengthening of the United Nations: an agenda for further change'*, UN Doc. A/58/351, 5 September 2003, para 6.
358 Background document prepared by the UN Secretariat, *Methods of Work relating to the State Reporting Process*, UN Doc. HRI/ICM/2003/3, 11 April 2003, para 49 f.
359 Ibid, para 51 f.
360 Ibid, para 54.
361 Permanent Representative of Liechtenstein to the United Nations, *Annex to the letter dated 13 June 2003 from the Permanent Representative of Liechtenstein to the United Nations addressed to the Secretary-General*, Report of a meeting on reform of the human rights treaty body system, Malbun, Liechtenstein, 4–7 May 2003, UN Doc. A/58/123, para 20.

III. Unified Standing Treaty Body, 2006

In preparation for the 2005 Review of the United Nations Millennium Declaration of 2000, the Secretary-General submitted a follow-up report on the outcome of the Millennium Summit to the 59th session of the General Assembly.[362] In his report, he called upon the UN High Commissioner for Human Rights to prepare a plan of action, which the UN High Commissioner for Human Rights[363] delivered on 26 May 2005.[364]

The plan of action showed that the challenges of the system did not diminish. Rather, the High Commissioner for Human Rights pointed to the prospective aggravation of the situation in the case of the – nevertheless aspired – universal ratification.[365] Since 2002, changes had been underway. Treaty Bodies began to harmonize their reporting guidelines which, once finalized and implemented, were intended to make the Treaty Bodies function as a unified system.[366] However, in the opinion of the High Commissioner for Human Rights, this process should have been advanced further until finally the work of the Treaty Bodies would be consolidated under one unified standing Treaty Body.[367] A comparable proposal was made by Mr. Alston in his interim report, but not as prominently. The option for Treaty Body reform towards a unified Treaty Body were presented in 2006, when the High Commissioner for Human Rights published her 'Concept Paper on the High Commissioner's Proposal for a Unified Standing Treaty Body'[368]. In the concept paper, she first explained the difficulties and challenges the system faced. Apart from the already identified reasons for the challenges of the system, for example lack of political will or ability of states to comply with the reporting obligation[369] or the missing coordination of reporting[370], she also emphasized the issue of non-visibility of the Treaty Bodies[371]. In the concept paper she concluded, that 'the lack

---

[362] Report of the Secretary-General, *In larger freedom: towards development, security and human rights for all*, UN Doc. A/59/2005, 21 March 2005.
[363] By this time Ms. Louise Arbour (2004–2008), see: <https://www.ohchr.org/EN/AboutUs/Pages/LouiseArbour.aspx> [accessed 02 December 2019].
[364] Report of the Secretary-General, *In larger freedom: towards development, security and human rights for all*, UN Doc. A/59/2005, 21 March 2005.
[365] *Ibid*, para 99.
[366] *Ibid*.
[367] *Ibid*.
[368] Report by the Secretariat, *Concept Paper on the High Commissioner's Proposal for a Unified Standing Treaty Body*, UN Doc. HRI/MC/2006/2, 22 March 2006; for a critique of that paper see O'Flaherty & O'Brien, '*Reform of UN Human Rights Treaty Monitoring Bodies: A Critique of the Concept Paper on the High Commissioner's Proposal for a Unified Standing Treaty Body*' (2007) 7 HRLR 141, 142 ff.
[369] Report by the Secretariat, *Concept Paper on the High Commissioner's Proposal for a Unified Standing Treaty Body*, UN Doc. HRI/MC/2006/2, 22 March 2006, para 16.
[370] *Ibid*, para 23.
[371] *Ibid*, para 21 f.

of visibility, authority and access [...] will persist'³⁷², if the system was not reformed and channeled into a unified Treaty Body. A unified standing Treaty Body would have the advantage of permanent availability, the possibility of quick responses to violations, consistent jurisprudence, and ability to continuously assist state parties with expert support in implementing human rights.³⁷³ Keeping in mind the integrated implementation of human rights the High Commissioner for Human Rights considered a comprehensive and cross-cutting monitoring and assistance desirable.³⁷⁴ The unified standing Treaty Body could come with a single reporting procedure, which already in previous proposals was considered to be encouraging towards states to report and to hereby enhance the effectivity of the whole monitoring and implementation process.³⁷⁵ Further options for reporting would be the consideration of reports under the different treaties by one body (essentially the current system with submission to only one committee), the submission of an expanded core document supplemented by shorter treaty specific reports or reports on specific lists of issues instead of periodic reports.³⁷⁶ The issue of overlapping regulations would be addressed, as a unified standing Treaty Body could interpret and comment on substantively similar provisions in different treaties in a coherent manner.³⁷⁷ In summary, the High Commissioner for Human Rights attributed the benefits of '[...] a holistic, comprehensive and cross-cutting assessment of human rights situations, eliminat[ing] duplication and potential inconsistent interpretations, reduc[ing] the reporting burden, underlin[ing] the indivisibility of rights, create[ing] visibility for the system and improv[ing] access for stakeholders[...]' to her proposal.³⁷⁸

The concept paper also addressed the various concerns of different stakeholders. The lack of specificity³⁷⁹, which was already an issue with regard to the single state report, the determination of membership and ratification, expertise of the Treaty Body members and the legal establishment of such a unified body³⁸⁰ appeared to be the most pressing

---

372   Ibid, para 27.
373   Ibid, para 27.
374   Ibid, para 28.
375   Ibid, para 28.
376   Ibid, para 46.
377   Ibid, para 30.
378   Ibid, para 43.
379   The issue of specificity again was discussed during the 'Malbun II' expert meeting, see Permanent Representative of Liechtenstein to the United Nations, *Letter dated 14 September 2006 from the Permanent Representative of Liechtenstein to the United Nations addressed to the Secretary General*, Annex (Chairperson's summary of a brainstorming meeting on reform of the human rights treaty body system ('Malbun II'), 18 September 2006, UN Doc. A/61/351, para 27.
380   The legal options are explored in United Nations Secretariat, *Preliminary non-paper on legal options for a unified standing treaty body*, <https://www.ohchr.org/EN/HRBodies/HRTD/Pages/FirstBiennial ReportbySG.aspx#SingleReport> [accessed 02 December 2019] and again addressed in Permanent

matters.[381] The concept paper unfortunately did not provide satisfying answers to those challenges; rather, the challenges were acknowledged and complemented with provisional ideas or suggestions.[382] In an expert meeting, the proposal to create a unified standing Treaty Body only received little support.[383] Instead, the experts expressed their approval for the harmonization of guidelines, the common core document and the list of issues.[384] It was agreed that non-reporting posed a serious problem to the system, however the favored solution was technical assistance rather than institutional change.[385]

IV. Harmonized Reporting Guidelines, 2006

After almost twenty years of reform proposals, the Inter-Committee Technical Working Group adopted the 'Harmonized guidelines on reporting under the international human rights treaties, including guidelines on a common core document and treaty-specific documents'.[386] The number of treaties that required periodic reports grew steadily and the Treaty Bodies themselves decided to ease the reporting burden by coordinating and streamlining the whole procedure to the benefit of the state parties.[387] They aimed for the improvement of compliance, increased dialogues – including the national level –

Representative of Liechtenstein to the United Nations, *Letter dated 14 September 2006 from the Permanent Representative of Liechtenstein to the United Nations addressed to the Secretary General*, Annex (Chairperson's summary of a brainstorming meeting on reform of the human rights treaty body system ('Malbun II'), 18 September 2006, UN Doc. A/61/351, paras 31 ff.

381 Report by the Secretariat, *Concept Paper on the High Commissioner's Proposal for a Unified Standing Treaty Body*, UN Doc. HRI/MC/2006/2, 22 March 2006, para 59.
382 *Ibid*, paras 59 ff.
383 Permanent Representative of Liechtenstein to the United Nations, *Letter dated 14 September 2006 from the Permanent Representative of Liechtenstein to the United Nations addressed to the Secretary General*, Annex (Chairperson's summary of a brainstorming meeting on reform of the human rights treaty body system ('Malbun II'), 18 September 2006, UN Doc. A/61/351, para 12.
384 *Ibid*, paras 17 ff.
385 *Ibid*, para 22; for a detailed assessment on the Unified Standing Treaty Body see Johnstone, 'Cynical Savings or Reasonable Reform – Reflections on a Single Unified UN Human Rights Treaty Body' (2007) 7 HRLR 173, 190 ff.
386 Report of the Inter-Committee Technical Working Group, *Harmonized guidelines on reporting under the international human rights treaties, including guidelines on a common core document and treaty-specific documents*, UN Doc. HRI/MC/2006/3, 10 May 2006 (reprinted in Report of the Secretary-General, Compilation on the form and content of reports to be submitted by States parties to the international human rights treaties, UN Doc. HRI/GEN/2/Rev.6, 3 June 2009).
387 Report of the Inter-Committee Technical Working Group, *Harmonized guidelines on reporting under the international human rights treaties, including guidelines on a common core document and treaty-specific documents*, UN Doc. HRI/MC/2006/3, 10 May 2006, para 12.

and a broader implementation of the treaties. The guidelines followed a draft presented by the UN Secretariat in 2004.[388]

The harmonized reporting guidelines were intended to apply to seven treaties.[389] The procedure would consist of the preparation of a common core document, providing all the necessary general information relevant to all of the (then) seven Treaty Bodies, and treaty specific documents.[390] The content of the common core document was supposed to help the Treaty Bodies understand the situation within the country. It required information about the population, the state system, the legal system, the culture, policies and the human rights obligations of the state.[391] If there were changes to any of those areas of interest, the common core document had to be updated.[392]

The additional treaty specific documents would follow the periodicity as prescribed in the relevant treaties.[393] In addition to the general information contained in the common core document, the treaty specific documents would elaborate on recent developments concerning the specific area of interest and follow up on previous dialogues and Concluding Observations as well as developments in the Treaty Bodies in general.[394]

V. Treaty Body Strengthening Process, 2009–2014

Due to the increasing amount of human rights treaties, the efficiency of the Treaty Body system deteriorated further. To reverse the process and strengthen rather than weaken the whole process, the High Commissioner for Human Rights[395] in 2009 called upon all stakeholders to reflect on the system and initiate the strengthening of the Treaty Body system.[396] Answering said call, a group of current and former Treaty Body members

---

388 Report of the Secretariat, *Guidelines on an expanded core document and treaty-specific targeted reports and harmonized guidelines on reporting under the international human rights treaties*, UN Doc. HRI/MC/2004/3, 9 June 2004; the draft was presented following a request by the second inter-committee meeting and fifteenth meeting of chairpersons of human rights treaty bodies, *ibid*, 1.

389 Namely ICCPR, ICESCR, ICERD, CEDAW, CAT, CRC, CMW, see Report of the Inter-Committee Technical Working Group, *Harmonized guidelines on reporting under the international human rights treaties, including guidelines on a common core document and treaty-specific documents*, UN Doc. HRI/MC/2006/3, 10 May 2006, para 1.

390 *Ibid*, para 17.

391 *Ibid*, paras 27, 31 ff.

392 *Ibid*, para 18.

393 *Ibid*, 17.

394 *Ibid*, paras 28, 60.

395 Then: Ms. Navanethem Pillay, see <https://www.ohchr.org/EN/AboutUs/Pages/NaviPillay.aspx> [accessed 02 December 2019].

396 Note by the Secretary-General, *United Nations reform: measures and proposals*, UN Doc. A/66/860, 26 June 2012, 9.

authored and published a statement in support of this process ('Dublin Statement').[397] The call by the High Commissioner and the Dublin Statement triggered various dialogues with different stakeholders on possibilities for improvement. One of the focus areas of these dialogues was the state reporting process. The dialogues reflected on ideas and options to strengthen the system and the compliance of states with their reporting obligations.[398] The outcome of those ideas were presented in the report of the UN High Commissioner for Human Rights on the strengthening of the human rights Treaty Bodies in June 2012.[399] During this strengthening process, before as well as after the High Commissioner's report on the outcome of the dialogues, the stakeholders were engaged by publishing documents which explained their view on the situation.

1. Report of the Secretary-General, 2011

In September 2011, the Secretary-General[400] issued a report reflecting on the progress of the strengthening process. The report 'Measures to improve further the effectiveness, harmonization and reform of the Treaty Body System'[401] evaluated the situation of the Treaty Bodies in 2011, following the establishment of further human rights treaties. By that time, the amount of treaties and optional protocols had risen to 17.[402] Although not all of them required periodic reporting, the workload for states now being party to every relevant instrument reached the all-time high of ten initial and eight periodic reports.[403]

Even though by this time only one third of the state parties was in compliance with their obligations, the Treaty Bodies already struggled severely with the consideration of the submitted reports.[404] With the envisaged improvement of compliance, this was expected to become an issue of increasing relevance, which is why the Secretary-General proposed the coordination of reporting to and review by all Treaty Bodies in one calendar, either interim (to tackle the existing and prevent further backlog) or permanent.[405] The

---

397 Human Rights Law Centre of the University of Nottingham, *The Dublin Statement on the Process of Strengthening of the United Nations Human Rights Treaty Body System*, 29 November 2009, accessible: <https://www.ohchr.org/en/hrbodies/hrtd/pages/documents.aspx> [accessed 02 December 2019].
398 UN Secretary-General, *Measures to improve further the effectiveness, harmonization and reform of the treaty body system*, UN Doc. A/66/344, 7 September 2011, para 41.
399 UN Secretary-General, United Nations reform: measures and proposals, Note by the Secretary-General, UN Doc. A/66/869, 26 June 2012.
400 Then: Mr. Ban Ki-moon, see <https://www.un.org/sg/en/content/former-secretaries-general> [accessed 02 December 2019].
401 UN Secretary-General, *Measures to improve further the effectiveness, harmonization and reform of the treaty body system*, UN Doc. A/66/344, 7 September 2011.
402 *Ibid*, para 7.
403 *Ibid*, para 8 (Table 1).
404 *Ibid*, para 21.
405 *Ibid*, paras 22 ff.

Secretary-General favored the option of a permanent reporting calendar. He considered this option would enable the Treaty Bodies to reduce their backlog, as well as increase compliance of the state parties with their reporting obligations due to the strict nature of such a calendar. In his opinion, it would even allow reviews in absence of a report.[406]

2. Consultations with Stakeholders, 2010–2012

Several stakeholder meetings were conducted to achieve the best possible results for the Treaty Body strengthening process. States parties, Treaty Bodies, academics, National Human Rights Institutions and civil society organizations were invited to put forward their ideas during various discussions.[407] The results of those consultations share as their least common denominator the strife for further harmonization of the procedure and the establishment of a review in absence of a report.

a. National Human Rights Institutions

In June 2010 various National Human Rights Institutions, Treaty Body experts and representatives of the Office of the High Commissioner for Human Rights met in Marrakech (Morocco) to discuss the status of the Treaty Body system from their point of view.[408] They recommended the streamlining of the system along the harmonized reporting guidelines and insisted on the usage of the simplified reporting procedure and cross-referencing.[409]

b. Treaty Bodies

In September 2010 an expert meeting was held in Poznan (Poland). The active participants were current and former members of Treaty Bodies[410], who recommended for the Treaty Bodies a harmonized, streamlined and focused procedure to improve the effectivity of the process. To implement this recommendation, they referred to the usage of the list of issues prior to reporting as well as the common core document. For the state

---

406 *Ibid*, para 29.
407 See for all documents Homepage of the Office of the High Commissioner for Human Rights, Treaty Body Strengthening – Outcome documents, reports, and statements, accessible <https://www.ohchr.org/EN/HRBodies/HRTD/Pages/Documents.aspx> [accessed 02 December 2019].
408 Advisory Council on Human Rights of Morocco, *Marrakesh Statement on strengthening the relationship between NHRIs and the human rights treaty bodies system*, 10 June 2010, <https://www.ohchr.org/en/hrbodies/hrtd/pages/documents.aspx> [accessed 02 December 2019], reprinted in Netherlands Quarterly of Human Rights 28 (2010), 121–27.
409 *Ibid*, para 16.
410 International Seminar of Experts on the Reforms of the United Nations Human Rights Treaty Body System, *The Poznan Statement on the Reforms of the United Nations Human Rights Treaty Body System*, 28–29 September 2010, <https://www.ohchr.org/en/hrbodies/hrtd/pages/documents.aspx> [accessed 02 December 2019].

parties, they encouraged better support by the Treaty Bodies, national consultations and frameworks as well as the inclusion of non-governmental organizations.[411]

c. Non-Governmental Organizations

Twenty non-governmental organizations (NGOs) presented in November 2010 their joint response[412] to the 2009 Dublin Statement. This response questioned the usefulness of the common core document[413] but welcomed the usage of the list of issues prior to reporting[414]. Their main recommendations concerning the reporting procedure were a reporting schedule on the consideration of state reports and the proper establishment of a mechanism to review state parties in absence of a report.[415]

In April 2011, international and national NGOs met in Seoul (South Korea) to discuss and subsequently respond to the initiative of the UN High Commissioner for Human Rights.[416] Apart from a call on the UN to accept NGOs as valid stakeholders in the reporting process and a greater inclusion of their input, the representatives recommended an inclusive consultation process by centered mechanisms established by the state party.[417] Concerning previous proposals, they supported the list of issues prior to reporting as a potentially valuable tool for focused and timely reporting. However, they saw the need for further assessment of the effectivity of this procedure.[418] Regarding non-reporting states, the participants expressed their approval of the review in absence of a report and suggested that the Treaty Bodies harmonize this procedure, include members of civil society in their review, hold the meetings in public sessions and generally make more use of the review in absence of a report.[419]

A consultation with members of the civil society held in Pretoria (South Africa) on 20 and 21 June 2011 intended to examine and complement previous consultations.[420] The members of civil society supported the previous recommendation of an advanced

---

411 Ibid, paras 7 ff.
412 Advocates for Human Rights et al., *Dublin Statement on the Process of Strengthening the United Nations Human rights Treaty Body System: Response by non-governmental organizations*, November 2010, <https://www.ohchr.org/EN/HRBodies/HRTD/Pages/Documents.aspx> [accessed 02 December 2019].
413 Ibid, para 18.
414 Ibid, para 19.
415 Ibid, 9 (para 20), 14.
416 National Human Rights Commission of Korea and the Korea Foundation, *Seoul Statement on Strengthening the UN Human Rights Treaty Body System*, 19–20 April 2011, <https://www.ohchr.org/EN/HRBodies/HRTD/Pages/Documents.aspx> [accessed 02 December 2019].
417 Ibid, paras 3, 4.
418 Ibid, para 5.
419 Ibid, para 8.
420 Centre for Human Rights, Faculty of Law, University of Pretoria, *Pretoria Statement on the Strengthen-*

review schedule[421] and the review in absence of a report[422]. They recommended the development of best practice guidelines for the engagement of state parties with Treaty Bodies[423], country webpages for an improved overview over the state compliance[424] and the increased and early involvement of NGOs[425]. Compliance with reporting obligations was recommended as a criterion to be considered while electing members of the Human Rights Committee.[426] To improve the overall functioning of the process, the participants of the civil society consultation recommended the division of the Treaty Bodies into chambers to increase the number of reports being considered in one session.[427]

After the initiation of an intergovernmental process for strengthening the Treaty Body system by the UN General Assembly[428], a group of 26 NGOs made a joint contribution on the developments including their recommendations not only for the inter-governmental process, but on the overall development of the Treaty Body strengthening.[429] Concerning state reporting, their main recommendations for the inter-governmental process were the provision of technical assistance[430] and early involvement of civil society during the reporting process, especially in the preparation phase.[431]

d. State Parties

The technical consultation organized on 12 and 13 May 2011 in Sion (Switzerland) invited state parties to exchange ideas on and concerns with the ideas presented up to this point following the 2009 call of the UN High Commissioner for Human Rights. The outcome document[432] provides detailed insight into the discussions in the different

---

    ing and Reform of the UN Human Rights Treaty Body System, 20–21 June 2011, <https://www.ohchr.org/EN/HRBodies/HRTD/Pages/Documents.aspx> [accessed 02 December 2019], para 1.1.
421 *Ibid*, para 4.2
422 *Ibid*, para 6.2.
423 *Ibid*, para 4.5.
424 *Ibid*, para 4.6.
425 *Ibid*, para 4.7, 4.8, 6.1.
426 *Ibid*, para 6.4.
427 *Ibid*, para 12.1.
428 UN General Assembly, *Strengthening and enhancing the effective functioning of the human rights treaty body system*, UN Doc. A/Res/68/268, 21 April 2014, preambulatory clause 4.
429 Alkarama et al, *Issues for the inter-governmental process on strengthening the effective functioning of the human rights treaty body system, A Joint NGO Contribution*, 12 April 2012, <https://www.ohchr.org/EN/HRBodies/HRTD/Pages/Documents.aspx> [accessed 02 December 2019].
430 *Ibid*, 3.
431 *Ibid*, 3.
432 Office of the High Commissioner for Human Rights, *Report of the Informal Technical Consultation with States parties in Sion, Informal Technical Consultation for States parties on Treaty Body Strengthening,*

V. Treaty Body Strengthening Process, 2009–2014

panels. In the panel on the topic 'Strengthening the preparation of States parties' reports', experts from different Treaty Bodies gave presentations on proposals made during the strengthening process. Representatives of the state parties responded to and discussed those presentations afterwards. The presentations especially highlighted the simplified reporting procedure under the harmonized reporting guidelines[433] and, rather as an alternative, the new list of issues prior to reporting[434]. Most speakers for the state parties welcomed the proposals, particularly the list of issues prior to reporting,[435] although some voiced concerns, such as the question of reliability of the sources on which the list of issues prior to reporting should be based[436]. Generally, the state parties emphasized their prominent role in the Treaty Body system, stressing that they were the creators of the underlying treaties[437] and those responsible for their implementation. Therefore, their views should be given great weight, and the reforms should reduce the pressure weighing on them from the treaties.[438]

Approximately one year after this first consultation, in February 2012, the Office of the High Commissioner for Human Rights invited states to Geneva (Switzerland) to resume the discussion from Sion.[439] Apart from budgetary issues and reassurances, that the state parties are indeed the creators and duty bearers of the system, many participants were greatly interested in a comprehensive reporting calendar.[440] However, criticism on the proposal addressing e.g. the lack of capacities to submit two reports every year and increase of meeting time was voiced as well.[441] Contrary to discussions with other stakeholders, the review in absence of a report received little or no support.[442] Regarding non-reporting, the participants proposed to research on the reasons of non-reporting and ways to lighten the reporting burden.[443] The search for methods differing from the 'classical' reporting in general was taken up positively.[444] Already existing

---

Sion, Switzerland, 12–13 May 2011, <https://www.ohchr.org/EN/HRBodies/HRTD/Pages/Documents.aspx> [accessed 02 December 2019].
433 *Ibid*, 4.
434 *Ibid*, 5.
435 *Ibid*, 7.
436 *Ibid*, 7.
437 *Ibid*, 6.
438 *Ibid*, 6.
439 Office of the High Commissioner for Human Rights, *Consultation for States on Treaty Body Strengthening*, Geneva, 7 &8 February 2012, <https://www.ohchr.org/EN/HRBodies/HRTD/Pages/Documents.aspx> [accessed 02 December 2019].
440 *Ibid*, para 18.
441 *Ibid*.
442 *Ibid*.
443 *Ibid*, para 20.
444 *Ibid*, para 43 f.

alternatives, such as the list of issues prior to reporting or the common core document, were taken up cautiously, but mainly positively.[445]

In April 2012, shortly before the release of the High Commissioner for Human Rights' report on the Treaty Body strengthening process, state parties were invited to a two-day consultation to New York (NY, USA). The outcome document[446] is a comprehensive report covering two days of discussions. Concerning the reporting process, the discussions evolved mainly around the list of issues prior to reporting, the further development of an aligned reporting process, with focus on the establishment of a comprehensive reporting calendar and the increase of support by technical cooperation and capacity building with the assistance of the Treaty Bodies. The idea of a review *in absentia* received little attention and even less support by the state parties.[447] New ideas on the handling of non-reporting states were introduced by the states themselves, namely the creation of a General Assembly working group concerned with consistent non-reporting states,[448] and a Treaty Body member, who was proposing *in-situ* visits.[449]

e. Academia

In October 2011 an academic consultation was hosted in Lucerne (Switzerland). Various academics and experts interested in the Treaty Body system were invited to respond to the call of the UN High Commissioner for Human Rights. Those consultations were concluded with a concluding report.[450] The participants discussed different proposals for the strengthening of the existing reporting procedure and came up with the following recommendations: to further harmonize the process beyond the lowest common denominator, the Treaty Bodies should adopt a consistent terminology, strengthen the role of the chairpersons as coordinators and be open to innovations.[451] The list of issues prior to reporting should be examined regarding its effectivity towards the improvement of reporting compliance.[452] To reduce costs and increase the amount of reviewed reports it was proposed that Treaty Bodies could work in smaller

---

445 *Ibid,* paras 44 ff.
446 Office of the High Commissioner for Human Rights, *Report on the Third Consultation for States parties,* New York, 2 & 3 April 2012, <https://www.ohchr.org/EN/HRBodies/HRTD/Pages/Documents.aspx> [accessed 02 December 2019].
447 *Ibid,* para 45.
448 *Ibid,* para 46.
449 *Ibid,* para 51.
450 Centre of Human Rights Education (PHZ Lucerne), *Lucerne Academic Consultation on Strengthening the United Nations Treaty Body System,* 24–25 October 2011, <https://www.ohchr.org/EN/HRBodies/HRTD/Pages/Documents.aspx> [accessed 02 December 2019].
451 *Ibid,* 5.
452 *Ibid,* 5.

chambers, establish preparation groups or have one member review a report and write a draft Concluding Observation, which, if approved by the Treaty Body, would conclude the process.[453]

Generally, the participants held that the existing system had to be maintained due to the specific rights protected under the different treaties. Nevertheless, to make the system sustainable and effective, they saw the need of integrating the work of the various committees.[454] It was proposed to divide the organization of the system into full-time standing members and a pool of non-permanent experts to support the review of specific reports within their expertise.[455]

f. United Nations Entities

The strengthening process also sparked inter-agency discussions between various entities and specialized agencies within the UN framework.

Resulting from a consultation on 28 November 2011, the entities and agencies published a document on their proposals for the strengthening of the Treaty Bodies.[456] Their proposals recommended measures such as information letters prior to reporting deadlines, combined reports by states (in the extreme even unified reporting), the engagement with national parliaments and the general use of the list of issues prior to reporting (with responses to it as a substitute of the report).[457]

g. Multi-Stakeholder Meetings

In November 2011, a multi-stakeholder seminar organized by the Maastricht Centre for Human Rights was conducted. In their outcome document[458] the participants proposed to focus a reporting cycle on specified issues (not more than four) in order to streamline and deepen the information reported by the state parties, the development of a synchronized 'master calendar', consolidated reporting on issues similar in substance

---

453   Ibid, 6.
454   Ibid, 8
455   Ibid, 9.
456   Office of the High Commissioner for Human Rights, *Consultation on treaty body strengthening with UN entities and specialized agencies*, 28 November 2011, <https://www.ohchr.org/EN/HRBodies/HRTD/Pages/Documents.aspx> [accessed 02 December 2019].
457   Ibid, 2–4.
458   Maastricht Centre for Human Rights, *The Universal Periodic Review Process and the Treaty Bodies: Constructive Cooperation or Deepening Divisions? Recommendations arising from the seminar held on 25 November 2011*, Maastricht, The Netherlands, <https://www.ohchr.org/EN/HRBodies/HRTD/Pages/Documents.aspx> [accessed 02 December 2019].

although regulated under different treaties and the overall application of the list of issues prior to reporting.[459]

The Human Rights Law Centre of the University of Nottingham facilitated a multi-stakeholder meeting involving chairpersons, Treaty Body members, conveners of the previous consultations and additional experts in 2011. The outcome document[460] of this meeting reflected on the recommendations and provided a cumulative view on the process including own proposals. Recommendations concerning state reporting were numerous. The participants reiterated the creation of a comprehensive reporting calendar to allow advance planning, the cooperation between the Treaty Bodies to support the state parties and harmonize their procedures, the development of a comparable process for review in absence of a report and the active involvement of members of civil society.[461] Furthermore, they agreed that a focused starting point for the reporting cycle, meaning specific issues previously identified for the state party, would greatly assist in the improvement of reporting.[462] Also, they considered alternatives to the 'classical' reporting, such as the partly used list of issues prior to reporting, the consideration of reports in chambers, cross-referencing and the extended usage of the common core document.[463] On the organizational side, they proposed to include compliance as a criterion for the election of Treaty Body members[464], joint statements on coinciding content[465], the build-up and strengthening of national frameworks[466] as well as the increased capacity building and technical assistance by the OHCHR[467].

3. Report of the High Commissioner for Human Rights, 2012

After three years of consultations, the High Commissioner for Human Rights[468] presented a first summary of those proposals she held to be the most promising. In her comprehensive report 'Strengthening the United Nations human rights treaty body

---

459   Ibid, 1 f.
460   Dublin II Meeting, *Strengthening the United Nations Human Rights Treaty Body System*, Outcome Document, 10–11 November 2011, <https://www.ohchr.org/EN/HRBodies/HRTD/Pages/Documents.aspx> [accessed 02 December 2019].
461   Ibid, paras 63 ff.
462   Ibid, para 65.
463   Ibid, paras 66–68, 72.
464   Ibid, para 77.
465   Ibid, para 73.
466   Ibid, para 79 f., 87.
467   Ibid, paras 84.
468   Then: Ms. Navanethem Pillay, see <https://www.ohchr.org/EN/AboutUs/Pages/NaviPillay.aspx> [accessed 02 December 2019].

system'[469], she reflected on the ongoing process and identified those proposals which gained the most support amongst all stakeholders. The report discussed every area of the Treaty Body System as well as the background and development of the strengthening process.

As can already be seen in the introduction, her key proposals concerning the reporting procedure were the establishment of a comprehensive reporting calendar, the increase of technical assistance and capacity building, the usage of a simplified reporting procedure and the strict limitation of the extent of the documents.[470]

The basis for her proposals was an in-depth analysis of the then given situation, which, with regard to non-reporting state parties, showed no great improvement in comparison to previous years. In 2010 and 2011 only 16 % of the reports were submitted on time.[471] Even with a generous timeframe of one year, two-thirds of the reports were still overdue.[472] Those numbers showed that despite the strengthening and reform process, which had already been in place for over twenty years, the previous changes to the system did not improve the situation.

To finally change this situation, the High Commissioners' proposals were backed up with the ideas derived from the stakeholder consultations conducted beforehand so they had the best chance to be accepted by every party involved in the system.[473] Also, the High Commissioner had her office calculate the cost of each proposal.

The comprehensive reporting calendar was proposed. This calendar came up in almost every one of the previous consultations and was expected to give the procedure a strict structure and nature. The expectation was, that by its introduction, states would be more engaged with their reporting to adhere to the strict deadline.[474] Especially combined with the Universal Periodic Review calendar, the High Commissioner expressed great approval for this idea.[475] She proposed a five-year circle, with a report on two treaties per year.[476]

The debated proposal of a review in absence of a report was not given much attention, mainly because by this time, almost all Treaty Bodies had established a procedure to

---

469   Note by the Secretary-General, *United Nations reform: measures and proposals*, UN Doc. A/66/860, 26 June 2012.
470   *Ibid*, 11.
471   *Ibid*, 21 f.
472   *Ibid*, 21.
473   *Ibid*, 10.
474   *Ibid*, 39.
475   *Ibid*, 37 ff.
476   *Ibid*, 37.

Chapter 2: Previous Reform Proposals

review non-reporting states without a report.[477] Hence, this measure seemed to be *de facto* implemented.

Apart from this increased streamlining, the High Commissioner proposed the simplification of the whole process. She recommended the general introduction of a 'simplified reporting procedure'.[478] In 2010, this procedure was partially used by Treaty Bodies, but only on an optional and/or trial basis.[479] The simplified reporting procedure was intended to be the successor to the list of issues prior to reporting. The idea was to have a questionnaire sent to the state parties, to which they should answer in a report. Such report would then be the basis of the dialogue. Thereby, the usual reporting cycle would be shortened by one step and the reporting cycle for a state party could be finished faster.[480]

In order to simplify the procedure, the High Commissioner, with reference to the harmonized reporting guidelines of 2006[481], recommended the usage of the common core document. This document was supposed to paint the bigger picture of a state with information relevant to all Treaty Bodies.[482] She expected the common core document to significantly shorten and focus the periodic reports as lots of cross-cutting information would be submitted with this basic document whereby unnecessary duplication of information would be avoided.[483]

A more technical issue was the call upon the state parties to adhere to the page limitations introduced by the harmonized reporting guidelines in 2006.[484] According to the High Commissioners' report, more than 60 % of the periodic reports exceeded the introduced limitation of 40 pages, which not only resulted in an ever increasing workload for the Treaty Bodies that considered those reports, but also had a great impact on the budget due to the translation costs.[485]

---

477 Ibid, 39.
478 Ibid, 48 ff.
479 Ibid, 49.
480 Ibid, 50.
481 Report of the Inter-Committee Technical Working Group, *Harmonized guidelines on reporting under the international human rights treaties, including guidelines on a common core document and treaty-specific documents*, UN Doc. HRI/MC/2006/3, 10 May 2006, and Report of the Inter-Committee Technical Working Group, *Harmonized Guidelines on reporting under the International human Rights Treaties, Including Guidelines on a Common Core Document and Treaty-Specific Documents*, Corrigendum, UN Doc. HRI/MC/2006/3/Corr. 1, 11 July 2006.
482 Note by the Secretary-General, *United Nations reform: measures and proposals*, UN Doc. A/66/860, 26 June 2012, 53.
483 Ibid, 53.
484 Ibid, 54.
485 Ibid, 55.

The call for support by the state parties, be it technical assistance or capacity building, was also addressed by the High Commissioner: she promised support to the maximum possible extent.[486]

The last proposal concerned with reporting called upon the states to establish a national standing reporting and coordination mechanism.[487] Such mechanism would be the central contact point for any question concerned with the Treaty Body. It would be responsible for preparing the reports, to follow up on them, to facilitate inquiries and individual communications.[488]

VI. Review 2020

The current process following the reform proposals of the past decades is the General Assembly Review 2020. The process was initiated by General Assembly Resolution 68/268[489], which scheduled a review of the whole Treaty Body system and obliged the Secretary-General to submit a biennial report on the developments in the strengthening process. Two biennial reports have been submitted so far, with the third currently being prepared.[490]

1. General Assembly Resolution 68/268, 2014

In April 2014, the UN General Assembly reflected on the Treaty Body strengthening process in its Resolution 68/268.[491] In the preambulatory clauses to this resolution, the General Assembly emphasized the great importance of the strengthening process and expressed its satisfaction with the initiatives taken so far.[492] The operative clauses mainly encouraged the implementation of various proposals made during the foregoing consultations, such as the offer and acceptance of the simplified reporting procedure, the usage of the common core document, the introduction of a strict word limit, the further harmonization of the reporting procedure or the increased capacity building on national level and cooperation with regional mechanisms. Apart from those more

---

486   Ibid, 84.
487   Ibid, 86.
488   Ibid, 87 f.
489   UN General Assembly, *Strengthening and enhancing the effective functioning of the human rights treaty body system*, UN Doc. A/Res/68/268, 21 April 2014.
490   For an overview see Homepage of the Office of the High Commissioner for Human Rights, Human Rights Bodies, on Treaty Body Strengthening: <https://www.ohchr.org/EN/HRBodies/HRTD/Pages/TBStrengthening.aspx> [accessed 02 December 2019].
491   UN General Assembly, *Strengthening and enhancing the effective functioning of the human rights treaty body system*, UN Doc. A/Res/68/268, 21 April 2014.
492   Ibid, preambulatory clauses 1 ff.

general clauses, three operative clauses of this resolution are especially relevant: 32, 40 and 41. Operative clause 32 offers state parties the possibility to get rid of their backlog with one combined report.[493] Even though this option could only be exercised in agreement with the relevant Treaty Body, it displays the increasing difficulties to achieve compliance and eliminate the already existing backlog. In operative clause 40, the General Assembly tasked the Secretary-General with submitting biennial reports on the progress of the strengthening process.[494] Finally, operative clause 41 introduces a review of the human rights Treaty Body system no later than 2020.[495] Those clauses read in conjunction established the recent strengthening process.

2. Biennial Reports

Since 2014, two biennial reports – as requested by the General Assembly – were submitted accordingly. Concerning state reporting, not much has changed. Overall compliance with the reporting obligation is still below 20%, despite a slight increase. Following the second biennial report in August 2018, the General Assembly in Resolution 73/162[496] re-emphasized its commitment to the strengthening process and requested the third and last biennial report to be submitted in January 2020, before the actual review would start.[497]

a. First and Second Biennial Report

In compliance with the request of the General Assembly in Resolution 68/268, the Secretary-General[498] submitted his first biennial report on 18 July 2016.[499] Regarding the State Reporting procedure, and especially the reporting compliance by State parties, information is scarce. What we learn from this report is that by January 2016 only 13% of the States were in full compliance with all of their reporting obligations, and that some non-complying states had not reported for more than 10 years.[500] Furthermore, five of the committees had experienced a decrease in the average number of reports received per year.[501] This information leads to the conclusion that there had been no improvement

---

493 *Ibid*, operative clause 32.
494 *Ibid*, operative clause 40.
495 *Ibid*, operative clause 41.
496 UN General Assembly, *Human rights treaty body system*, UN Doc. A/RES/73/162, 8 January 2019.
497 *Ibid*, operative clause 10.
498 Then Mr. Ban Ki-moon, see <https://www.un.org/sg/en/content/former-secretaries-general> [accessed 02 December 2019].
499 Report of the Secretary-General, *Status of the human rights treaty body system*, UN Doc. A/71/118, 18 July 2016.
500 *Ibid*.
501 *Ibid*, para 19.

in compliance. This contradicts the overall positive improvement of the system's effectivity, as concluded by the Secretary-General.[502]

The second biennial report pursuant to Resolution 68/268, which covered the period of 1 January 2016 to December 2017, was submitted by the Secretary-General[503] on 6 August 2018.[504] During that period, the overall reporting compliance increased to 17 %.[505] However, every Treaty Body experienced a decrease in the average number of reports submitted.[506] Hence, an improvement of the situation was not observed. In contrast to the overall encouragement to use the simplified reporting procedure, the Secretary-General held a skeptical position towards this approach. With reference to lacking empirical evidence of its effectivity and sustainability regarding resources, he recommended cautious consideration, especially in light of expected increase in ratifications and associated increased need for resources.[507] Nevertheless, in his future perspective, he considered ways to facilitate the whole review process.[508] This did not necessarily include the simplified reporting procedure, but seemed to imply the (partially conducted) review in absence of a report.

b. Preparation for the Third Biennial Report

In preparation for the third biennial report by the Secretary-General on the current reform process, the Office of the High Commissioner for Human Rights called for contributions and comments by states and other stakeholders.[509] Following this call, several states as well as NGOs and academia submitted proposals.

Until the deadline of 1 May 2019, several states answered the call of the Office of the High Commissioner on Human Rights.[510] The proposals submitted addressed for the

---

502 *Ibid*, para 87.
503 Then Mr. António Guterres, see: <https://www.un.org/sg/en/content/sg/biography> [accessed 02 December 2019].
504 Report of the Secretary-General, *Status of the human rights treaty body system*, UN Doc. A/73/309, 6 August 2018.
505 *Ibid*, para 19.
506 *Ibid*, para 21.
507 *Ibid*, para 44.
508 *Ibid*, para 84.
509 Office of the High Commissioner for Human Rights, *Questionnaire in relation to General Assembly Resolution 68/268*, 31 January 2019, <https://www.ohchr.org/EN/HRBodies/HRTD/Pages/3rdBiennialReportbySG.aspx> [accessed 02 December 2019].
510 See Office of the High Commissioner for Human Rights, Homepage Office of the High Commissioner for Human Rights, Third biennial report by the Secretary-General, <https://www.ohchr.org/EN/HRBodies/HRTD/Pages/3rdBiennialReportbySG.aspx> [accessed 02 December 2019]; in the following, the replies of the states are listed by the state's name for reasons of clarity; the full title can

most part issues which had been raised continuously in the previous reforms, which shows that there was little changes in the procedure until today. The majority of states is supportive of the simplified reporting procedure and a considerable number is already using it.[511] Some stakeholders even called upon the Treaty Bodies to establish the simplified reporting as the common procedure for reporting.[512] Word limits for reports were partially welcomed.[513] The coordination of the submission of reports and the subsequent review, mainly in form of a calendar or timetable, were requested by almost every submitting state.[514] Often the states criticized the short time periods between the reviews.[515]

Generally, states called for a heightened streamlining and harmonization of the process.[516] Specifically, no new obligations should be created in the process and the Treaty Bodies were reminded to remain within their mandate.[517] A great number of states pointed out that state parties are obliged to report to the international committees, as well as to the regional committees, the Universal Periodic Review mechanism and other special procedures. Those numerous obligations and their overlaps create difficulties for full compliance and should be taken into account in the reform process.[518] Overlaps per

---

be found in the Index of Authorities; for a better understanding, the indicator 'p.' for page is included exceptionally.

511 See for example reply by Australia (p. 4), Estonia (p. 1), Finland (p. 1, 4), Holy See (p. 2), Japan (p. 3), Liechtenstein (p. 3), Netherlands (p. 1), Philippines (p. 1), Poland (p. 1), Portugal (p. 1 f.), Republic of Korea (p. 1), Slovenia (p. 1), Sweden (p. 3), Thailand (p. 1), Turkey (p. 1); replies accessible: <https://www.ohchr.org/EN/HRBodies/HRTD/Pages/3rdBiennialReportbySG.aspx> [accessed: 02 December 2019].

512 See for example reply by Canada (p. 2), Estonia (p. 1), Liechtenstein (p. 2), Norway (p. 3), Switzerland (p. 2), Thailand (p. 1), Israel (p. 2), Palestine (p. 3); replies accessible: <https://www.ohchr.org/EN/HRBodies/HRTD/Pages/3rdBiennialReportbySG.aspx> [accessed: 02 December 2019].

513 For example replies by Turkey (p. 1) and Finland (p. 2), accessible: <https://www.ohchr.org/EN/HRBodies/HRTD/Pages/3rdBiennialReportbySG.aspx> [accessed: 02 December 2019].

514 See for example reply by Australia (p. 2), Bulgaria (p.1), Brazil (p. 2), Canada (p. 1), Finland (p. 5), Netherlands (p. 1), Pakistan (p. 2), Portugal (p. 3), Sweden (p. 5), Switzerland, (p. 2), Thailand (p. 2), Turkey (p. 2); replies accessible: <https://www.ohchr.org/EN/HRBodies/HRTD/Pages/3rdBiennialReportbySG.aspx> [accessed: 02 December 2019].

515 See for example reply by the Netherlands (p. 2), Israel (p 2), Finland (p. 5), Estonia (p. 2); replies accessible: <https://www.ohchr.org/EN/HRBodies/HRTD/Pages/3rdBiennialReportbySG.aspx> [accessed: 02 December 2019].

516 See for example reply by Japan (p. 4), Bulgaria (p. 1), Brazil (p. 1), Finland (p. 4), the Group of Small States (p. 4), Liechtenstein (p. 2), Israel (p. 3); replies accessible: <https://www.ohchr.org/EN/HRBodies/HRTD/Pages/3rdBiennialReportbySG.aspx> [accessed: 02 December 2019].

517 See for example reply by the Holy See (p. 2); reply accessible: <https://www.ohchr.org/EN/HRBodies/HRTD/Pages/3rdBiennialReportbySG.aspx> [accessed: 02 December 2019].

518 See for example reply by Bulgaria (p. 1), Brazil (p. 2), Estonia (p. 1), Finland (p. 7), the Group of Small States (p. 3 f.), Netherlands (p. 1), Japan (p. 2), Sweden (p. 5 f.; 7.), Thailand (p. 2), Norway

VI. Review 2020

se were even considered to reduce the credibility of the Treaty Bodies themselves.[519] To reduce those overlaps, combined reports[520] were positively mentioned.

On administration, the states proposed a bicameral system for the committees[521] or a clustering of the reports[522] following the proposal of the 2018 Report 'Optimizing the UN Treaty Body System, Academic Platform Report in the 2020 Review' published by the Geneva Academy of International Humanitarian Law and Human Rights[523], back-to-back examinations[524], a template for the report[525], a Secretariat for the reporting procedure[526] and joint reviews[527].

Apart from states, seven other stakeholders contributed to the preparation with written submissions.[528] The proposals concerned with the state reporting procedure were divergent:

The submission of the Center for Reproductive Rights considered different issues of the Treaty Body System,[529] such as resource constraints and individual communications.

(p. 3), Switzerland (p. 3), Pakistan (p.2); replies accessible: <https://www.ohchr.org/EN/HRBodies/HRTD/Pages/3rdBiennialReportbySG.aspx> [accessed: 02 December 2019].

519 Reply by Bulgaria (p. 1), reply accessible: <https://www.ohchr.org/EN/HRBodies/HRTD/Pages/3rdBiennialReportbySG.aspx> [accessed: 02 December 2019].

520 See for example reply by the Holy See (p. 2), accessible: <https://www.ohchr.org/EN/HRBodies/HRTD/Pages/3rdBiennialReportbySG.aspx> [accessed: 02 December 2019].

521 See reply by Republic of Korea (p. 2), Sweden (p. 5), Germany (p. 2 f.); replies accessible: <https://www.ohchr.org/EN/HRBodies/HRTD/Pages/3rdBiennialReportbySG.aspx> [accessed: 02 December 2019]

522 Reply by Germany (p. 3), accessible: <https://www.ohchr.org/EN/HRBodies/HRTD/Pages/3rdBiennialReportbySG.aspx> [accessed: 02 December 2019].

523 Geneva Academy of International Humanitarian Law and Human Rights, *Optimizing the UN Treaty Body System, Academic Platform Report in the 2020 Review*, 7 May 2018, <https://www.geneva-academy.ch/news/detail/121-optimizing-the-un-treaty-bodies-system> [accessed 02 December 2019].

524 See only reply by Germany (p. 2), accessible: <https://www.ohchr.org/EN/HRBodies/HRTD/Pages/3rdBiennialReportbySG.aspx> [accessed: 02 December 2019].

525 See only reply by the Group of Small States (p. 4), accessible: <https://www.ohchr.org/EN/HRBodies/HRTD/Pages/3rdBiennialReportbySG.aspx> [accessed: 02 December 2019]

526 See only reply by the Group of Small States (p. 5), accessible: <https://www.ohchr.org/EN/HRBodies/HRTD/Pages/3rdBiennialReportbySG.aspx> [accessed: 02 December 2019].

527 See reply by Israel (p. 2 f.), accessible: <https://www.ohchr.org/EN/HRBodies/HRTD/Pages/3rdBiennialReportbySG.aspx> [accessed: 02 December 2019].

528 Those are: Center for Reproductive Rights; Geneva Academy of International Humanitarian Law and Human Rights; GQUAL; International Service for Human Rights; Jacob Blaustein Institute for the Advancement of Human Rights; Joint-NGOs; Norwegian Centre for Human Rights, see <https://www.ohchr.org/EN/HRBodies/HRTD/Pages/3rdBiennialReportbySG.aspx> [accessed 27 November 2019].

529 Center for Reproductive Rights, *Submission from Center for Reproductive Rights to OHCHR Questionnaire in relation to General Assembly resolution 68/268: Comments on the state of the human rights treaty*

Chapter 2: Previous Reform Proposals

On the issue of compliance with reporting obligations, the Center stressed the importance of reporting for the participation of members of the civil society and commended the *in absentia* reviews as well as reviews without a report. The Center considered the reduction of the frequency of reporting as risky and overlaps between committees desirable due to the specificities of the individual treaties. Furthermore, they rejected the consolidation and clustering of reports due to the risk of reduced visibility of civil society contributions, the marginalization of vulnerable groups, and the potential decrease of the quality of the reports and dialogues.[530] Finally, the Center supported the idea of a comprehensive reporting calendar as well as the harmonization of working methods, especially the increased use of the simplified reporting procedure.[531]

The Geneva Academy of International Humanitarian Law and Human Rights provided a short summary of their 2018 report 'Optimizing the UN Treaty Body System'[532] The main recommendations concerned the consolidation of reports and state reviews, either by producing a single state report to be reviewed every eight years or by having a partial consolidation through clusters with a review every four years.[533]

The International Service for Human Rights recommended the simplified reporting procedure as compulsory to increase understanding and usage of this helpful instrument.[534]

The Jacob Blaustein Institute for the Advancement of Human Rights emphasized that a reduction of the reporting burden will not lead to the desired result; rather, the overlaps should be tackled by leaving the consideration of specialized topics to the specialized committees (such as the Committee on the Rights of the Child) and have general topics

---

body system in view of the upcoming review by 9 April 2020, of the effectiveness of the measures taken in order to ensure the sustainability (of treaty bodies), and, on any further action to strengthen and enhance the effective functioning of the human rights treaty body system, <https://www.ohchr.org/EN/HRBodies/HRTD/Pages/3rdBiennialReportbySG.aspx> [accessed 02 December 2019].

530   *Ibid*, 3f.
531   *Ibid*, 5.
532   Geneva Academy of International Humanitarian Law and Human Rights, *Optimizing the UN Treaty Body System, Academic Platform Report in the 2020 Review*, 7 May 2018, <https://www.geneva-academy.ch/news/detail/121-optimizing-the-un-treaty-bodies-system> [accessed 02 December 2019].
533   Geneva Academy of International Humanitarian Law and Human Rights, *Submission by the Geneva Academy of International Humanitarian Law and Human Rights to the Questionnaire in Relation to General Assembly Resolution 68/268 circulated by OHCHR, academic input into the 2020 review*, <https://www.ohchr.org/EN/HRBodies/HRTD/Pages/3rdBiennialReportbySG.aspx> [accessed 02 December 2019].
534   International Service for Human Rights, *ISHR submission to OHCHR Questionnaire in relation to General Assembly resolution 68/268*, May 2019, <https://www.ohchr.org/EN/HRBodies/HRTD/Pages/3rdBiennialReportbySG.aspx> [accessed 02 December 2019], 10.

be exclusively considered by committees with a broad mandate (such as the Human Rights Committee).[535]

The Norwegian Centre for Human Rights proposed to introduce a 'Technical Review of Impact and Progress' to monitor the situation within a state between the reviews, preferably in the form of country visits. Furthermore, the establishment of a reporting schedule is supported. They also recommended that, as an underlying principle, the synergy between the Treaty Body system and other human rights mechanisms should be increased.[536]

c. Third Biennial Report

On 10 January 2020 the Secretary-General[537] submitted the third and (for now) last biennial report on the status of the human rights treaty body system.[538] According to his report, there were only 38 State parties (equals 19 per cent) in full compliance with their reporting obligations.[539] The committees experienced a slight but overall insignificant increase in the average number of submitted reports of 1.1 per cent.[540] The report contains brief sections on the simplified reporting procedure[541] and on proposals which the Chairs to the Committees agreed on implementing.[542] What becomes clear from this report is that over the course of the past six years, the situation concerning the submission of state reports and herewith the compliance with the reporting obligation did not improve.

---

535 Jacob Blaustein Institute for the Advancement of Human Rights, *Recommendations for the Third Biennial Report of the UN Secretary-General on the Status of the Human Rights Treaty Body System*, 24 April 2019, <https://www.ohchr.org/EN/HRBodies/HRTD/Pages/3rdBiennialReportbySG.aspx> [accessed 02 December 2019], 1.
536 Norwegian Centre for Human Rights, *Response by the Norwegian Centre for Human Rights (NCHR), Faculty of Law, University of Oslo, to the Questionnaire on the implementation of General Assembly resolution 68/268 on 'Strengthening and enhancing the effective functioning of the human rights treaty body system'*, 18 March 2019, <https://www.ohchr.org/EN/HRBodies/HRTD/Pages/3rdBiennialReportbySG.aspx> [accessed 02 December 2019], 3.
537 Then Mr. António Guterres, see: <https://www.un.org/sg/en/content/sg/biography> [accessed 18 June 2020].
538 Report of the Secretary-General, *Status of the human rights treaty body system*, UN Doc. A/74/643, 10 January 2020.
539 *Ibid*, para 11.
540 *Ibid*, para 13.
541 *Ibid*, paras 35 f.
542 *Ibid*, para 61 f.; for further detail see *Report of the Chairs of the human rights treaty bodies on their thrirty-first annual meeting*, 30 July 2019, UN Doc. A/74/256, Annex III.

VII. Conclusion

Even though the Treaty Body system has been under review and ideas for its improvement have been exchanged for over 30 years, the proposals are still evolving – in one form or another – around the same issues: lighten the reporting burden, streamline the procedures, simplify the process and increase the support by the Treaty Bodies. Most of the proposals which have been and are still discussed until today had already been brought forward in the Alston Proposals, for example the flexibility of the reporting periodicity, the consolidation of reporting guidelines, cross-referencing and the review in absence of a report. The constant review of the process makes it clear, that so far, either the will or the capacities were missing to actually implement what has been proposed for years. There are proposals, such as the simplified reporting procedure, which were repeatedly welcomed by various stakeholders; and yet, the procedure remains mainly optional.[543]

From proposals made over the course of 30 years of reform and strengthening process, which introduced a great variety of ideas on how to improve the Treaty Body system, only very few ideas were taken up and implemented. The call for a more streamlined procedure amongst the Treaty Bodies was handled by adopting harmonized reporting guidelines in 2006.[544] With these reporting guidelines, the procedure was renewed, now consisting of the common core document and the treaty specific documents. A further addendum was the simplified reporting procedure. However, due to its optional nature, it is only applied if the relevant state party agrees to it.[545] Furthermore, almost all Treaty Bodies established a procedure to review non-complying state parties in absence of a

---

543 At its 126th session in July 2019 the Human Rights Committee decided to move from an opt-in to an opt-out model, making the simplified reporting procedure obligatory if the State party does not indicate that it wishes to further use the standard reporting by 31 December 2019. Simplified reporting will in the future be applied to initial reports as well (Human Rights Committee, *Decision on additional measures to simplify the reporting procedure and increase predictability*, 1–26 July 2019 (will be reflected in the Committee's annual report (UN Doc. A/75/40, to be issued in 2020), accessible: <https://www.ohchr.org/EN/HRBodies/CCPR/Pages/PredictableReviewCycle.aspx> [accessed 02 December 2019]).

544 Report of the Inter-Committee Technical Working Group, *Harmonized guidelines on reporting under the international human rights treaties, including guidelines on a common core document and treaty-specific documents*, UN Doc. HRI/MC/2006/3, 10 May 2006.

545 Human Rights Committee, *Focused reports based on replies to lists of issues prior to reporting (LOIPR): Implementation of the new optional reporting procedure (LOIPR procedure)*, UN Doc. CCPR/C/99/4, 29 September 2010; for the Human Rights Committee see: Human Rights Committee, *Decision on additional measures to simplify the reporting procedure and increase predictability*, 1–26 July 2019 (will be reflected in the Committee's annual report (UN Doc. A/75/40, to be issued in 2020), accessible: <https://www.ohchr.org/EN/HRBodies/CCPR/Pages/PredictableReviewCycle.aspx> [accessed 02 December 2019].

VII. Conclusion

report.[546] This step was not taken as a coordinated measure, but introduced by each committee individually.

Every proposal implemented so far was an addendum to the already existing system. Thereby, the reform and strengthening process created an increasingly intransparent, confusing and burdensome environment.[547] Furthermore, the system itself grew to now eight treaties and two Optional Protocols obliging state parties to report periodically. Those, however, are only the obligations created within the human rights system of the UN. The past reform and strengthening process did not lead to a solution, which actually improved the situation, as can be seen in the recent numbers on non- and late reporting states[548], as well as in the Second Biennial Report by the Secretary-General in 2018[549]. Considering the overall situation, the whole process, all the proposals, including those few that were actually implemented without changing the system itself, one can conclude that the parties involved were overcautious in their effort to make the system more efficient. Radical changes to the system were frequently proposed. Proposals such as the complete unification of the system by introducing a unified standing Treaty Body or the production of only one single state report were based on the premise that the system as it was was not practicable and needed a complete and utter reform. Nevertheless, although being well thought through, each proposal was rejected, primarily for the reason that they would require a change of the whole treaty system which would either be costly or might diminish the protection of specific rights, especially those of vulnerable groups.

It appears like the parties involved only saw the two extremes, namely to radically change everything (as can be seen in the example of the proposal of a unified standing Treaty Body in 2006) or to do so little that the influence is barely measurable (introducing page limits without enforcing them; introducing a new procedure, but making it optional). However, what becomes obvious from the course of the reforms is that the stakeholders can agree on certain minimum denominators. As a result from the examination of the process in this Chapter, it can be inferred that these lowest common denominators are (1) to increase the flexibility of the system, (2) to further streamline

---

546 See also Oette, *'The UN Human Rights Treaty Bodies: Impact and Future'*, 102; for the Human Rights Committee see *General Comment No. 30*, UN Doc. CCPR/C/21/Rev.2/Add.12, 18 September 2002, para 4.
547 See on the same challenge in the African Human Rights System Heyns, *'The African Regional Human Rights System: The African Charter'* (2003), 108 Penn St L Rev,679, 702
548 By April 2019, 36 out of 197 States parties were in compliance with their reporting obligations, see: United Nations Treaty Body Database, <https://tbinternet.ohchr.org/_layouts/TreatyBodyExternal/LateReporting.aspx> [accessed 02 December 2019].
549 Report of the Secretary-General, *Status of the human rights treaty body system*, UN Doc. A/73/309, 6 August 2018, para 19 f.

Chapter 2: Previous Reform Proposals

the reporting procedure, (3) to reduce the reporting burden to increase compliance but with respect to regulations of special protection and (4) to be implementable without eradicating or fundamentally changing the existing system.

It becomes similarly clear that the previous efforts did not change the system in accordance with these factors. Therefore, the following Chapter provides a proposal based on the identified minimum denominators in accordance with the relevant treaties. It shall adhere to the criteria put forward by Philip Alston of '*i) minimizing the burden placed on States and ii) maximizing the effectiveness of measures to ensure respect for human rights*'[550].

---

550 Note by the Secretariat, *Status of Preparation of Publications, Studies and Documents for the World Conference, Interim report on updated study by Mr. Philip Alston*, Addendum, UN Doc. A/CONF.157/PC/62/Add.11/Rev.1, 22 April 1993, para 126.

Chapter 3:
Integrative Reporting 'Bottom-Up' and Sanctions under International Law for the Breach of the State Reporting Obligation
Integrative Application and the Possibility to Sanction

Despite the troublesome past and the unclear future of the state reporting procedure, it still represents the most long-standing instrument for continuous human rights monitoring and one of two universal monitoring mechanisms.[551] Especially due to its mandatory nature by becoming obligatory immediately with the ratification of a treaty, it has the potential to effectively monitor compliance with human rights in the long-term. Furthermore, it is preferable to prevent human rights violations through constant monitoring to only punishing violations.[552] The procedure as such should be maintained to enable oversight committees to evaluate the situation based on reliable data.[553]

However, as the previous Chapters show, the status quo of the system cannot be upheld. Reform proposals, which have been discussed for 30 years and counting, did not improve the situation. On the contrary, most changes to the system made the already intransparent situation more chaotic, increased the reporting burden for the states and made the conditions of the working environment for the Treaty Bodies worse.

There is consensus among the stakeholders on certain characteristics that they consider relevant for the functioning of the Treaty Body system. With a focus on state reporting, they require the system to be flexible, consolidated (at least the reporting guidelines), simple (i.e. by using cross-references and the simplified reporting procedure) and – within limitations – enforceable (i.e. by conducting reviews in absence of a report). Only a few stakeholders insisted to uphold the full and unimpeded sovereignty of the state parties; generally, limitations to the sovereignty of states were considered acceptable to increase the effectivity of the Treaty Body system.[554] Although this can only be deducted from the considerations of stakeholders on the international level, one can

---

551 Kälin, 'Examination of state reports', 17.
552 See also Tomuschat, 214.
553 Also in favor of maintaining the procedure see for example Centre of Human Rights Education (PHZ Lucerne), *Lucerne Academic Consultation on Strengthening the United Nations Treaty Body System*, 24–25 October 2011, <https://www.ohchr.org/EN/HRBodies/HRTD/Pages/Documents.aspx> [accessed 02 December 2019], 5; cf Kälin, 'Examination of state reports', 71 f.; Report of the Secretary-General, *Status of the human rights treaty body system*, UN Doc. A/73/309, 6 August 2018, para 89.
554 Cf Oette, 'The UN Human Rights Treaty Bodies: Impact and Future', 98.

infer the same for the regional level based on the wide consensus amongst the states on the international level.

The main criteria that seem to underlie every proposal made are still those formulated by Philip Alston in 1993 requesting the system to minimize the burden on states and maximize the effectivity.[555] Based on this premise and the considerations made in the previous Chapters, the proposals made in this Chapter are twofold:

First, a new form of reporting: the integrative reporting procedure[556]. The streamlining of the reporting process is increased by the creation of a permanent basis, accessible by all relevant stakeholders, consisting of a baseline report on the general situation within the state and a bottom-up review of the legislative framework protecting human rights. Double reporting is expected to decrease through the integration of the various treaties from the international as well as the regional sphere. The comprehensive periodic report shall be completely replaced by a periodic Q&A based on the pre-existing database.

Second, as a measure of last resort, the possibility of sanctioning persistent non-reporting states is discussed. In the absence of treaty specific sanctions recourse is taken to customary rules of international law.

I. Integrative Reporting

Over the course of the reform process, it became clear that proposals must be implementable within the existing treaty system.[557] Such proposals encounter widespread acceptance of the states (which consented to the existing treaty framework) as well as the Treaty Bodies and do not require vast amounts of money for their implementation. Keeping this in mind, and taking recourse to the common denominators identified in the previous chapter, the presented proposal is based on the following criteria:

---

555 Note by the Secretariat, *Status of Preparation of Publications, Studies and Documents for the World Conference, Interim report on updated study by Mr. Philip Alston*, Addendum, UN Doc. A/CONF.157/PC/62/Add.11/Rev.1, 22 April 1993, para 126.
556 A comparable procedure is (partially) used to identify value creation by organizations in the process of corporate reporting. A framework for integrated reporting (<https://integratedreporting.org/how-practical-advice-and-tools/> [accessed 02 December 2019]) was developed by the International Integrated Reporting Council, a global not-for-profit organization, and published in December 2013. For more information see <https://integratedreporting.org/> [accessed 02 December 2019]. The proposal made in this thesis is based on this framework and translates it into the State reporting system due to the comparability of the underlying idea.
557 Report of the Secretary-General, *Status of the human rights treaty body system*, UN Doc. A/73/309, 6 August 2018, para 82; see also for example *Japan's comments on the Questionnaire in relation to General Assembly resolution 68/268*, <https://www.ohchr.org/EN/HRBodies/HRTD/Pages/3rdBiennialReportbySG.aspx> [accessed 02 December 2019].

Chapter 3: Integrative Reporting 'Bottom-Up' and Sanctions under International Law

(1) to increase the flexibility of the system, (2) to further streamline the reporting procedure, (3) to reduce the reporting burden to increase compliance but with respect to regulations of special protection and (4) to be implementable without eradicating or fundamentally change the existing system.

The result of the previous considerations is the proposal of integrative reporting 'bottom-up'. It shifts the focus from the individual treaties ('top-down') to the state parties by introducing a mandatory comprehensive baseline report focused on the national situation and legislation ('bottom-up') while encompassing every treaty which contains a state reporting obligation in the regional and international human rights sphere the state in question is party to. The baseline report is complemented by a bottom-up review of the legislative framework of the relevant state party and a periodic Q&A consisting of a list of issues on treaty-specific regulations which the state is obliged to reply to in order to fulfill the reporting obligation. This procedure is intended to encompass regional and international regulations to create a comprehensive reporting system, which is why in this thesis the procedure is termed 'Integrative Reporting'. It is expected that an integrative procedure would be in the interest of all stakeholders. First approaches to create a rather holistic reporting environment can be seen in the positive stand on cross-referencing practice[558] as well as references to regional and international oversight committees, respectively[559]. As an individual concept it has not yet been proposed.

1. The Concept of Integrative Reporting

Every human rights treaty, international as well as regional, requests for its report a great amount of information similar to such required under the other treaties. This had already been recognized in previous proposals and resulted in the proposal (and partial adoption) of the harmonized reporting guidelines[560] as well as the simplified reporting

---

558 See for example Note by the Secretary General, *Effective implementation of international instruments on human rights, including reporting obligations under international human rights*, 8 November 1989, UN Doc. A/44/668, 8 November 1989, para 48 ff.; Advisory Council on Human Rights of Morocco, *Marrakesh Statement on strengthening the relationship between NHRIs and the human rights treaty bodies system*, 10 June 2010, accessible: <https://www.ohchr.org/en/hrbodies/hrtd/pages/documents.aspx> [accessed 02 December 2019], reprinted in Netherlands Quarterly of Human Rights 28 (2010), 121–27, para 16; Dublin II Meeting, *Strengthening the United Nations Human Rights Treaty Body System*, Outcome Document, 10–11 November 2011, <https://www.ohchr.org/EN/HRBodies/HRTD/Pages/Documents.aspx> [accessed 02 December 2019], para 72.

559 See for example Inter-American Commission on Human Rights, *Guidelines for Preparation of Progress Indicators in the Area of Economic, Social and Cultural Rights*, OAS Doc. OEA/Ser.L/V/II.132, Doc. 14, 19 July 2008, para 13.

560 Report of the Inter-Committee Technical Working Group, *Harmonized guidelines on reporting under the international human rights treaties, including guidelines on a common core document and treaty-specific documents*, UN Doc. HRI/MC/2006/3, 10 May 2006, para 4.

I. Integrative Reporting

procedure[561]. The harmonized reporting guidelines expect the state to submit a common core document entailing general information relevant for every Treaty Body. The requested information concerns government structure, history, ethnicity and the implementation or status of a few principles which were enshrined in almost every treaty, e. g. non-discrimination.[562] When using the optional simplified reporting procedure, the state would receive a list of issues based on which it is supposed to prepare the periodic report in the form of a written reply.[563] Such reports are deemed to be more precise and less burdensome for the state.[564] Since the procedure piloted in 2010, it has gained increasing support and is considered to assist the improvement of the system.[565] However, due to the optional nature of these procedures, the reporting system and especially the simplified reporting procedure has not yet unfolded its full potential.

The major distinctiveness of the procedure proposed in this thesis lies (1) in its mandatory nature and (2) in the comprehensive integration of both the international and the regional human rights treaties. The comprehensive integration is derived from the fact that the majority of international and regional human rights treaties regulate similar, if not the same content, most just vary slightly in their focus.[566] This lead to difficulties and

---

561 *Committee against Torture*, Report of the Committee against Torture, UN Doc. A/62/44, 6–24 November 2006 and 30 April-18 May 2007, para 23 f.; Human Rights Committee, *Focused reports based on replies to lists of issues prior to reporting (LOIPR): Implementation of the new optional reporting procedure (LOIPR procedure)*, UN Doc. CCPR/C/99/4, 29 September 2010; the Committee on Migrant Workers in 2011, the Committee on the Rights of Persons with Disabilities in 2013, the Committee on Economic, Social and Cultural Rights, the Committee on the Elimination of Racial Discrimination and the Committee on the Elimination of Discrimination against Women in 2014, and the Committee on the Rights of the Child in 2016. A total of 8 out of the 10 treaty bodies currently thus offer this procedure (Human Rights Committee, *Simplified reporting procedure*, Report of the Working Group, UN Doc. CCPR/C/123/3, 6 December 2018, para 33).

562 Report of the Inter-Committee Technical Working Group, *Harmonized guidelines on reporting under the international human rights treaties, including guidelines on a common core document and treaty-specific documents*, UN Doc. HRI/MC/2006/3, 10 May 2006, paras 27, 31 ff.

563 Human Rights Committee, *Focused reports based on replies to lists of issues prior to reporting (LOIPR): Implementation of the new optional reporting procedure (LOIPR procedure)*, UN Doc. CCPR/C/99/4, 29 September 2010, paras 1, 11.

564 *Ibid*, para 2.

565 See for example Human Rights Committee, *Simplified reporting procedure*, Report of the Working Group, UN Doc. CCPR/C/123/3, 6 December 2018, Summary; UN General Assembly, *Strengthening and enhancing the effective functioning of the human rights treaty body system*, UN Doc. A/Res/68/268, 21 April 2014, para 110; for the Human Rights Committee see: Human Rights Committee, *Decision on additional measures to simplify the reporting procedure and increase predictability*, 1–26 July 2019 (will be reflected in the Committee's annual report (UN Doc. A/75/40, to be issued in 2020), accessible: <https://www.ohchr.org/EN/HRBodies/CCPR/Pages/PredictableReviewCycle.aspx> [accessed 02 December 2019].

566 A table of overlapping treaty obligations in the UN Treaty Body System was already produced in the 1990 s, see Report of the Secretariat, *Guidelines on an expanded core document and treaty-specific targeted*

Chapter 3: Integrative Reporting 'Bottom-Up' and Sanctions under International Law

overlaps, which created a landscape of multiple applicable norms[567] and the potential of conflict.[568]

One could try to solve such conflicts and overlaps by taking recourse to the well-established conflict-solution techniques of *lex specialis derogat legi generali* and *lex posterior derogat legi priori*.[569] However, the application of those maxims proves difficult in the sphere of multilateral human rights treaties: *first*, it is questionable among whom those rules should be applied[570] – only between those two parties, who dispute the norm, or among all parties party to the relevant treaties? This question is especially challenging when a state is only party to one of the treaties in question, while the other is party to several, as this situation might be in conflict with the principle of *pacta tertiis nec nocet nec prosunt*.[571] *Second*, the application of *lex posterior* is a challenge due to the varying times of 'conclusion' of a multilateral treaty.[572] This challenge is also closely interconnected with the *lex specialis* question concerning the applicable rules in the relation between the state parties – in the case of an application vis-à-vis the entirety of states party to the treaties in question instead of a one-to-one application, the applicability may vary with each state party. *Third*, apart from the general difficulties of the *lex specialis* rule[573], its applicability to multilateral human rights treaties could spark two specific problems: one, it could disrupt the universality of human rights. The same act might violate the ICCPR and the CEDAW – by applying *lex specialis*, the violation of the ICCPR as the more general treaty would be subsidiary, if not excluded. Hence, there would be a fragmented application of treaties depending on the issue instead of a holistic picture of the violation. Two, it carries the risk of rendering the UN treaties meaningless, as most

---

reports and harmonized guidelines on reporting under the international human rights treaties, UN Doc. HRI/MC/2004/3, 9 June 2004, 9 f.
567   Or Multi-Sourced Equivalent Norms, as they are termed by Broude & Shany, see: *Multi-Sourced Equivalent Norms in International Law* (2011).
568   On resolutions of conflicts resulting from the fragmentation of international law: Peters, 'The refinement of international law: From fragmentation to regime interaction and politicization' (2017), I•CON, Vol. 15 (3), 671–704.
569   For a detailed study on those maxims see Report of the Study Group of the International Law Commission, Finalized by Martti Koskenniemi, *Fragmentation of International Law: Difficulties Arising from the Diversification and Expansion of International Law*, UN Doc. A/CN.4/L.682, 13 April 2006, paras 46–122; critical towards the application of *lex specialis* and *lex posterior* in international law Peters, 'The refinement of international law: From fragmentation to regime interaction and politicization' (2017), I•CON Vol. 15 No. 3, 682 f.
570   On this question Linderfalk, 'Who Are 'the Parties'? Article 31 Paragraph 3(c) of the 1969 Vienna Convention, and the 'Principle of Systemic Integration' Revisited' (2008) 55 NILR 343.
571   On the same challenge concerning conflict clauses Merkouris, 'Article 31(3)(c) VCLT and the Principle of Systemic Integration – Normative Shadows in Plato's Cave' (2015), 144 (with further references.).
572   Ibid, 158 (with further references)
573   For an overview see *Ibid*, 168 f.

states today are party to a corresponding regional human rights treaty, which, due to its specific scope, would enjoy preference. All of the above contradicts the idea of indivisible and universal human rights.

To prevent the deteriorating effect the application of the general conflict-rules could have on human rights protection, the integration of international and regional human rights treaties into the state report follows the idea of systemic integration. Hereby, the increasing fragmentation of human rights[574] protection shall be prevented and the universality of human rights upheld.

Systemic integration is a concept applied to prevent the so-called fragmentation of international law. Since the report of the Study Group of the International Law Commission (finalized by Martti Koskenniemi) on fragmentation in 2006[575] plenty of scholarship has been produced on this issue.[576] Systemic integration is primarily deducted from Art. 31 (3) VCLT[577], which obliges the interpreter of an international norm to consider other international documents in force between those two parties, who dispute the interpreted norm[578]. As an instrument for the interpretation of

---

574 For a comprehensive assessment of fragmentation in International Human Rights law see Ajevski, *Fragmentation in International Human Rights Law – Beyond Conflict of Laws* (2014), 32 NJHR 87, 87–98.
575 Report of the Study Group of the International Law Commission, Finalized by Martti Koskenniemi, *Fragmentation of International Law: Difficulties Arising from the Diversification and Expansion of International Law*, UN Doc. A/CN.4/L.682, 13 April 2006.
576 See for example Rachovitsa, '*The Principle of Systemic Integration in Human Rights Law*', 66 ICLQ 557 (2017), 557–588; McLachlan, '*The Principle of Systemic Integration and Article 31(3)(c) of the Vienna Convention*' (2005) 54 ICLQ 279; Merkouris, *Article 31(3)(c) VCLT and the Principle of Systemic Integration – Normative Shadows in Plato's Cave* (2015); Linderfalk, '*Who Are 'the Parties'? Article 31 Paragraph 3(c) of the 1969 Vienna Convention, and the 'Principle of Systemic Integration' Revisited*' (2008) 55 NILR 343; d'Aspremont, '*The Systemic Integration of International Law by Domestic Courts: Domestic Judges as Architects of the Consistency of the International Legal Order*' in Nollkaemper & Fauchald (eds), *The Practice of International and National Courts and the (De-) Fragmentation of International Law* (2012), 141–165.
577 Report of the Study Group of the International Law Commission, Finalized by Martti Koskenniemi, *Fragmentation of International Law: Difficulties Arising from the Diversification and Expansion of International Law*, UN Doc. A/CN.4/L.682, 13 April 2006; McLachlan, '*The Principle of Systemic Integration and Article 31(3)(c) of the Vienna Convention*' (2005) 54 ICLQ 279, 280; d'Aspremont, '*The Systemic Integration of International Law by Domestic Courts: Domestic Judges as Architects of the Consistency of the International Legal Order*' in Nollkaemper & Fauchald (eds), *The Practice of International and National Courts and the (De-) Fragmentation of International Law* (2012), 141–165; Merkouris, *Article 31(3)(c) VCLT and the Principle of Systemic Integration – Normative Shadows in Plato's Cave* (2015).
578 This rule is widely regarded as reflecting customary international law, see Report of the Study Group of the International Law Commission, Finalized by Martti Koskenniemi, *Fragmentation of International Law: Difficulties Arising from the Diversification and Expansion of International Law*, UN Doc. A/CN.4/L.682, 13 April 2006, para 427 (with further references).

Chapter 3: Integrative Reporting 'Bottom-Up' and Sanctions under International Law

international law, systemic integration may only be applied while interpreting international obligations enshrined in interstate treaties[579] which contain rules applicable in the relations between the parties[580].

The object and purpose of systemic integration in international law is to cater for the intertwined nature of international law by solving normative conflicts.[581] International law cannot be split up into its individual sources; rather, it increasingly creates an interconnected system.[582] Following from this, the interpretation of a norm cannot be properly conducted without considering other similar obligations of the state party in question. The herewith achieved rapprochement of obligations in specific relationships of a disputed character can be joint into a holistic fundament for international legal practice, because if a norm has to be interpreted in light of other similar norms equally binding on the state in question, the same has to be valid for the legal practice. A state has to fulfill all its obligations enshrined in different treaties in order for it not to be in breach of international law.[583] The proposal of an integrative report is not an issue of interpretation, which is why the concept of systemic integration cannot be applied directly. Therefore, the underlying idea as well as the object and purpose of systemic integration is applied to the practice of international treaty law to create an integrative practice and strengthen the holistic concept of human rights.

Resulting from these considerations, integrative reporting is based on the herewith introduced concept of "integrative compliance". This concept is the practical consequence and advancement of systemic integration. It shall apply to the parallel fulfillment of similar or equal obligations under international law by a single action. This concept creates the basis for integrative reporting, covering regional and international obligations as far as they are overlapping.

Integrative compliance as a concept is consistent with and serves the enforcement of international law. States party to more than one of the relevant treaties consented to be

---

579 Schmalenbach, in Dörr & Schmalenbach (eds), *VCLT Commentary*, Art. 1 para 1.
580 In case of multilateral treaties, 'the parties' are not further specified – it could be between the parties in dispute or all parties to the treaty; see Report of the Study Group of the International Law Commission, Finalized by Martti Koskenniemi, *Fragmentation of International Law: Difficulties Arising from the Diversification and Expansion of International Law*, UN Doc. A/CN.4/L.682, 13 April 2006, para 426(c).
581 Cf Report of the Study Group of the International Law Commission, Finalized by Martti Koskenniemi, *Fragmentation of International Law: Difficulties Arising from the Diversification and Expansion of International Law*, UN Doc. A/CN.4/L.682, 13 April 2006, para 420.
582 Cf *ibid*, para 414.
583 If an international obligation is not fulfilled the State commits an internationally wrongful act according to Art. 2 *Draft articles on Responsibility of States for Internationally Wrongful Acts* [ILC Ybk 2001, / II(2), 26 (also available as Report on the work of the fifty-third session (2001), UN Doc. A/56/10 + Corr. 1, IV. E., 32 ff.)].

I. Integrative Reporting

bound by the regulations of each treaty individually, including the obligation to report. Therefore, according to the principle *pacta sunt servanda*, they are obliged to fulfill all of those obligations in good faith.[584] If several regulations require the same action for their fulfillment, and those actions can be merged into one action that fulfills several obligations satisfactorily, it is in the interest of efficiency and harmonization – both considered desirable for the Treaty Body system – to allow one action as the fulfillment of all corresponding obligations. This procedure would be sensitive to the specificities of the different treaties, as only such obligations could be subject to integrative compliance that regulate the same content. Lastly, as can be seen by comparing different reports of the same state to different committees, a great amount of similar information about compliance with treaty regulations is submitted to various oversight committees to show compliance with a specific obligation.[585]

Therefore, the concept of integrative compliance as the practical dimension of systemic integration is in line with international law and can therefore be applied to international and regional human rights treaties. It establishes the theoretical foundation for the integrative reporting procedure which is described in the following.

2. Rationale of Integrative Reporting

In the continuously growing framework of human rights and the growing fragmentation accompanying this growth it is necessary to promote cohesive approaches to integrate the various obligations and to thereby create a comprehensive framework of protection. Integrative reporting is an instrument to harmonize the various reporting obligations to create a cohesive monitoring environment which serves the purpose of integrative compliance as well as the indivisibility of (especially) human rights law. To serve this purpose, integrative reporting follows a certain rationale that is supposed to guide the state parties in the fulfillment of their reporting obligations.

First, the report is supposed to show the most pressing issues the state has to tackle in general. This could concern for example difficulties in providing adequate education to everyone, healthcare, violence of state organs against civilians or even armed insurgents threatening to overthrow the state. The report should indicate how the state intends to tackle those problems in the near future.

---

584 As enshrined in Art. 26 VCLT and reflected in the principle of *pacta sunt servanda*.
585 A table of overlapping treaty obligations in the United Nations Treaty Body System was already produced in the 1990s, see Report of the Secretariat, *Guidelines on an expanded core document and treaty-specific targeted reports and harmonized guidelines on reporting under the international human rights treaties*, UN Doc. HRI/MC/2004/3, 9 June 2004, 9f.

Chapter 3: Integrative Reporting 'Bottom-Up' and Sanctions under International Law

Second, the report must provide information on the interconnectivity of the different authorities that are mandated with the implementation of human rights in the national sphere. Especially important is the information on the cooperation between the different actors to evaluate whether human rights protection is provided as all-encompassing as intended.

Third, the report shall provide information on the relation between the state and other stakeholders, most importantly the beneficiaries of human rights protection, meaning individuals. Here, the state party is supposed to provide information on its human rights record, for example past and pending cases in front of national, regional and international courts or individual complaints pending at or concluded by oversight committees. The state is supposed to show how decisions are implemented and how victims of human rights violations are taken care of in the national framework and how the state makes sure that such violations will not be repeated.

Fourth, the report shall provide information on challenges that hinder the state in complying with its obligations. Such information could be the lack of financial or human resources, systemic defaults, overburdening or comparable difficulties that the state is unable to solve by itself. This does not only help to assess whether the state party is unwilling or in fact unable to comply, but also to provide tailored assistance to increase compliance.

Fifth, the report should be succinct. It should not contain information that is not absolutely necessary to understand the human rights situation within the country. The word limit introduced for the common core document is a good point of orientation; however, as the bottom-up reviewed legislative part (see *infra*, part two, chapter 3, I. 3. b.) will already be of a considerable length, it prospectively cannot be upheld for integrative reports and needs to be extended. The word limit would need to be determined by practice.

Sixth, information provided in the report must be verifiable and conclusive. Information given by the states must be free from material errors. This does not mean that the report must be free of any mistakes, but the state is obliged to provide the requested information in good faith. The procedures used and the oversight applied to the gathering of information should be conducted as thoroughly as possible to lower the risk of any misinformation. Conclusive information means that the state shall not only provide positive information, but also challenges and difficulties. It should include information provided by members of the civil society to provide a holistic insight into the national situation.[586]

---

586 The involvement of Civil Society was already considered desirable in the 90 s, see Gaer, 'First Fruits: Reporting by States under the African Charter on Human and Peoples' Rights' (1992) 10 NQHR 29, 34 (with further references).

Seventh, the information given in the report shall be presented in a form that allows a comparative evaluation with the processes of other state parties. Even though every state party is individual in its way of implementing and protecting human rights, there might be the possibility to carve out best practices from positive reports that could be suggested to other states in Concluding Observations or even General Comments.

This rationale should be used by the state party to prepare the report. It specifies the relevant information while leaving enough flexibility for the state party to decide which information is especially important and must be included. Nevertheless, by following this rationale, the state cannot evade producing information vital for the understanding of the human rights situation within the respective state party, which results in the improvement of the report's content. That again caters for the solution of the challenge of inadequate reporting identified as a breach of international law (see *supra*, part two, chapter 1, IV. 1.). Furthermore, it gives effect to the objectives of the reporting procedure.[587]

The rationale of integrative reporting is reflected in the content components. Those are specified in the following.

3. Content Components of an Integrative Report

Integrative reporting consists of three parts, which cumulatively fulfill every reporting obligation a state is bound by. Two parts form a constant basis of information which functions as the point of reference for the periodic reports required under each of the aforementioned (*supra*, chapter 1, II.) treaties. The first part is called 'Baseline Report'. It consists of answers to a questionnaire of ten questions with the purpose to comprehensively, but also concisely inform every oversight committee about the organization, structure, goals, human rights 'performance' and other viable elements to understand the relationship of the respective state with human rights law. The second part is the 'Bottom-Up Review'. It gives insight into the legislative framework of the state party in relation to human rights protection. The majority of norms and regulations in human rights treaties need to be transferred into the national legislation. Hence, the enacted legislation of a state is a first indicator for its compliance rate. The review concerns the whole legal landscape and shall identify norms that violate treaty regulations as well as treaty regulations that are not implemented in national legislation. The outcome of the review is not only of assistance to easily detect breaches of treaties, but also for reform efforts by the states. The third and last part is not permanent but periodic. A periodic Q&A between oversight committee and state party to constantly evaluate the process

---

587 For the object and purpose of the reporting procedure see *supra*, Part Two, Chapter 1, III. 2.

Chapter 3: Integrative Reporting 'Bottom-Up' and Sanctions under International Law

made in implementing goals, eradicating violations and improving the situation within the country concludes the integrative reporting procedure. As the general and legislative framework, hence the theoretical foundation, are dealt with in the first two parts of the integrative report, the periodic Q&A shall display the practical implementation of human rights.

a. Baseline Report

The first part of the integrative report follows a set of questions, which the state party shall answer under consideration of the rationale. The order of the questions is recommended to serve the seventh rationale of comparability. If the order is not followed, the state party should give a reason for the deviation in the introduction of the document. The components of the report are designed to provide sufficient insight into the organization and performance of a state to create a comprehensive basis for the considerations of every oversight committee. The basic content then shall be complemented by periodic updates on the progress of implementation based on a questionnaire designed by the oversight committees. To have the states answer questions instead of giving information following abstract requests derives from the consideration that answers to questions tend to be more focused and precise,[588] which again serves the fifth rationale of succinctness. The questions to be answered are as follows:

One: How is the state structured and organized?

The answer to this question shall contain information on state territory, population, governmental structure, authorities, historical development, culture, legal system, members/representatives of the civil society and any further information the state deems important for the understanding of its structure.

Two: How does the state structure allow for the implementation and protection of human rights?

Here, the state shall give information on the interconnectivity and cooperation between the relevant authorities and the authorities and members of the civil society as well as individuals. Furthermore, information on the legal landscape in general as well as the method of implementing international law into the national legal framework (e. g. monism or dualism, transfer, adoption) shall be given under this point. Information on

---

588 A set of questions was indicated as a challenge especially for developing States introducing the 're-formed' reporting procedure, see the example of Timor Leste by Devereux & Anderson, *'Reporting under International Human Rights Treaties: Perspectives from Timor Leste's Experience of the Reformed Process'* (2008), 8 HRLR 69, 94 f.

national court cases, decided or pending, and on further institutions mandated with the protection of human rights (for example ombudsman) are of interest.

Three: In which environment does the state operate?

Information of interest for this question is the external relationship of the state. Which international and regional treaties are signed, to which alliances is it party, are there border disputes or animosities towards certain states, is there an economic or even armed conflict, are there agreements which bind the state with respect to the performance of specific human rights (e. g. concerning the admission or rejection of refugees, visa facilitations, open borders).

Four: What are the challenges for human rights protection in the state?

This question interconnects with the first and fourth rationale. The state is supposed to show what issues concerning the protection of human rights are pending, and which are the most pressing. If possible, the source of or the reason for the challenge should be named. If, for example, there is a challenge concerning the freedom of religion in certain parts of the state which is caused by rebellious groups suppressing certain religious beliefs, this information would be relevant in this part.

Five: What are the best-practices of human rights protection in the state?

Here, the state shall give information on practices, policies and comparable actions that improved the human rights situation in the country. This may not only concern far reaching reforms in legislation or the state system but may include, for example, support for NGOs, precedential cases, the adoption of a new strategy for the protection of a vulnerable group. As this part could be flooded with information the state party shall especially pay attention to the rationales number five (succinctness) and seven (comparability).

Six: What are the goals of the state concerning human rights?

To understand the process of implementation and the prioritization of actions of a state one has to understand the goals a state has concerning implementation and protection of human rights. Even though full implementation and a clean human rights protection record should be the goal of every state, this goal is illusory. Hence, the state party shall indicate short- and long-term goals in light of the challenges and best-practices described in the report. This will help the oversight committee in deciding whether the state has improved its human rights performance and to create a focused periodic questionnaire. The goals set by the state party will also assist with the Concluding Observations and follow-ups. Last but not least, it will give the state party guidance for improving its human rights protection.

Chapter 3: Integrative Reporting 'Bottom-Up' and Sanctions under International Law

Seven: To what extent has the state party achieved these goals?

For this part, the human rights 'record' of the state is of interest. Information on court cases decided by or pending at regional and international courts and tribunals, communications and complaints with any oversight committee, implementation of decisions and judgments, care for victims of human rights violations as well as strengthening cooperation between authorities, sensitizing governmental institutions and organs, awareness raising amongst the population or regulating work conditions are relevant. The information has to be focused on either the short- or long-term goals the state has described in the report. The state of achievements will be of assistance in assessing what further action is required to fully achieve the set goals which could be conducted during a constructive dialogue between the oversight committee and the state party.

Eight: Which and how many resources are allocated to the implementation and protection of human rights?

As many states claim not to have adequate resources for the implementation and protection of human rights it is important to know which and how many resources of the state are allocated to this topic in comparison to other topics. Human rights protection can concern various parts of the governmental structure, wherefore the allocation of resources to a great variety of institutions could be of interest. Here again, the state is asked to prioritize and focus the information relating to the information contained in the report.

Nine: How does the state intend to achieve the goals set, and which challenges is the state likely to encounter in the future?

In this part, the state is requested to provide information about policies, plans and ideas that are pursued to improve the human rights situation in the country. The ideas should follow the set goals and should tackle the challenges explained in the report while taking into account the best-practices. The future activities shall be analyzed critically to identify challenges which might surface during their implementation. By identifying such challenges beforehand, every stakeholder is informed about difficulties that might occur and may prepare to either lower the risk of the challenge to actually materialize into a real problem in practice or to at least lower the impact it might have. Furthermore, it would give the oversight committees the possibility to provide resources if it becomes clear that the state will not be able to manage the difficulties by itself.

Ten: How does the state decide which matters are communicated to the oversight committee? Which authority is responsible for gathering and providing the relevant information?

It is of interest how the state party decides which information shall be provided and which should not. This part does not need to be of substantial length. It should contain

I. Integrative Reporting

sufficient information to inform the oversight committee which authority or authorities are responsible for the gathering and sorting of information and which authority authored the report. Hereby, the oversight committees are given the opportunity to request further information from the competent authorities if needed.

The answers to the aforementioned questions create the first part of the integrative report which is termed in this thesis the 'Baseline Report'. It depicts the core framework of human rights protection in the respective state party and provides every information relevant to understand its human rights performance. Furthermore, it creates the basis for a streamlined communication and a reference for constructive dialogues amongst all stakeholders. To foster these dialogues – and herewith support the achievement of parts of the object and purpose of reporting – the Baseline Report must be made publicly available and accessible.[589] Depending on the situation in the respective state, this might be done by publishing it online or providing access to printed copies in various institutions throughout the country. Countries with a high rate of illiterate persons should consider recording the report to play it out for the affected individuals.

The second part of the integrative report consists of a 'Bottom-Up' review, which is described in the following.

b. Bottom-Up Review

In the Bottom-Up Review, the second part of the integrative report, the whole legislation of the state party covering human rights after being reviewed from a bottom-up perspective is included. Bottom-up in this context means that the basis of the review is not one specific international or regional treaty in relation to the whole national legislation ('top-down'), but rather the specific national legislation with regard to the entirety of human rights treaty obligations of the said state ('bottom-up').[590] Depending on the way of implementation of international law a state follows, the Bottom-Up Review will impose a greater or lighter burden on the state party. Obviously, dualist states have more material to review than monist states, which could simply refer to the ratification of the relevant treaty. However, as this difference is based upon the sovereign decision of the respective states, it may not be invoked to render this approach invalid.

---

589 As opposed to the practice of some State, as assessed by Heyns & Viljoen, 'The Impact of the United Nations Human Rights Treaties on the Domestic Level', 23 HRQ 3, 483, 506.
590 The terminology of top-down and bottom-up was already used in earlier publications (see e. g. Hampson, *Overview of the Reform of the UN Human Rights Machinery*, 7 HRLR 7 (2007), 13), however addressing the practical impact which in this thesis is encompassed by the Periodic Q&A.

Chapter 3: Integrative Reporting 'Bottom-Up' and Sanctions under International Law

What becomes obvious from assessments of the current state reporting procedure is the often inadequate quality of the submitted reports.[591] Many reports simply recite national legislation[592] which covers the relevant provision in the respective treaty. This, however, is not the information the periodic report should provide. Instead, balanced information including information on the *de facto* situation is of interest for the oversight committees.[593] The Bottom-Up Review does not only tackle the challenge concerning the quality of the state reports; it also provides a solution to the difficulty of double-reporting due to overlapping norms in different human rights treaties. A table of overlapping treaty obligations was already produced in the 1990s, covering the then existing UN human rights treaties.[594] The overlaps in the UN treaty sphere increased since then, and the overlaps with regional treaties are not even considered in this table. Those overlaps can be identified, displayed and reported to within one document to avoid double-reporting.

The idea of the Bottom-Up Review is the review of the entire legislation in force.[595] This part is concerned with the states' binding laws and their compliance with the relevant

---

591 Note by the Secretary-General, *Effective Implementation of International Instruments on Human Rights, Including Reporting Obligations under International Instruments on Human Rights*, UN Doc. A/44/668, 8 November 1989, para 34; Broecker & O'Flaherty, 'The Outcome of the General Assembly's Treaty Body Strengthening Process: An Important Milestone on a Longer Journey', Policy Brief Universal Rights Group, June 2014, <https://www.universal-rights.org/urg-policy-reports/the-outcome-of-the-general-assemblys-treaty-body-strengthening-process-an-important-milestone-on-a-longer-journey/> [accessed 02 December 2019], 7; Report by the Secretariat, *Concept Paper on the High Commissioner's Proposal for a Unified Standing Treaty Body*, UN Doc. HRI/MC/2006/2, 22 March 2006, para 24 f.; cf Steiner, Alston & Goodman, *International Human Rights in Context* (3rd edn, 2007), 850 (on reports to the ICCPR Committee); Smith, 156; Bayefsky, *The UN Human Rights Treaty System: Universality at the Crossroads* (2001), 22.
592 Bayefsky, *The UN Human Rights Treaty System: Universality at the Crossroads* (2001), 22; Smith, 156; Steiner, Alston & Goodman, *International Human Rights in Context* (3rd edn, 2007), 850 (on reports to the ICCPR Committee).
593 Harmonized guidelines on reporting under the international human rights treaties, including guidelines on a common core document and treaty-specific documents, Report of the Inter-Committee Technical Working Group, *Harmonized guidelines on reporting under the international human rights treaties, including guidelines on a common core document and treaty-specific documents*, UN Doc. HRI/MC/2006/3, 10 May 2006, para 24 ff.; Kälin, 'Examination of state reports', 60 f.
594 Report of the Secretariat, *Guidelines on an expanded core document and treaty-specific targeted reports and harmonized guidelines on reporting under the international human rights treaties*, UN Doc. HRI/MC/2004/3, 9 June 2004, 9 f.
595 Such a review complies with the first objective of reporting under the ICESCR, see Committee on Economic, Social and Cultural Rights, *General Comment No. 1: Reporting by States Parties*, UN Doc. E/1989/22, 24 February 1989, 87 f. (Annex III), reprinted in *Compilation of General Comments and General Recommendations*, adopted by Human Rights Treaty Bodies, UN Doc. HRI/GEN/1/Rev.6 at 8, 12 May 2003, para 2; furthermore, such reviews are already practiced, see for example Italy in its Reply to the Questionnaire on implementation of GA Res. 68/268 of 21 April 2014: 'With an

international and regional treaties.⁵⁹⁶ The idea is to create a comprehensive framework which enables every Treaty Body to immediately recognize compliance or non-compliance with the formal implementation of the relevant treaty provisions. It reduces the issue of overlapping obligations by focusing on the underlying national provision regulating a specific right instead of singled out treaty provisions.

To create this greater picture, states will have to identify legislation which concerns human rights, and conduct a comparative study on their compliance with every international and regional treaty. Initially, this will be an increase of work. However, as soon as this study is conducted, it provides a comprehensive picture of the legislative framework of human rights protection and is only subject to changes following changes in the national legislation. Concurrently, the state party can review whether the legislation in force on its territory is in accordance with its international obligations.

aa. Identification of Relevant Legislation

Compliance with an international obligation can first and foremost be monitored by examining the legislative framework of a state. If an international treaty gives clear instructions on the prohibition or legalization of certain conduct, those instructions must be mirrored in the laws passed by the state party.⁵⁹⁷ Hence, the legislative framework provides the basis for every further compliance monitoring.

The relevant norms are identified under the following criteria: (1) the law in question must be in force or about to be passed. This prevents unnecessary reviews of laws that are not and will never be relevant for human rights protection due to their lack of enforceability. (2) The regulations under review must be authoritative norms with a binding legal force. Laws, which are laws as defined by the respective country, are predestined for being reviewed. In the context of the selection of the relevant laws subject to the review, it is

---

inter-ministerial and participatory approach, CIDU as the standing national reporting and follow-up mechanism performs the following tasks: a) review of all laws, regulations and administrative acts adopted at the national and local levels concerning pledges taken at the international level in the area of human rights,[…]' (Ministry of Foreign Affairs and International Cooperation, Inter-ministerial Committee for Human Rights, Italy's Contribution, In Light of Questionnaire on UN General Assembly Resolution 68/268, 30 April 2019, accessible: <https://www.ohchr.org/EN/HRBodies/HRTD/Pages/3rdBiennialReportbySG.aspx> [accessed 02 December 2019], 1 f.).

596 The majority of the regulations in international human rights law need some form of enactment, sometimes even in monist States, cf Kadelbach, 'International Law and the Incorporation of Treaties into Domestic Law, (1999), 42 Ger YIL 66, 81 f.

597 An example would be Art. 4 CAT: '1. Each State Party shall ensure that all acts of torture are offences under its criminal law. The same shall apply to an attempt to commit torture and to an act by any person which constitutes complicity or participation in torture. 2. Each State Party shall make these offences punishable by appropriate penalties which take into account their grave nature.'.

Chapter 3: Integrative Reporting 'Bottom-Up' and Sanctions under International Law

necessary to point out the difficulty arising in federal states. Laws in federal states might be laws passed by the individual states or the federal state as a whole. As the legislative competence can lie with the federal state as a whole or the individual states, the laws of both have to be considered. Hence, in federal states a mechanism for the cooperation regarding the reporting needs to be established. (3) The regulation must implement the material (meaning substantive) part of the treaty. In most cases those will be the rights and duties to which the individual is the addressee. It might have the form of a subjective right or duty, or provide the legislative framework for the implementation of the substantive provisions of the treaty.[598] This excludes from the review for example procedural regulations and regulations of organizational nature. Hence, only a certain part of regulations enshrined in the national law are of relevance for the review.[599]

Essentially every piece of legislation in force within the jurisdiction of the state party is relevant and can be subject to review.[600] The comprehensive nature and the focus on the national legal regulation provides the reviewer with the possibility to not only identify direct violations but also indirect violations or violations by legislative acts which do not seem to be connected with the regulation under review. The process of identification therefore is part of the whole review procedure. It is recognized that the amount of legislation to be considered might be immense. With modern technology, however, relevant laws could be pre-selected by a program working with an algorithm that follows the aforementioned criteria. This would reduce the amount of regulations under review to a manageable number. The identification of relevant legislation and the subsequent review should first and foremost be the duty of the respective state party. Even though it could be of great assistance for the implementation and for sensitization of those working with human rights on a daily basis if the relevant public sector entities would conduct the review of the laws they are working with, it carries the risk of having specific laws reviewed multiple times, while others might not be reviewed at all. Hence, it is preferable if one office or interdepartmental institution coordinates the review process.[601] In the context of federal states, vesting the responsibility of reporting in one office could solve

---

598 As for example a framework legislation as recommended in Committee on Economic, Social and Cultural Rights, *General Comment No. 14: The Right to the Highest Attainable Standard of Health (Art. 12)*, 11 August 2000 (Contained in Document E/C.12/2000/4), para 56.
599 For an example of a relevant rule and the subsequent procedure see *infra*, Part Two, Chapter 3, I., 1., b., bb.
600 For examples of legislation influenced by international human rights treaties see Heyns & Viljoen, 'The Impact of the United Nations Human Rights Treaties on the Domestic Level', 23 HRQ 3, 483, 500 ff.
601 As in for example Egypt, Mexico, Philippines or Canada, see Heyns & Viljoen, 'The Impact of the United Nations Human Rights Treaties on the Domestic Level', 23 HRQ 3, 483, 505; such coordination would clarify the responsibility for reporting within a state as considered positive by Devereux & Anderson, 'Reporting under International Human Rights Treaties: Perspectives from Timor Leste's Experience of the Reformed Process' (2008), 8 HRLR 69, 99 ff.

I. Integrative Reporting

the difficulties arising from the shared legislative competence by mandating this office with collecting and compiling the relevant information into one representative report.

bb. Procedure of the Bottom-Up Review

The procedure of the review consists of four steps. *First*, the relevant law to be reviewed is split up in its individual norms carrying an individual right or duty. *Second*, the individual norms are compared to the substantive provisions of every international and regional treaty to which the respective state is a party. Violations of any treaty by insufficient or contravening content of the reviewed norm is noted. *Third*, those international and regional obligations which are not implemented into the national legislation are identified. *Fourth*, the results are combined and depicted.

The report on the results of the review shall not contain information on every norm which was reviewed. Only those norms shall be included which are not in compliance with the international treaties. Furthermore, those provisions of any regional or international treaty shall be included in the report which are not implemented in the national legislation. Thereby, non-compliance with the binding norms of the international and regional treaties is documented and clearly displayed. It is expected that this procedure and the form of the report not only assist the Treaty Bodies in their work, but also to give the states the opportunity to harmonize their legislative framework with their treaty obligations.

To clarify the procedure, it is exemplarily shown by reviewing previous § 13(2) of the German Federal Elections Act:

> *Example: § 13(2) German Federal Elections Act (f. e.) (Bundeswahlgesetz [BWahlG], a. F.)*

In the following, the procedure is demonstrated on a previous national regulation from the German Federal Elections Act (*Bundeswahlgesetz* [BWahlG])[602], namely § 13 no. 2 BWahlG (a. F.). This norm prescribes an exclusion of persons subject to full legal guardianship from federal elections.[603]

---

602 Bundeswahlgesetz, 7 May 1956, Bundesgesetzblatt Nr. 21, Teil I, 383 ff. in the version promulgated on 23 July 1993 (BGBl. 1288, 1594), most recently amended by Art. 2 of the law of 10 July 2018 (BGBl. I 1116); the Bundeswahlgesetz most recently was amended by Article 1 of the law of 18 June 2019 (BGBl. I 834), changing Article 13. However, as the former article provides a good example, it is used in this context.

603 On 29 January 2019, the Constitutional Court of Germany decided on the constitutionality of § 13 no. 2, no. 3 BWahlG and declared that the norms in question are incompatible with the German Basic Law. The German legislation was obliged to adjust the federal law for it to be in compliance with the German Constitution (which it did on 18 June 2019, see BGBl. I S. 834). In the judgement, regulations from international human rights treaties were analyzed to identify whether they contain a different threshold for a violation than the relevant rights from the German Basic Law; ultimately, the

Chapter 3: Integrative Reporting 'Bottom-Up' and Sanctions under International Law

The relevant part of the norm reads as follows:

> § 13 Ausschluß vom Wahlrecht
>
> Ausgeschlossen vom Wahlrecht ist,
>
> [...]
>
> 2. derjenige, für den zur Besorgung aller seiner Angelegenheiten ein Betreuer nicht nur durch einstweilige Anordnung bestellt ist; dies gilt auch, wenn der Aufgabenkreis des Betreuers die in § 1896 Abs. 4 und § 1905 des Bürgerlichen Gesetzbuchs bezeichneten Angelegenheiten nicht erfaßt, [...]

The wording can be translated as

> § 13 Disqualification from the Right to Vote
>
> A person is disqualified from the right to vote, if
>
> [...]
>
> 2. a custodian has been appointed not only through a restraining order to attend to all his or her affairs; this also applies when the custodian's sphere of duties does not include the affairs set forth in Article 1896, Paragraph (4) and Article 1905 of the Civil Code (Bürgerliches Gesetzbuch).[604]

As the *first step*, § 13 no. 2 BWahlG has been identified as the individual norm subject to review.

In the *second step*, this individual norm has to be compared to the regional and international treaties ratified by Germany. Germany is party to all relevant international and regional human rights treaties. Of those treaties, the following regulations could be of relevance in this case: Art. 25 ICCPR[605], Art. 29 (1) a CRPD[606] and Art. 3 of Protocol No. 1 to the Convention for the Protection of Human Rights and Fundamental

---

senate decided that the threshold is the same. The BVerfG held that the regulation violates Art. 38 subsection 1 sentence 1 and Art. 3 subsection 3 sentence 2 of the German Basic Law. There was no decision on the violation of international law. See BVerfG, Order of the Second Senate of 29 January 2019–2 BvC 62/14 -, paras (1–142), <http://www.bverfg.de/e/cs20190129_2bvc006214en.html> [accessed 02 December 2019].

604 Translation taken from: German Law Archive, edited by Prof. Dr. Gerhard Dannemann, accessible: <https://germanlawarchive.iuscomp.org/?p=228> [accessed 02 December 2019].

605 Art. 25 (b) ICCPR: 'Every citizen shall have the right and the opportunity, without any of the distinctions mentioned in article 2 and without unreasonable restrictions:
[...] (b) To vote and to be elected at genuine periodic elections which shall be by universal and equal suffrage and shall be held by secret ballot, guaranteeing the free expression of the will of the electors; [...]'.

606 Art. 29 (1) (a) CRPD: 'States Parties shall guarantee to persons with disabilities political rights and the opportunity to enjoy them on an equal basis with others, and shall undertake to:

I. Integrative Reporting

Freedoms[607]. To decide whether § 13 no. 2 BWahlG (a. F.) violates the identified international human rights obligations, the scope and content of those regulations has to be analyzed.

According to the Human Rights Committee, Art. 25 ICCPR does not contain an unrestrictable right. However, restrictions of Art. 25 ICCPR must be proportionate, meaning that restrictions are possible when introduced by law following objective and reasonable criteria.[608] The European Court of Human Rights interprets Art. 3 of the Protocol No. 1 to the Convention for the Protection of Human Rights and Fundamental Freedoms in a comparable manner: a restriction of the right to vote is lawful as long as it has a legitimate aim and adheres to the principle of proportionality.[609] In contrast, the Committee on the Rights of Persons with Disabilities, the relevant oversight committee for the CRPD, holds Art. 29 (1) a CRPD to be of an absolute nature. According to the committee, restrictions to the right to vote of persons with disabilities are not allowed.[610]

When applying the scope of those international obligations to the restriction of the right to vote as enshrined in § 13 no. 2 BWahlG (a. F.) the following conclusions are drawn:

The exclusion of persons who are considered to be restricted in their legal capacity to the extent that they have been appointed a custodian in all their affairs is incompatible with Art. 29 (1) (a) CRPD. This does not only derive from the fact that according to

> (a) Ensure that persons with disabilities can effectively and fully participate in political and public life on an equal basis with others, directly or through freely chosen representatives, including the right and opportunity for persons with disabilities to vote and be elected, inter alia, by:
> (i) Ensuring that voting procedures, facilities and materials are appropriate, accessible and easy to understand and use;
> (ii) Protecting the right of persons with disabilities to vote by secret ballot in elections and public referendums without intimidation, and to stand for elections, to effectively hold office and perform all public functions at all levels of government, facilitating the use of assistive and new technologies where appropriate;
> (iii) Guaranteeing the free expression of the will of persons with disabilities as electors and to this end, where necessary, at their request, allowing assistance in voting by a person of their own choice; […]'.

607 Art. 3 Protocol No. 1 to the Convention for the Protection of Human Rights and Fundamental Freedoms: 'The High Contracting Parties undertake to hold free elections at reasonable intervals by secret ballot, under conditions which will ensure the free expression of the opinion of the people in the choice of the legislature.'.
608 Human Rights Committee, *General Comment No. 25: The right to participate in public affairs, voting rights and the right of equal access to public service*, UN Doc. CCPR/C/21/Rev. 1/Add. 7, 12. July 1996, para 4.
609 See for example ECHR, Case of Hirst v The United Kingdom (No.2), Application no. 74025/01, paras 72 ff.
610 Committee on the Rights of Persons with Disabilities, *General comment No. 1 (2014): Article 12: Equal recognition before the law*, 19 May 2014, UN Doc. CRPD/C/GC/1, paras 12 ff. i. c. w. 48.

the responsible oversight committee no restrictions are permissible,[611] but also from the conclusion that such a restriction is in any case not proportionate. Even if one finds a legitimate aim for restricting the right to vote, such as upholding the integrative function of elections or the prevention of the abuse of the right to vote by the custodian[612], the restriction as included in § 13 no. 2 BWahlG is neither appropriate nor necessary to achieve said aim. § 13 no. 2 BWahlG is (also) applicable to persons who are capable to take part in and to undergo the political decision-making process.[613] This capability is not part of the decision to be appointed a custodian and is not to be taken into consideration before the custodian gets appointed.[614] Hence, to exclude them from the right to vote is inappropriate. Even if it was appropriate, there would be less restrictive means to achieve the identified legitimate aims, such as increased criminal sanctions for the abuse of the right to vote by the custodian.[615] In any case, the restriction is based on an arbitrary differentiation: if a person is excluded from the right to vote or not is solely dependent on whether or not the person requiring care has assistance other than a legally appointed custodian. In such assistance from relatives of trusted persons is possible, § 13 no. 2 BWahlG is not applicable, even though the person requiring care might be in the exact same condition as a second person without the option to get assistance from relatives or other trusted persons.[616] Consequently, the exclusion from the right to vote as enshrined in § 13 no. 2 BWahlG does not only contravene Art. 29 (1) (a) CRPD (and this irrespective of whether one agrees with the interpretation of the Committee on the Rights of Persons with Disabilities or not) but also Art. 25 ICCPR and Art. 3 of Protocol No. 1 to the Convention for the Protection of Human Rights and Fundamental Freedoms. This finding concludes the second step of the review.

As this review only concerns an individual norm, the *third step* can only be explained theoretically. If the review concerned the whole Federal Elections Act, the obligations relating to elections which are enshrined in the relevant (ratified) international and regional treaties and are not included in this law would have to be identified.

---

611 Contra this opinion BVerfG, Order of the Second Senate of 29 January 2019–2 BvC 62/14 -, <http://www.bverfg.de/e/cs20190129_2bvc006214en.html> [accessed 18 June 2020], para 77.
612 BVerfG, Order of the Second Senate of 29 January 2019–2 BvC 62/14 -, <http://www.bverfg.de/e/cs20190129_2bvc006214en.html> [accessed 18 June 2020], paras 92, 94.
613 *Ibid*, para 95.
614 *Ibid*.
615 Cf. *ibid*, para 92.
616 *Ibid*, paras 101 ff.

I. Integrative Reporting

As *the fourth* and last step, the finding of the review needs to be included in a report on the relevant law in the following form:

> *The restriction of the right to vote of persons with disabilities enshrined in § 13 no. 2 BWahlG (a. F.) contradicts Art. 25 b ICCPR, Art. 29 (1) a CRPD and Art. 3 of the Protocol No. 1 to the Convention for the Protection of Human Rights and Fundamental Freedoms.*

The focus in this finding lies on the national regulation, hence within the legal sphere state party, and not in the international law sphere. In the forms of review currently conducted, the focus lies on the regulations of the relevant individual international and regional treaties. The impact of the international treaties in the Bottom-Up Review is measured viewed from the situation within the state party, from 'the ground'-hence, bottom-up.

The findings of the review of the national legislation shall then be presented as the second part (bottom-up reviewed legislation) complementary to the Baseline Report. Should a norm which was previously identified as violating one or several international obligations be revised or cease to exist, the relevant passage can be deleted.

The findings of the individual reviews form the second part of the integrative report. It is suggested that the structure follows the alphabetical order of the names of the reviewed codes. Within the individual code reviews, it is suggested to include a first part which entails violations against relevant treaty obligations following the order of the provisions of the code (chronologically) and a second part describing those obligations which are not (yet) implemented. Another possible structure would be to sort the identified violations according to their gravity. Even though this would require an increased effort, the report could be used by the state party as a guideline for reforms. It could take care of those violations first, which are considered grave in order to prevent international responsibility for – in the worst case – a material breach of a treaty.

c. Periodic Q&A

The periodic report as required by most of the state reporting obligations enshrined in the relevant treaties cannot and should not be eradicated. Not only is a periodic update advantageous and necessary for constant monitoring, it is also explicitly requested by the wording of the provisions. Therefore, a periodic document submitted by the state party must be included in the procedure. To fulfill this requirement, a periodic Q&A is proposed.[617] The periodic Q&A consists of a questionnaire send by the oversight committee with focused questions on recent issues concerning the human rights

---

617 A comparable proposal was made by Morijn, *'Reforming United Nations Human Rights Treaty Monitoring Reform'* (2011) 58 NILR 295, 326.

situation in the respective state and the state's answer. The periodic Q&A should contain information on the practical implementation and the actual impact of the treaties for the beneficiaries of the relevant treaties. Hence, it complements the theoretical approach to legislation in the Bottom-Up Review with information on the practical impact of the respective treaties.[618]

The questionnaire should be developed in light of the Baseline Report, the Bottom-Up Review and previous consultations between the state and the relevant oversight committee. It should contain no more than twenty individual questions,[619] each concerned with the actual impact and the effects the treaties have on the life of the individuals living in the respective state. As the simplified reporting procedure, based on a questionnaire as well, was taken up positively by those states using it and seemed to have the effect of increasing compliance[620], the number of questions is considered to be satisfactory to achieve the aim of the procedure. Due to the extended form of the Baseline Report and the Bottom-Up Review which contain a number of information currently requested by the periodic reports, the limitation to twenty questions is justified. By limiting the oversight committees to twenty questions, the whole process is expected to be streamlined and focused (which is also beneficial to the object and purpose of the reporting procedure, meaning to establish and uphold a constructive dialogue between the state party, members of the civil society and the oversight committee).

The answer of the state party should only contain information on the twenty questions asked by the oversight committee. If the state feels the need to discuss further issues, it may attach a request for discussion or for an extension of the word limit. The length of the answer should be 40 pages, which is the page limit that is already recommended for periodic reports by the international committees.[621] This limit is recommended to be used by every oversight committee to establish a comparability of the relevant reports and thereby comply with the seventh rationale (comparability). This would facilitate the cooperation between the regional and international committees as information provided in a comparable form can be exchanged more easily. The specific questions of the

---

618 The clear distinction between 'theory' and 'practice' of the implementation improves the clarity of the required information, which under the current reporting procedure was identified as problematic, see Devereux & Anderson, *'Reporting under International Human Rights Treaties: Perspectives from Timor Leste's Experience of the Reformed Process'* (2008), 8 HRLR 69, 95.
619 The recommendation of this number is guided by the recommendation of 25 questions by the Working Group in their report Human Rights Committee, *Simplified reporting procedure*, Report of the Working Group, UN Doc. CCPR/C/123/3, 6 December 2018, para 120 (a).
620 *Ibid*, paras 86 ff.
621 Report of the Inter-Committee Technical Working Group, *Harmonized guidelines on reporting under the international human rights treaties, including guidelines on a common core document and treaty-specific documents*, UN Doc. HRI/MC/2006/3, 10 May 2006, para 19.

committees will streamline and focus the report of the state party. Especially pressing aspects could be highlighted. It is expected that the answer will contain more detailed information on the recent situation with respect to human rights. As the legislative situation is moved to the second part of the integrative report, states would not be able to evade the question of the practical impact by enlisting their newly enacted laws and regulations.[622] Hereby, the quality of the reports is expected to increase significantly. Often oversight committees are dissatisfied with the quality of state reports because the reports do not provide sufficient information on the actual impact of the treaty.[623] As has been shown above, the submission of reports of inadequate quality constitutes a breach of the international law obligation of the respective state party. Due to the nature and focus of the answer, the risk of breaching the obligation by providing insufficient information would be minimized, if not eradicated.

As the periodic Q&A would be significantly shorter than the current periodic reporting procedure (at least concerning the UN Treaty Bodies), and an improvement of the timely processing of state reports can already be seen with the introduction of the simplified reporting procedure (which is still more work-intensive than the procedure proposed in this thesis), the periodicity of the Q&A could follow the periods indicated in the individual treaties. The overburdening of the states mainly results from the extensive and time-consuming preparation of the reports which would be significantly reduced by applying the integrative reporting procedure.

4. Evaluation of the Integrative Reporting Procedure

Taking into consideration the concept of integrative compliance based on systemic integration as well as the previously established criteria for a system which could satisfy the majority of stakeholders, the integrative reporting procedure is expected to establish a suitable system in the long-run. Previous considerations had and recent ones still claim as a common denominator that the flexibility of reporting and the consolidation of the reporting guidelines be increased, that cross referencing be used more extensively and that the simplified reporting procedure be used generally. The increased coordination and the predictability of the reporting process is considered desirable also by the

---

[622] Such enumeration would not satisfy the requirements for reports, see Report of the Secretariat, *Guidelines on an expanded core document and treaty-specific targeted reports and harmonized guidelines on reporting under the international human rights treaties*, UN Doc. HRI/MC/2004/3, 9 June 2004, 23, para 33.

[623] Note by the Secretary-General, *Effective Implementation of International Instruments on Human Rights, Including Reporting Obligations under International Instruments on Human Rights*, UN Doc. A/44/668, 8 November 1989, para 34; Report by the Secretariat, *Concept Paper on the High Commissioner's Proposal for a Unified Standing Treaty Body*, UN Doc. HRI/MC/2006/2, 22 March 2006, para 24 f.; cf Steiner, Alston & Goodman, *International Human Rights in Context* (3rd edn, 2007), 850 (on reports to the ICCPR Committee); cf Smith, 156.

General Assembly.[624] Furthermore, all those criteria should be implemented within the existing framework.[625]

The integrative reporting procedure provides extended and sufficient consolidation through its Baseline Report and Bottom-Up Review so that massive overlaps and thereby the very burdensome double-reporting of states can be reduced. The periodic Q&A caters for the specific needs of the individual treaties. Especially by asking focused questions, the protection of vulnerable groups within a state could even be increased through on-point information which could subsequently be used by Treaty Bodies as well as members of the civil society. The questionnaire provides the oversight committees with great flexibility concerning the topics which can be discussed. Hereby, the questionnaire can be adapted to the current situation and the most pressing issues concerning the respective state party. By introducing the integrative reporting procedure as the mandatory procedure for all oversight committees, including the regional ones,[626] the consolidation of the reporting guidelines would be maximized. This would satisfy the recently increasing calls for a harmonized and streamlined procedure including the reduction of overlaps and repetitive information.[627] Generally, the integrative reporting procedure would support the implementation of the object and purpose of state reporting, especially the object of evaluating the actions of the competent authorities[628] as well as the objective to provide the oversight committee with a comprehensive review of the national legislation, administrative rules and procedures and practices[629].

---

624 UN General Assembly, *Strengthening and enhancing the effective functioning of the human rights treaty body system*, UN Doc. A/Res/68/268, 21 April 2014, para 34.
625 Report of the Secretary-General, *Status of the human rights treaty body system*, UN Doc. A/73/309, 6 August 2018, para 82.
626 The reporting system in the Inter-American context was already considered as being complementary to the procedure of the United Nations Committee on Economic, Social and Cultural Rights by the Inter-American Commission on Human Rights itself (see for example Inter-American Commission on Human Rights, *Guidelines for Preparation of Progress Indicators in the Area of Economic, Social and Cultural Rights*, OAS Doc. OEA/Ser.L/V/II.132, Doc. 14, 19 July 2008, para 13). Hence, it is expected that an integrative approach would be taken up positively by the regional committees; the African Charter on the Rights and Welfare of the Child is an example for international-regional cooperation, see Lauer, *Die Implementierung menschenrechtlicher Verträge in Afrika* (2018), 153 f.
627 See for example Reply to the Questionnaire on implementation of GA Res. 68/268 of 21 April 2014 by Finland (p. 4), Israel (p. 2 f.), Australia (p. 4), replies accessible: <https://www.ohchr.org/EN/HRBodies/HRTD/Pages/3rdBiennialReportbySG.aspx> [accessed: 02 December 2019]; Human Rights Committee, *Simplified reporting procedure*, Report of the Working Group, UN Doc. CCPR/C/123/3, 6 December 2018, para 107 (a); cf Status of the human rights treaty body system, Report of the Secretary-General, *Status of the human rights treaty body system*, UN Doc. A/73/309, 6 August 2018, paras 44, 52.
628 See also Kälin, *'Examination of state reports'*, 36 f.
629 Committee on Economic, Social and Cultural Rights, *General Comment No. 1: Reporting by States Parties*, UN Doc. E/1989/22, 24 February 1989, 87 f. (Annex III), reprinted in *Compilation of General*

I. Integrative Reporting

Furthermore, the Baseline Report and the Bottom-Up Review would be an adequate replacement for the initial report and the common core document. Requirements for the initial report are for example described by the Human Rights Committee.[630] It is supposed to 'establish the constitutional and legal framework for the implementation of Covenant rights, explain the legal and practical measures adopted to give effect to Covenant rights [and to] demonstrate the progress made in ensuring enjoyment of Covenant rights by the people within the state party and subject to its jurisdiction'[631]. The report should include legal norms which adopt the articles of the Covenant and information on their application, including remedies for their violation. Furthermore, information on the incorporation and enforceability of the Covenant rights and the responsible authorities as well as the relevant legal texts as Annexes are required.[632] Those requirements are fulfilled with the Baseline Report and the Bottom-Up Review. A common core document, which already was submitted by 163 states[633], could satisfactorily be restructured and merged into the Baseline Report. The information provided in the common core documents would only need to be restructured and supplemented. That way, the work put into the common core document would not go to waste and the work needed for the Baseline Report would be reduced.

Apart from the aspects of easy implementation and compliance with the common denominators called for throughout the reform process, the integrative report, especially the Bottom-Up Review, has a positive practical impact. By creating a document which examines and clearly displays the compliance rate of the national legislation with international and regional human rights, the respective state is given a roadmap for reforms.[634] Having a legislative framework compliant with every human rights obligation should be a desirable goal for any state. Hence, by producing the Bottom-Up Review,

---

Comments and General Recommendations, adopted by Human Rights Treaty Bodies, UN Doc. HRI/GEN/1/Rev.6 at 8, 12 May 2003, para 2.
630 UN Secretary-General, Compilation of Guidelines on the Form and Content of Reports to be submitted by States Parties to the International Human Rights Treaties, UN Doc. HRI/GEN/2/Rev. 6, 3 June 2009, 43 f.
631 Ibid, 43
632 Ibid, 44.
633 See Homepage of the Office of the High Commissioner for Human Rights, Treaty Body Database, Core Documents, <https://tbinternet.ohchr.org/_layouts/15/TreatyBodyExternal/CoreDocuments.aspx> [accessed 02 December 2019].
634 This roadmap would provide authoritative advice to the state towards increased conformity with human rights; such function was already considered desirable by earlier authors, see e. g. Morijn, 'Reforming United Nations Human Rights Treaty Monitoring Reform' (2011) 58 NILR 295, 312; O'Flaherty & O'Brien, 'Reform of UN Human Rights Treaty Monitoring Bodies: A Critique of the Concept Paper on the High Commissioner's Proposal for a Unified Standing Treaty Body' (2007) 7 HRLR 141, 164.

the state creates a catalogue of where reforms are needed. The practical impact of the Bottom-Up Review is raising awareness and eventually initiating reform processes. The benefit of the Bottom-Up Review could even be increased by sorting the violations of the treaty regulations according to their gravity, meaning that the report could contain a section with serious violations that need immediate attention by the legislative power, and violations that should be attended to in the near future.[635] A third section could contain those treaty regulations that are missing from the legal framework, meaning those, where the state is obliged to pass an implementing regulation according to the treaty in question, but has not yet done so. Hereby, the legislative power would be enabled to establish an agenda to attend to the problems in their legislation according to their urgency. A further practical benefit is the easy identification of indirect and eventually hidden violations of international law. Due to the all-encompassing nature of the Bottom-Up Review even such violations, which do not become obvious on first sight, can be detected. The periodic Q&A complements this advantage by providing the possibility to detect indirect and hidden violations in the human rights practice of the state through specific and focused questions.

Finally, the integrative reporting procedure can be introduced within the existing framework. None of the relevant reporting regulations provides a strict definition on how reporting must be conducted. Apart from the periodicity prescribed in some regulations (which can be upheld with the periodic Q&A), the Treaty Bodies are free to decide on the procedure.[636] Hence, it is well within the possibilities of the current system to introduce a streamlined procedure as proposed. As some regional bodies already use a comparable procedure,[637] the regional oversight committees would not even have to introduce a new procedure to implement the streamlined process with the UN oversight committees.

---

635 Such prioritization is partially practiced by United Nations Treaty Bodies in der Concluding Observations, see assessment by O'Flaherty, *'The Concluding Observations of United Nations Human Rights Treaty Bodies'* (2006) 6 HRLR 27, 45 f.; O'Flaherty, however, considers prioritization risky, *ibid*, 46.

636 The possibility to single-handedly change the reporting procedure can be seen in the recent decision of the Human Rights Committee which introduced the simplified reporting procedure as mandatory subject to veto, see Human Rights Committee, *Decision on additional measures to simplify the reporting procedure and increase predictability*, 1–26 July 2019 (will be reflected in the Committee's annual report (UN Doc. A/75/40, to be issued in 2020), accessible: <https://www.ohchr.org/EN/HRBodies/CCPR/Pages/PredictableReviewCycle.aspx> [accessed 02 December 2019], para 2.

637 See for example Group of Experts on Action against Violence against Women and Domestic Violence (GREVIO), *Questionnaire on legislative and other measures giving effect to the provisions of the Council of Europe Convention on Preventing and Combating Violence against Women and Domestic Violence (Istanbul Convention)*, 11 March 2016, GREVIO/Inf(2016).

As the past reform proposals, which were implemented, were simply added to the procedure, which made the situation even more intransparent, the integrative reporting procedure should be implemented instead of the various procedures currently in force and should be made the standard procedure used by every committee and mandatory for every state party. Only with a full replacement, the simplification as the positive incentive for the state parties is expected to materialize. To just add another procedure to the already existing framework would rather deteriorate than improve the situation.

To conclude, the proposed integrative reporting procedure fulfills the common criteria regularly called for by stakeholders of the state reporting procedure and is expected to be an adequate solution for the current challenges of the state reporting system.[638]

II. Sanctions for the Breach of the State Reporting Obligation under International Law

A considerable number of states persistently refuse to report under their international and regional obligations. Even though they signed and ratified the relevant treaties, some never even submitted their initial report.[639] Some of those reports have been overdue for more than ten years.[640] In cases in which the state party is unable to fulfill its reporting obligation – due to financial and/or structural deficiencies – assistance should be and (as far as possible) is granted to support the compliance of the willing state.[641] However, when there is a lack of political will to report and the state is ultimately refusing to comply with the obligation it accepted by ratifying the treaty,[642] support is not a viable measure.

Already in the earlier stage of the reform process, the need for sanctions was repeatedly recognized. In 1997, the Secretary-General stated that

> *[…] a lack of political will translates essentially into a calculation by the State concerned that the consequences, both domestic and international, of a failure to report are*

---

638 In favor of integration, however in the form of an Integrated Treaty Body System, Lhotský, *Human Rights Treaty Body Review 2020*, 53 ff.
639 6 States that are members to the African Union have not submitted any report, see <https://www.achpr.org/statereportsandconcludingobservations> [accessed 02 December 2019].
640 United Nations Secretary-General, *Status of the human rights treaty body system, Report of the Secretary-General, Supplementary information: 24 statistical annexes*, UN Doc. A/73/309 (Annexes), 6 August 2019, Annex II, Table 5 and Table 6.
641 Report of the Secretary-General, *Status of the human rights treaty body system*, UN Doc. A/73/309, 6 August 2018, paras 29, 93.
642 Dublin II Meeting, *Strengthening the United Nations Human Rights Treaty Body System*, Outcome Document, 10–11 November 2011, <https://www.ohchr.org/EN/HRBodies/HRTD/Pages/Documents.aspx> [accessed 02 December 2019], para 63.

Chapter 3: Integrative Reporting 'Bottom-Up' and Sanctions under International Law

less important than the costs, administrative and political, of complying with reporting obligations. In that case, the only viable approach on the part of the treaty bodies and/or the political organs is to seek to raise the 'costs' of non-compliance. A failure to devise appropriate responses of this nature has ramifications which extend well beyond the consequences for any individual State party. Large-scale non-reporting makes a mockery of the reporting system as a whole. It leads to a situation in which many States are effectively rewarded for violating their obligations while others are penalized for complying (in the sense of subjecting themselves to scrutiny by the treaty bodies), and it will lead to a situation in which a diminishing number of States will report very regularly and others will almost never do so.[643]

Today, the maximum 'sanction' for persistently non-reporting states is the now widely accepted review in absence of a report.[644] However, the review in absence is not considered as a sanction in the sense of a 'penalty or coercive measure applied resulting from a failure to comply with a law, rule or order'[645]. Other sanctions, namely those provided under Public International Law, have not been considered so far. However, due to the increasingly accepted limitation of the sovereignty of States, there could be a possibility to introduce further sanctions for non-compliance with reporting obligations in international law which would be backed by the consent of the states. In the following, the possibility to sanction a breach of the state reporting obligation under the international law available will be evaluated. Possible sources are international treaties, customary international law and general principles of international law.[646] In the specific case of state reporting, sanctions could be enshrined in the human rights treaties themselves, the VCLT[647], the customary international law rules underlying the VCLT and the customary international law rules represented in the Draft Articles on State Responsibility[648].

---

643   Note by the Secretary-General, *Effective Functioning of Bodies Established Pursuant to United Nations Human Rights Instruments*, 27 March 1997, UN Doc. E/CN.4/1997/74, para 44.
644   See for example Human Rights Committee, *General Comment No. 30*, UN Doc. CCPR/C/21/Rev.2/Add.12, 18 September 2002, para 4 (review in absence as a remedy rather than a sanction); United Nations reform: measures and proposals, Note by the Secretary-General, *United Nations reform: measures and proposals*, UN Doc. A/66/860, 26 June 2012, 39; Dublin II Meeting, *Strengthening the United Nations Human Rights Treaty Body System*, Outcome Document, 10–11 November 2011, <https://www.ohchr.org/EN/HRBodies/HRTD/Pages/Documents.aspx> [accessed 02 December 2019], paras 63 ff.; this procedure was already used in the 1990s, see Kornblum, '*A comparison of self-evaluating state reporting systems*' (1995) 304 IRRC 39, 49.
645   Black's Law Dictionary, 'sanction', 1145.
646   Those are the sources of international law as recognized in Art. 38 (1)(a)-(c) ICJ Statute.
647   VCLT, 22 May 1969, entry into force 27 January 1980, United Nations Treaty Series, vol. 115, 331.
648   *Draft articles on Responsibility of States for Internationally Wrongful Acts*, ILC Ybk 2001, /II(2), 26 (also available as Report on the work of the fifty-third session (2001), UN Doc. A/56/10 + Corr. 1, IV. E., 32 ff.)

II. Sanctions for the Breach of the State Reporting Obligation under International Law

As this part of the thesis only addresses the legal sources for the possible sanctioning of the violation of the state reporting obligation, and those source exist and may be applied parallel to each other, the order of the sources of international law is irrelevant.

1. International Treaties

To identify a state's obligations under international law, one should first consider the treaties signed and ratified by said state. As international law is a legal system based on consent, sanctions for breaches of international obligations are usually included in the treaty text. To evaluate the possible sanctions under treaty law *first* the specific international and regional human rights treaties and *second* general treaty law as enshrined in the VCLT needs to be considered.

a. International and Regional Human Rights Treaties and their Supplements

None of the international or regional human rights treaties provide an explicit 'hard' sanction for the breach of the reporting obligation.[649] However, some of the Rules of Procedure adopted by oversight committees make reference to the issue of non- and late-submission whilst introducing a consequence in form of a negative incentive for states not in compliance with their reporting obligation.[650] Examples are:

The **Rules of Procedure of the African Commission on Human and Peoples' Rights.** It regulates non-submission in it Rule 76. There it is stated that

> '1. *The Commission shall, at the beginning of each year, inform the States Parties which are not up to date with their obligations under Article 62 of the deadlines of their submission of their reports and the date at which they are expected to comply.*
>
> 2. *At the beginning of each Ordinary Session, the Secretary shall inform the Commission of all cases of non-submission of reports or of additional information requested by the Commission. In such cases, the Chairperson of the Commission may send a reminder, through the Secretary, to the State Party concerned;*

---

649 In the sense of the definition provided in fn 628, *supra;* see also Kälin, *'Examination of state reports'*, 32; already Kornblum, *'A comparison of self-evaluating state reporting systems'* (1995) 304 IRRC 39, 49; Schöpp-Schilling, *'Treaty Body Reform: The Case of the Committee on the Elimination of Discrimination against Women'* (2007) 7 HRLR 201, 203.
650 The discrepancy between the express consensus of the States not to include a sanction in the treaty text and the (indirect) sanctioning through the Rules of Procedure of the Committee is a critical point. However, research on this topic would exceed the scope of this dissertation.

Chapter 3: Integrative Reporting 'Bottom-Up' and Sanctions under International Law

> 3. *The Activity Report of the Commission shall point out the status of initial and Periodic Report of States Parties.'*[651]

This rule establishes an obligation to inform which is rather an obligation of the Commission than a sanction for a state party in breach. It provides the legal basis for 'naming and shaming' for non-compliance in the African Human Rights System.

Rule 17 (7) of the **Rules of Procedure of the Committee of Experts of the European Charter for Regional or Minority Languages**[652] (for reports that are more than twelve months late) and Rule 28 (3) of the **Rules of Procedure of the Group of Experts on Action against Violence against Women and Domestic Violence**, which regulate review in absence of a report.[653]

The **Rules of Procedure of the Governmental Committee of the European Social Charter** and the **European Code of Social Security**, which declare in Chapter II, Art. 17:

> *'A warning may also be addressed for not submitting a report within the time limit. In this case, the Party concerned shall be informed that if the requested information is not provided, a proposal for a recommendation may be discussed in the next cycle.'*[654]

This rule clearly does not contain a sanction, rather a warning and a postponement of the recommendation to the next cycle.

Rule 70 of the **Rules of Procedure of the Human Rights Committee**, which in subsection (1) states

> '1. In cases where the Committee has been notified under rule 69, paragraph 1, of the failure of a State to submit under rule 66, paragraph 3, of these rules, any report under article 40, paragraph 1 (a) or (b), of the Covenant and has sent reminders to the State party, the Committee may, at its discretion, notify the State party through the Secretary-General that it intends, on a date or at a session specified in the notification, to

---

651 African Commission on Human and People's Rights, *Rules of Procedure*, adopted 2–13 February 1988, revised 2–11 October 1995, approved 12–26 May 2010, <https://www.achpr.org/legalinstruments/detail?id=34> [accessed 02 December 2019].
652 Committee of Experts of the European Charter for Regional or Minority languages, *Rules of Procedure of the Committee of Experts of the European Charter for Regional or Minority languages*, 2001 (most recently modified 18 March 2019), MIN-LANG (2019) 7, <https://rm.coe.int/minlang-2019-07-comex-rules-of-procedure-final/1680954878> [accessed 02 December 2019].
653 Group of Experts on Action against Violence against Women and Domestic Violence (GREVIO), *Rules of Procedure*, 21–23 September 2015 (most recently amended 29–23 February 2018), GREVIO/Inf(2015)RoP-amdt3.
654 Governmental Committee of the European Social Charter and the European Code of Social Security, *Rules of procedure* (2016), GC(2016)16.

II. Sanctions for the Breach of the State Reporting Obligation under International Law

examine in a private session the measures taken by the State party to give effect to the rights recognized in the Covenant and to proceed by adopting provisional concluding observations which will be submitted to the State party.'[655]

Further rules containing regulations for non-submission of reports in the UN Treaty Body System are Rule 62 (3) of the **Rules of Procedure of the ICESCR**[656], Rule 67 of the **Rules of Procedure of CAT**[657], Rule 40 of the **Rules of Procedure of the CRPD**[658], Rule 66 of the **Rules of Procedure of CERD**[659], Rule 71 **Rules of Procedure of the CRC**[660], Rule 34 of the **Rules of Procedure of CMW**[661] and Rules 49 and 51 of the **Rules of Procedure of CEDAW**[662].

As can been seen from those examples, the non-submission and late submission of reports is increasingly regulated in the rules of procedure of different oversight committees. However, they only prescribe a certain conduct for the oversight committee and no hard sanctions for the state party in breach. Also, they do not address the submission of reports of inadequate quality. Hence, even though the measures of warnings or the review in absence of a report is increasingly included in the rules of procedure, still the human rights treaties do not provide the oversight committees with the possibility to sanction states in breach with their reporting obligation. At most could the review in absence of a report appear as a coercive measure to the respective state party. However, it can also be understood as a measure to uphold the functioning of the reporting system than a penalty for a non-reporting state party.[663] As determining the nature of the review in absence of a report would exceed the scope of this thesis, preference is given to the absence of a sanction in the treaty texts, i.e. what the state parties consented to. Therefore, no sanction can be deducted from the international and regional human rights treaties.

---

655 Rule 70 *Rules of Procedure of the Human Rights Committee*, 22 September 2005, UN Doc. CCPR/C/3/Rev.8.
656 Committee on Economic, Social and Cultural Rights, *Rules of Procedure of the Committee*, Provisional rules of procedure, 1 September 1993, UN Doc. E/C.12/1990/4/Rev.1
657 Committee against Torture, *Rules of procedure*, 1 September 2014, UN Doc. CAT/C/3/Rev.6.
658 Committee on the Right of Persons with Disabilities, *Rules of Procedure*, 10 October 2016, UN Doc. CRPD/C/1/rev.1.
659 Committee on the Elimination of Racial Discrimination, *Rules of Procedure*, UN Doc. CERD/C/35/Rev.3, 1 January 1989.
660 Committee on the Rights of the Child, *Rules of procedure*, 1 March 2019, UN Doc. CRC/C/4/Rev.5.
661 Committee on the Protection of the Rights of All Migrant Workers and members of Their Families, *Rules of Procedure*, 8 February 2019, UN Doc. CMW/C/2.
662 Committee on the Elimination of Discrimination against Women, *Rules of Procedure*, in: UN Secretariat, *International Human Rights Documents, Compilation of rules of procedure adopted by Human Rights treaty bodies*, UN Doc. HRI/GEN/3/Rev.3, 28 May 2008, 93 ff.
663 Cf Tomuschat, 231 f.

Chapter 3: Integrative Reporting 'Bottom-Up' and Sanctions under International Law

b. Vienna Convention on the Law of Treaties (1969)

The VCLT[664] is the basic international law document which regulates international treaty law. Its provisions regulating the breach of multilateral treaties, especially its Art. 60, is, according to Art. 50 (5), subsidiary to any more specific provision in other treaties. As shown above, there are no specific rules governing the breach of the reporting obligation in the relevant human rights treaty texts. Therefore, it is possible to take recourse to the rules of the VCLT.

The VCLT is the codification of previously practiced customary international law rules[665] and has 116 state parties[666]. The difficulty with applying the VCLT to multilateral treaties is that in a positivist reading it only applies when all parties to the conflict are parties to the VCLT and the treaty in question.[667] Furthermore, it does not apply retroactively[668], meaning that it does not apply to treaties that were concluded before the Vienna Convention entered into force for the relevant party. This, however, is only valid for the codified treaty norm, not the underlying customary rule.[669]

Questions of applicability only have to be considered in this thesis if the VCLT actually provides a sanction for the breach of the reporting obligation. A state being signatory to a treaty is obliged not to defeat the object and purpose of the treaty it signed. This obligation is reflected in Art. 18 VCLT.[670] After ratification, this obligation is upheld, as can be seen in Art. 60 VCLT: the violation of a provision essential to the accomplishment of the object or purpose of a treaty is a material breach of a treaty and gives the other party or parties the opportunity to sanction such behavior.[671]

The reporting obligation is a provision which is essential to the object and purpose of a treaty, because it establishes the opportunity to monitor the effective implementation of the rights agreed upon.[672] It is the only instrument compulsory in every relevant

---

664 VCLT, adopted 22 May 1969, 115 UNTS 331.
665 VCLT, 7th recital of the Preamble; see also Schmalenbach, in Dörr & Schmalenbach (eds), *VCLT Commentary*, Preamble, para 1.
666 See Homepage, United Nations Treaty Collection, Vienna Convention on the Law of Treaties, <https://treaties.un.org/Pages/ViewDetailsIII.aspx?src=TREATY&mtdsg_no=XXIII-1&chapter=23&Temp=mtdsg3&clang=_en> [accessed 02 December 2019].
667 Criticized by *Scheinin*, 'Human Rights Treaties and the Vienna Convention on the Law of Treaties – Conflict or Harmony', European Commission for Democracy through Law (Venice Commission), 8 September 2005, CDL-UD(2005)014rep, 2 f.
668 Art. 4 VCLT.
669 Schmalenbach, in Dörr & Schmalenbach (eds), *VCLT Commentary*, Article 4, para 1; cf ICJ, *Kasikili/Sedudu Island (Botswana/Namibia)*, Judgment, ICJ Rep 1999, 1045, para 18.
670 Art. 18 VCLT.
671 Art. 60 (3)(b) VCLT.
672 Tomuschat, 215.

II. Sanctions for the Breach of the State Reporting Obligation under International Law

human rights treaty and the only monitoring instrument applicable from the moment of ratification.[673] No reservations to this obligation are permissible.[674] If a state party does not comply with its reporting obligation by non-submission, late submission and/ or by inadequate submission it effectively defeats the object and purpose of the treaty it is supposed to report to.

Therefore, the breach of the state reporting obligation amounts to a material breach of the respective treaty.[675] The question following is, which consequences the VCLT provides for the breach of an obligation essential to the object and purpose of a treaty and whether such consequence is a viable sanction.

A material breach triggers the applicability of Art. 60 (3) b VCLT. According to this provision, the material breach of a multilateral treaty entitles the other state parties to suspend the operation of the treaty towards the breaching party or as a whole, Art. 60 (2) (a) VCLT. If applied *stricto sensu*, the state parties to human rights treaties would be able to suspend – by unanimous decision – the operation of a human rights treaty in relation to a state party that did not submit an adequate state report.[676] A single breach would suffice to trigger this provision.

However, this result contravenes *first* the idea of sanctions as a last resort and the general interest of preserving the stability of multilateral treaties and *second* the object and purpose of a human rights treaty in general.

First, although the idea of sanctioning breaches of the reporting obligation was approved by various stakeholders, it was only accepted by those stakeholders as the last resort against persistently non-reporting state parties.[677] As common practice and consensus has to be taken into account when interpreting a treaty[678], it has to be concluded that only a repeated and persistent violation in the sense of strict non-reporting could lead to such material breach as required under Art. 60 (3) (b) VCLT. However, as the general interest concerning multilateral treaties is to preserve their stability[679], the termination or even suspension of a treaty following the non-compliance with the state reporting obligations seems to be counterproductive.

---

673 *Ibid*, 215
674 *Ibid*, 215
675 According to Art. 60 (3)(b) VCLT.
676 Reference here is made to Art. 60 (2)(a) VCLT. The applicability of subsections (b) and (c) is considered to be highly unlikely, if not impossible in the context of State Reporting.
677 Note by the Secretariat, *Status of Preparation of Publications, Studies and Documents for the World Conference, Interim report on updated study by Mr. Philip Alston*, Addendum, UN Doc. A/CONF.157/PC/62/Add.11/Rev.1, 22 April 1993, paras 119 ff.
678 Dörr, in Dörr & Schmalenbach (eds), *VCLT Commentary*, Art. 31, para 77.
679 Giegerich, in Dörr & Schmalenbach (eds), *VCLT Commentary*, Art. 60, para 46.

Second, the first and foremost object and purpose of human rights treaties is the protection of the individual. Such provisions are especially protected under international law, as can be seen in Art. 60 (5) VCLT. Even though this subsection does not apply in the case of the state reporting obligation, as it is not a provision with the object and purpose of the protection of the human person, the underlying idea must be considered in relation to the interpretation of human rights treaties. Considering the special status human rights have in international law, the conclusion that a multilateral treaty between states for the benefit of the human being can be suspended because of the violation of a monitoring obligation by the state party contravenes the aforementioned ideas.[680]

Therefore, even though the wording of Art. 60 (3) (b) VCLT would provide a sanction for the breach of the state reporting obligation, such sanction is – in the light of the object and purpose of human rights treaties and the high level of protection human rights enjoy in international law – not viable.

c. Conclusion

Provisions that regulate sanctions for the violation of the state reporting obligations are not included in international or regional human rights treaties, only in the Rules of Procedure of the committees. When taking recourse to the VCLT, a sanction for the breach of a multilateral treaty can be found in Art. 60 (3) (b) VCLT. It provides that in case of a material breach of a multilateral treaty the other state parties may suspend the operation of the treaty in relation to the state in breach. However, this sanction contravenes the requirement of a sanction being the last resort as well as the overall object and purpose of a human rights treaty. Therefore, it is not viable.

Consequently, international treaty law does not provide a viable sanction for the breach of the state reporting obligation.

---

680   Of the same opinion concerning denunciation and withdrawal already United Nations Human Rights Committee, *CCPR General Comment No. 26: Continuity of Obligations,* 8 December 1997, UN Doc. CCPR/C/21/Rev.1/Add.8/Rev.1, para 5.

II. Sanctions for the Breach of the State Reporting Obligation under International Law

2. Draft Articles on Responsibility of States for Internationally Wrongful Acts

Customary international law rules arise, when states perform a specific behavior (*state practice*) while being convinced that they are obliged to do so under international law (*opinio juris*).[681] As soon as a customary international law rule emerges, it becomes binding on every state which is not persistently objecting to its binding force.[682]

Customary international law rules on the responsibility of states for a breach of an international obligation – and of course its consequences – are reflected in the Draft Articles on the Responsibility of States for Internationally Wrongful Acts[683] (ARS) as well as in those principles underlying the VCLT. The VCLT does not contain a viable sanction for the breach of the state reporting obligation, as was shown in the previous paragraphs.[684] Hence, this section will focus on the ARS.

The majority of regulations concerning the responsibility of states for breaches of international law are defined in the ARS. The ARS are not a binding treaty; however, parts of them put existing customary international law obligations on state responsibility into writing.[685] Therefore, regulations on the responsibility of states for internationally wrongful acts, especially the responsibility for the breach of an international treaty, is – due to its customary nature – binding on every state that is not a persistent objector to the relevant rule.

In their Art. 1, the ARS prescribe that every internationally wrongful act of a state triggers an international responsibility. According to Art. 2, such internationally wrongful act is given when a state, by act or omission, breaches an international obligation binding on it and such breach is attributable to that state. If those requirements are fulfilled, the consequences under international law are those set out in Art. 28–31 ARS, such as the duty to perform the act without a breach (Art. 29), the obligation to cease the wrongful conduct immediately (Art. 30) and the obligation to make reparations for the injury resulting from the breach (Art. 31). An injury, as defined in Art. 31 (2), is

---

681 For more information on Customary International Law see *Crawford*, 21 ff.
682 *Crawford*, 26.
683 *Draft articles on Responsibility of States for Internationally Wrongful Acts*, ILC Ybk 2001, /II(2), 26 (also available as Report on the work of the fifty-third session (2001), UN Doc. A/56/10 + Corr. 1, IV. E., 32 ff.); the *Draft Articles on Responsibility of States for Internationally Wrongful Acts* were never adopted as a binding treaty. However, they are considered to be the codification of rules accepted as customary international law (see for example
684 See *supra*, Part Two, Chapter 3, II. 1. b.
685 *Crawford*, 524.

'any damage, whether material or moral, caused by the internationally wrongful act of a State.'[686]

Applying these consequences as sanctions to the situation of persistently non-reporting states, the following is concluded:

The ARS are applicable to the breach of the state reporting obligation. An internationally wrongful act as required under Art. 2 ARS is the breach of the state reporting obligation. As has been shown in the previous chapters, the breach of the state reporting obligation is a breach of an international treaty obligation with regard to every challenge the system faces (non-reporting, late reporting and inadequate reporting).[687]

What follows would be the consequences set out in Art. 28–31 ARS. Even though it is questionable whether there would be an injury suffered which would give rise to a claim of reparations, in any case Art. 29 and 30 would be applicable.

Essentially, the sanction for the breach of the reporting obligation would be enforced by the initiation of proceedings in front of the International Court of Justice by (at least one of) the other state parties. The state in breach would prospectively be ordered to adhere to its obligation, which follows the idea of sanctioning as last resort and supports monitoring as part of the object and purpose of human rights treaties.[688] Such a judgement would be an aggravated form of the 'naming and shaming' which is one of the few possible quasi-sanctions that are already practiced by the committees.[689] The adequate reparation would be restitution (Art. 35 ARS) in the form of submission of the missing report(s) or satisfaction (Art. 37 ARS) in the form of acknowledgement of the breach, expression of regret and a formal apology (as provided in Art. 37 (2) ARS).

To conclude: under customary international law a possibility to sanction the breach of the state reporting is provided by the rules reflected in the ARS. As customary international law – once established and acknowledged – is binding on every state that is not a persistent objector, and the obligation is owed to the other state parties,[690] there is no difficulty with the application of the rules. In consequence, the other state parties could initiate proceedings in front of the International Court of Justice against the state party which does not adhere to its reporting obligation[691] – given that all jurisdiction

---

686 Art. 31(2) ARS (see fn 667 *supra*).
687 See *supra*, Part Two, Chapter 1, IV. 1.
688 As described *supra*, Part Two, Chapter 3, II. 1. b.
689 See *supra*, Part Two, Chapter 3, II. 1. a.
690 See *supra*, Part Two, Chapter 1, III. b.
691 Cf Schöpp-Schilling, *'Treaty Body Reform: The Case of the Committee on the Elimination of Discrimination against Women'* (2007) 7 HRLR 201, 203.

II. Sanctions for the Breach of the State Reporting Obligation under International Law

and admissibility criteria are fulfilled.[692] Following the consequences resulting from a breach which are enshrined in the ARS, the state party in breach would prospectively be ordered to cease its wrongful conduct immediately and provide reparations in the form of restitution or satisfaction. This option would amount to an aggravated form of 'naming and shaming', a quasi-sanction already used by the committees, which, in such an evolved form, would give rise to doubts concerning the trustworthiness of a state towards the fulfillment of its treaty obligations[693] which results in a coercive measure following the breaching behavior of the state (and hereby a sanction *per definitionem*).

3. Evaluation of Sanctioning According to the Rules of International Law

A possibility to sanction states which persistently do not comply with their reporting obligation can be found in international treaty law as well as customary law rules as reflected in the Draft Articles on State Responsibility. As the sanctions under international treaty law, more specifically as provided by the VCLT (including the customary rules underlying its provisions), are not in compliance with the object and purpose of human rights law as well as the idea of sanctions as a last resort (even the first non-submission would give rise to the consequences enshrined in Art. 60 of the VCLT), the only viable sanctions can be found in the customary international law rules reflected in the Draft Articles on State Responsibility. Because the sanctions identified in this Chapter are customary international law, they can be imposed without changing the individual treaties. Therefore, this option would fulfill the request to create sanctions for persistent non-reporting states without having to obtain the consent of the State parties for a change of the individual treaty text.

However, it is and remains questionable whether sanctions would bring the desired effect to increase compliance. Generally, it seems desirable to motivate States to comply with their reporting obligation by positive incentives. Sanctioning under international law often leads to an even more reserved behavior by the affected state. Nevertheless, if

---

692 Art. 34–38 ICJ-Statute.
693 Some authors consider the concern for damage to the reputation of a State as creating a great incentive to comply with international (human rights) obligations (rational choice model of reputation) because the State considers compliance as a security that other States will cooperate and contract with them in the future, see for example Krommendijk, 'The domestic effectiveness of international human rights monitoring in established democracies. The case of the UN human rights treaty bodies' (2015), 10 Rev Int Organ 489, 493; Schimmelfennig, 'Strategic calculation and international socialization: membership incentives, party constellations, and sustained compliance in Central and Eastern Europe' (2005), 59 International Organization 827, 831 f.; the reputation of a State concerning human rights is also considered as the main reason for the ratification of human rights treaties, see Heyns & Viljoen, 'The Impact of the United Nations Human Rights Treaties on the Domestic Level', 23 HRQ 3, 483.

this possibility is applied restrictively and exclusively as a last resort, after all other possibilities (call upon the state to comply, name persistent non-reporting states publicly, review in absence of a report) are exhausted, it could be an option to use proceedings in front of the International Court of Justice as a measure to enforce compliance.

Yet, on the note of practicability, it is doubtful that there would be a state party willing to initiate proceedings against a state in breach of its obligation. As can be seen from the statistics on compliance with the reporting obligations as published by the Treaty Bodies and frequently by the Secretary-General, almost every state is in breach by either non-submission, late submission or the quality of the submission.[694] Therefore, it is questionable whether a state would have an interest to initiate proceedings against another state on the basis of the violation of the reporting obligation.[695] Due to the high number of non- and late-reporting states, this scenario is highly unlikely.[696] Apart from this specific problem, it appears that states generally do not have a strong interest to hold other states responsible for breaches of human rights treaties.[697] However, theoretically, it would be possible to sanction the breach of the reporting obligation under international law and enforce the consequences by initiating proceedings in front the International Court of Justice.[698]

What could be feasible would be a compromise between the sanctioning by proceedings in front of the International Court of Justice and the current practice of reviewing a state in absence of a report. As the reputation of a State is of major relevance in the international sphere, the publication of the names of consistently non-reporting states on, for example, the homepage of the respective oversight committee and the explicit naming of the non-reporting states at the beginning of each session of the committee

---

694 See Homepage of the Office of the High Commissioner, UN Treaty Body Database, accessible: <https://tbinternet.ohchr.org/_layouts/15/TreatyBodyExternal/LateReporting.aspx> [accessed 02 December 2019]. The Homepage does not contain information on the quality of the respective reports, which is why the breach by inadequate quality is not mentioned here.

695 Krommendijk, *The domestic effectiveness of international human rights monitoring in established democracies. The case of the UN human rights treaty bodies* (2015), 10 Rev Int Organ 489, 491.

696 Also, there could be difficulties in the admissibility of such a claim due to the doctrine of 'clean hands'. However, the existence of this doctrine is still disputed and the International Court of Justice has not yet recognized it (see most recently ICJ, *Certain Iranian Assets (Islamic Republic of Iran v. United States of America)*, Preliminary Objections, Judgement, 13 February 2019, General List No. 164, paras 116 ff.). Therefore, this matter is not discussed in this thesis.

697 Hathaway, 'Do human rights treaties make a difference?' (2002), 111 Yale Law Journal 1935, 1938.
Also, there could be difficulties in the admissibility of such a claim due to the doctrine of 'clean hands' (see also *supra*, fn 671).

698 The admissibility of the claim would of course be subject to the admissibility criteria of art. 34, 35, 36, 40 ICJ Statute.; especially the question whether the respective States can be parties in the relevant case (art. 34, 35 ICJ Statute) would be of interest.

could circumvent the difficulties of a court procedure while approximating the outcome of a judgement. From the review of the various rules of procedure, it appears that the committees are able to introduce and enforce such publication in their respective rules. With such a public "naming and shaming", the states would have to take into consideration their appearance before the international community and the public which could motivate them to engage more actively with the oversight committees and fulfill their reporting obligation. Such a procedure would be absolutely independent from the states and within the power of the oversight committees.[699]

III. Résumé on the Considerations Made in this Chapter

This Chapter proposed a twofold solution to the low effectivity of the current reporting procedure with a focus on the written submission of the report – the 'first step' of the reporting cycle. The integrative reporting procedure is based on the findings resulting from the considerations of the previous Chapters and therefore takes up those requirements frequently put forward as desirable for a functional monitoring system to the human rights treaties.

The proposed integrative reporting procedure does not only provide a solution for the remaining challenges that have not yet been solved. It combines the fruitful ideas of previous reforms with considerations based on the lowest common denominators identified by those previous reform processes and is expected to be accepted by all relevant stakeholders. The Baseline Report could serve as a source not only for the oversight committees but also for members of the civil society and thereby increase the transparency and coherence of human rights protection in various systems and on all levels. The Bottom-Up Review supports legislation in compliance with human rights as it produces a roadmap for reforms while at the same time assists the oversight committees in the supervision of the state's implementation of the relevant treaty. The periodic Q&A eases the reporting burden significantly while assisting human rights protection through focused and targeted questions on the specific situation within the respective state. The integrative reporting procedure keeps focus on vulnerable groups, reduces the obligations for the state parties and is implementable within the existing framework. Furthermore, this procedure is expected to increase the cooperation of regional and international oversight committees due to the common basis they would be working with.

Should, despite the further simplification of the procedure, states still persistently refuse to report and/or cooperate with the oversight committees, they could be sanctioned under regulations of customary international law. The treaties enshrining the state

---

699 Some regional committees already use this form of "naming and shaming", see for example Rule 76 (2) of the Rules of Procedure of the African Commission on Human and Peoples' Rights.

reporting obligation do not foresee a sanction for the breach of the reporting obligation themselves. However, treaty regulations and regulations of customary international law can exist parallel to each other and are not mutually exclusive. It is therefore possible to hold a state accountable for a breach of an international treaty obligation despite the fact that the respective treaty does not entail a sanctioning clause. This possibility answers the repeated calls for an option to sanction as a measure of last resort. Obviously, it should not be possible to punish every state for even the slightest non-compliance with the reporting obligation, especially because the reason for non-compliance might derive from or be due to a complex issue that the breaching state party is unable to solve. Hence, sanctions for a breach of the reporting obligation should only be applied in exceptional circumstances and as a last resort. Even though there remains some doubt about the practicability of sanctioning due to the questionable requirement of a state instituting proceedings against another state party to enforce compliance, it provides a possible solution. A judgement on this matter would be an aggravated form of the 'naming and shaming' already practiced partly by several oversight committees. As a court procedure comes with several difficulties, a compromise between the absence in review of a report and a court procedure might be the more feasible option: the oversight committees should amend their rules of procedure in a way which allows them to publicly name the states which a not in compliance with their reporting obligation, for example on the respective homepage or at the beginning of each session. Hereby, the negative effect on the reputation of the relevant state which would come with a judgement could be approximated while proceedings in front of the International Court of Justice would be prevented. Furthermore, this compromise is independent from the states, as it is completely within the power of the oversight committee to amend their rules and publish the relevant names.

In conclusion, the twofold proposal made in this chapter is able to increase the compliance of state parties with their reporting obligations under international and regional human rights treaties by introducing the integrative reporting procedure and offers the possibility to sanction non-compliance.

Part Three:
Conclusion – Call to Uphold and Advance the State Reporting Procedure

The monitoring instrument of state reporting is the oldest and most frequently used procedure to monitor compliance of states with their treaty obligations. First introduced by the League of Nations and the International Labour Organization, it developed into one of the most prominent monitoring procedures in the human rights law sphere. When it was included in the first human rights treaty in the regional sphere in the 1950s[700] and the international sphere in the 1960s (Convention against All Forms of Racial Discrimination), it was the only means of monitoring the state parties could accept within their prevalent perception of the almost absolute sovereignty of states in international law. As the masters of the treaties, the majority of states refused to create an oversight body with forcible monitoring powers, which resulted in the state reporting procedure being included in the treaty texts as the lowest common denominator. As the major part of monitoring is conducted by the state itself, state reporting is very sensitive towards state sovereignty. Nevertheless, due to its inclusion in the treaty texts, the obligation to report becomes binding on every state immediately upon ratifying the respective treaty, which makes it the only procedure which is binding on the state parties irrespective of a further consent to be obtained from the states. Over the course of the decades following its first inclusion into a human rights treaty, the obligation to periodically report to a competent oversight committee today is enshrined in eight treaties and two optional protocols in the UN Treaty Body System as well as in several regional human rights treaties.

Despite its broad inclusion into human rights treaties as the one compulsory monitoring instrument, the content, purpose and nature of state reporting as an abstract instrument remained unclear. The obligation consists of three individual elements that have to be fulfilled cumulatively to satisfy the duty imposed on the state. Only if those obligations are fulfilled by the state party the object and purpose of state reporting can be fulfilled. This procedure serves the purpose of fostering a constructive dialogue between the state parties, members of the civil society and the oversight committees on the effective implementation and hence the improvement of human rights protection on the territory of the state. This dialogue shall be sparked by the self-evaluation of the state party, followed by a check or control of the oversight committee, with or without

---

700 As a reporting obligation upon request, Art. 57 Convention for the Protection of Human Rights and Fundamental Freedoms (4 November 1950, CETS No. 005).

Part Three: Conclusion – Call to Uphold and Advance the State Reporting Procedure

taking into account contributions by members of the civil society. Considering the object and purpose of the state reporting obligation, and taking into account that the state reporting procedure is an essential part of a human rights treaty (as part of its object and purpose due to the minimum amount of monitoring it provides), it becomes clear that the state reporting obligation is a primary (or substantive) obligation of a state which is owed the other states party to the respective treaties.

Although the state reporting procedure has now been used for over a century, monitoring through state reports cannot be considered a success story. The positive aspect of its wide acceptance due to its sensitivity towards state sovereignty is at the same time one of its biggest challenges. The lack of sanctions combined with a great overburdening of states parties to all relevant international as well as the relevant regional human rights treaties massively hinders the effectivity of the system, and has done so for decades. Full compliance with all reporting obligations is rare, most prominently when it comes to submission of the written reports. Those reports, which are submitted, are mostly not submitted on time. And even if they are submitted on time, most of them are of an inadequate quality. All these challenges certainly carry political problems with them. But, more importantly, these challenges are breaches of international law. Non-compliance with the state reporting obligation does not only breach an obligation imposed by the ratification of the respective treaty under international law, it also is a violation of the general principle of *pacta sunt servanda*, one of the most important principles in the international law sphere.

The challenges of the state reporting procedure, mostly in the context of the UN Treaty Body System, have been evaluated by scholarship and UN organs over the course of the past 30 years. The reform and strengthening process circulated around the same issues and although there were multiple proposals made to improve the situation, the challenges remain until today. Most of the proposals made were not implemented and some of the proposals, such as the single state report or a unified standing treaty body, were ultimately rejected. Only few proposals found their way into the Treaty Body System: the harmonized reporting guidelines, the simplified reporting procedure (including the list of issues prior to reporting) and page limits. As a review mechanism parallel to and intended to complement state reporting, a peer-reviewed mechanism, the Universal Periodic Review, was established. Also, over the course of the reform process, a great number of new treaties were concluded. All of the above led to an accumulation of the obligations the states had to fulfill as well as a decrease in the transparency of the system. Eventually, the reporting system became too complex to be effective and most states are incapable to comply with all their obligations. Even though this problem was well known amongst the Treaty Bodies, it seemed difficult to come to a solution due to the strong individualism of the committees and the increasing fragmentation of international human rights law. The

Part Three: Conclusion – Call to Uphold and Advance the State Reporting Procedure

instrument of state reporting came close to being dysfunctional, which initiated calls for its abolition.

Nevertheless, despite all the difficulties the state reporting procedure may have, it has to be upheld and advanced to serve the object and purpose it initially was created for. The state reporting procedure holds a lot of potential and caters for needs in the protection of human rights which would not be cared for should the procedure be abolished. First and foremost, the state reporting procedure is the only monitoring procedure a state cannot evade. It becomes compulsory with ratification, and no reservation is permissible to it. The state reporting procedure establishes a constant monitoring of implementation and protection of human rights within a specific country, as it is not subject to precondition such as, for example, a violation of a specific right protected under the relevant treaty. It is a preventive rather than regressive measure, and the only compulsory preventive measure enshrined in the treaty texts. The importance of the procedure and the ambitions to continue its application can be seen in the recent review process of the UN General Assembly, which was initiated in 2014. Over the course of the past five years, stakeholders of all kind sent contributions containing proposals for the improvement of the overall system, all of those containing a call to sustain the Treaty Body system and especially the reporting procedure – however, not in the current form. Recently, some states proposed to generally replace the 'conventional' reporting procedure with the simplified reporting procedure, making it the mandatory procedure for reporting under international human rights treaties. An increasing amount of UN Treaty Bodies use, or offer the usage of, the simplified reporting procedure[701], which is taken up positively by the states.[702] Many of the regional oversight committees use comparable procedures, mainly excluding the constructive dialogue, which, however, was not part of the research for this thesis.

The universal usage of the simplified reporting procedure is strongly supported in this thesis. However, the introduction of the simplified reporting procedure as the mandatory procedure alone does not suffice to tackle all the challenges the system faces.

---

701 The Human Rights Committee decided to have the simplified reporting procedure as their standard from 2020 on, see Human Rights Committee, *Decision on additional measures to simplify the reporting procedure and increase predictability*, 1–26 July 2019 (will be reflected in the Committee's annual report (UN Doc. A/75/40, to be issued in 2020), accessible: <https://www.ohchr.org/EN/HRBodies/CCPR/Pages/PredictableReviewCycle.aspx> [accessed 02 December 2019].

702 See for example reply to the Questionnaire in relation to General Assembly resolution 68/268 of the Office of the High Commissioner for Human Rights, 31 January 2019, by Australia (p. 4), Estonia (p. 1), Finland (p. 1, 4), Holy See (p. 2), Japan (p. 3), Liechtenstein (p. 3), Netherlands (p. 1), Philippines (p. 1), Poland (p. 1), Portugal (p. 1 f.), Republic of Korea (p. 1), Slovenia (p. 1), Sweden (p. 3), Thailand (p. 1), Turkey (p. 1); replies accessible: <https://www.ohchr.org/EN/HRBodies/HRTD/Pages/3rdBiennialReportbySG.aspx> [accessed: 02 December 2019].

Part Three: Conclusion – Call to Uphold and Advance the State Reporting Procedure

An advanced version of the simplified reporting procedure, backed up by sanctions for non-compliance, is considered to be of great advantage for the state reporting instrument. It is necessary to establish a comprehensive and integrative form of reporting to further streamline the process and ease the reporting burden of states.

Integrative reporting, as proposed in this thesis, is a procedure designed to handle the challenges evolving from the increasing fragmentation of international law, and especially human rights law, by creating an all-encompassing basis for reports to regional and international oversight committees. It consists of three parts: a Baseline Report, a Bottom-Up Review and a periodic Q&A.

The first part of the permanent basis, the Baseline Report, is a comprehensive document accessible to every relevant stakeholder, first and foremost to international and regional oversight committees but also the general public. It serves as the foundation for the monitoring of regional and international oversight committees.

The Bottom-Up Review, as the second permanent part, is an addendum valuable for the improvement of the quality of the reports. Its focus lies on the individual state (contrary to 'top-down', focus on the individual treaty) by reviewing the legislative framework of the respective state. This part contains a full catalogue of the laws in force and their compatibility with the international and regional treaties. With this, the long-standing difficulty the committees are facing because of states whose periodic reports solely consist of an enlistment of enacted legislation would be eliminated.

The Baseline Report and the Bottom-Up Review are only subject to changes within the state and its legislation. The Baseline Report shall also serve as – and thereby replace – the initial report required under the majority of treaties. It shall be made publicly available.

The third – periodic – part of the integrative report is the periodic Q&A in the form of a questionnaire sent by the respective oversight committee and an answer by the relevant state, comparable to the procedure used as the list of issues prior to reporting. Due to the comprehensive content of the permanent parts a maximum of twenty questions per oversight body should suffice. Those questions should be focused on the *de facto* situation within the country and shall consider recent developments in the respective state. They should not be of a general nature but rather force the state party to provide information on the practical implementation of the relevant treaty. It is expected to streamline and focus the discussion between state party and oversight committee, as well as the discussions between state and members of the civil society and oversight committee and members of the civil society, respectively. The answer of the state party shall serve as the periodic report. It is expected to be significantly shorter and with focused

Part Three: Conclusion – Call to Uphold and Advance the State Reporting Procedure

information. As a positive side-effect, it is expected that the state parties will be enabled to adhere to the page limit of 40 pages, which, despite being requested by the oversight committees for periodic reports, currently is not respected in the majority of reports.

Integrative reporting would support a streamlining of the reporting process not only within the system of the UN Treaty Bodies, but also the cooperation between the Treaty Bodies and the regional human rights committees. At the same time, it preserves the individuality of the respective committees and thereby upholds the protection necessary for the vulnerable groups which could be affected the most by a streamlined and harmonized process. Also, it is supportive towards the states (as it eases the reporting burden) and the regional committees (as the majority is already using a comparable procedure). The simplification of the procedure serves as an incentive for the state parties to present them as trustworthy affiliates.

Should the further simplification of the procedure not suffice as an incentive to increase reporting compliance, persistent non-reporting states can be held liable and be subject to sanctions under international law. Although the treaties themselves do not provide a sanction for the breach of the reporting obligation, such sanction can be deducted from customary international law. Oversight committees – and increasingly state parties – express their approval for the sanctioning of states which are persistently in breach. However, sanctions should be introduced as a measure of last resort.

A quasi-sanction already widely practiced is 'naming and shaming', meaning that non-submission is made public by or at least in front of the relevant oversight committee. Furthermore, an increasing number of oversight committees established rules to proceed with a review in absence of a report, which is already considered a measure of last resort. Those, however, are the maximum consequences currently applied against breaching states. Even though those consequences served the purpose of moving some the breaching state towards actually submitting a report, in most of the cases the report was still inadequate. Sometimes, even the review in absence did not motivate the breaching state party at all.

For those cases of persistent refusal, a hard sanction can be deducted from the customary international law rules as enshrined in the Draft Articles on the Responsibility of States for Internationally Wrongful Acts: they provide that the commission of an internationally wrongful act obliges the state in breach to immediately cease its wrongdoing and make reparations. The breach of the state reporting obligation is, without doubt, an internationally wrongful act. The customary law rules underlying the ARS are binding upon every state that is not a persistent objector to them. They are applicable to multilateral human rights treaties and can be claimed in front of the International Court of Justice. Hence, since the state reporting obligation is owed to the other states parties

Part Three: Conclusion – Call to Uphold and Advance the State Reporting Procedure

to the respective multilateral treaty, it would be possible for at least one of the other states to initiate proceedings against the relevant state on the basis of the breach of the reporting obligation. Such a claim could result in the duty of restitution (Art. 35 ARS) in the form of the ordered submission of the report or, as the preferred option, satisfaction in the form of acknowledgement of the breach, expression of regret and a formal apology (as provided for in Art. 37 (2) ARS). The order of satisfaction could be a viable instrument as it attacks the trustworthiness of the state in question and might lead to an increased motivation to adhere to the treaty obligations it pledged to comply with. It has to be stressed though that states which are unable to comply with their reporting obligation due to restrictions in their human, structural or financial resources may not be subject to the aforementioned sanctions. Such cases have to be assessed individually.

However, despite the availability of such a sanction and the consideration that this sanctioning could actually increase compliance of persistent non-complying states it unfortunately is highly unlikely that a state will actually initiate proceedings in front of the International Court of Justice to enforce compliance. Most states are not in compliance, so they would risk having proceedings initiated against themselves on the same basis. Furthermore, most states will not have an interest in the compliance of other states with their respective state reporting obligation. Nevertheless, it is worth considering the use of this sanctioning option.

The current state of the human rights system is the stage of implementation.[703] More than 70 years after the Universal Declaration of Human Rights the system has grown in means of acceptance and scope of protection. While it is commendable that more specialized treaties are underway, it is equally desirable to stabilize compliance with the existing treaties and reach universal ratification while at the same time stabilize the monitoring framework. As all the other monitoring instruments are subject to the consent of the state parties and only state reporting is compulsory, and while monitoring the protection and implementation of human rights in the respective states is an essential part of the human rights system in the UN as well as in the regional systems, the strengthening process must be concluded successfully. The UN General Assembly Review 2020 is the next opportunity for the international community to turn from creating human rights to implementing them. Even if the proposals of this thesis are not considered in the 2020 Review, the nature of the state reporting obligation as well as the legal challenges identified in this thesis are recommended to be taken into account by all stakeholders in order to create a functioning and effective human rights monitoring system.

---

703 Heyns & Viljoen, 'The Impact of the United Nations Human Rights Treaties on the Domestic Level', 23 HRQ 3, 483, 483; Keller & Ulfstein, 'Introduction', in: Keller & Ulfstein, *UN Human Rights Treaty Bodies: Law and Legitimacy* (2012) 1, 1.

Index of Authorities

If not indicated otherwise, all internet sources were last accessed on 02 December 2019.

A

Additional Protocol to the American Convention on Human Rights in the Area of Economic, Social and Cultural Rights ('Protocol of San Salvador'), 17 November 1988, OAS Treaty Series No. 69

Advisory Committee on the Framework Convention for the Protection of National Minorities, Outline for State Reports to be submitted under the second monitoring Cycle, in conformity with Article 25 Paragraph 1 of the Framework Convention for the Protection of National Minorities, adopted by the Committee of Ministers on 15 January 2003, at the 824th meeting of the Ministers' Deputies, CoE Doc. ACFC/INF(2003)001

Advisory Council on Human Rights of Morocco, Marrakesh Statement on strengthening the relationship between NHRIs and the human rights treaty bodies system, 10 June 2010, accessible: <https://www.ohchr.org/en/hrbodies/hrtd/pages/documents.aspx>, reprinted in Netherlands Quarterly of Human Rights 28 (2010), 121–27

Advocates for Human Rights et al., Dublin Statement on the Process of Strengthening the United Nations Human rights Treaty Body System: Response by non-governmental organizations, November 2010, accessible: <https://www.ohchr.org/EN/HRBodies/HRTD/Pages/Documents.aspx>

African Charter on Democracy, Elections and Governance, 30 January 2007, accessible: <https://au.int/en/treaties/african-charter-democracy-elections-and-governance>

African Charter on Human and People's Rights, 27 June 1981, OAU Doc. CAB/LEG/67/3 rev. 5, 21 International Legal Materials 58 (1982)

African Charter on the Rights and Welfare of the Child, 1 July 1990, OAU Doc. CAB/LEG/24.9/49 (1990)

African Charter on the Values and Principles of Decentralisation, Local Governance and Local Development, 27 June 2014, accessible: <https://au.int/en/treaties/african-charter-values-and-principles-decentralisation-local-governance-and-local>

African Commission for Human and Peoples' Rights, Homepage of the African Commission for Human and Peoples' Rights, <https://www.achpr.org/reportingprocedure>

Index of Authorities

African Commission for Human and Peoples' Rights, Homepage of the African Commission on Human and People's Rights, State Reports and Concluding Observations, <https://www.achpr.org/statereportsandconcludingobservations>

African Commission on Human and People's Rights, Rules of Procedure, adopted 2–13 February 1988, revised 2–11 October 1995, approved 12–26 May 2010, accessible: <https://www.achpr.org/legalinstruments/detail?id=34>

African Commission on Human and Peoples' Rights, State Reporting Procedures and Guidelines, accessible <https://www.achpr.org/statereportingproceduresandguidelines>

African Committee of experts on the Rights and Welfare of the Child, Revised Rules of Procedure of the African Committee of Experts on the Rights and Welfare of the Child, accessible <https://www.acerwc.africa/working-documents/revised-rules-of-procedures-final/>

African Union Convention for the Protection and Assistance of Internally Displaced Persons in Africa (Kampala Convention), 23 October 2009, UN Registration No. 52375

African Union Convention on Preventing and Combating Corruption, 1 July 2003, accessible: <https://au.int/en/treaties/african-union-convention-preventing-and-combating-corruption>

Ajevski, Marjan, Fragmentation in International Human Rights Law – Beyond Conflict of Laws, Nordic Journal of Human Rights (2014), 32:2, 87–98, DOI: 10.1080/18918131.2014.897795

Alfredsson, Gudmundur et al. (eds.), International Monitoring Mechanisms: Essays in Honour of Jacob Th. Möller. 2nd revised edition, Brill 2009

Alkarama et al., Issues for the inter-governmental process on strengthening the effective functioning of the human rights treaty body system, A Joint NGO Contribution, 12 April 2012, accessible: <https://www.ohchr.org/EN/HRBodies/HRTD/Pages/Documents.aspx>

Alston, Philip, Against a World Court for Human Rights, Ethics&International Affairs, 28(2) (2014), 197–212

American Convention on Human Rights ('Pact of San Jose, Costa Rica'), 22 November 1969, OAS Treaty Series, No. 36.

Association of Southeast Asian Nations, Declaration on Human Rights, ASEAN Human Rights Declaration, adopted 18 November 2012, accessible <https://asean.org/asean-human-rights-declaration/>

Index of Authorities

Australian Mission to the United Nations, 2020 Review of the United Nations Treaty Body System – Comments on the Australian Government's implementation of General Assembly resolution 68/268, including those provisions addressed to States, accessible: <https://www.ohchr.org/EN/HRBodies/HRTD/Pages/3rdBiennialReportbySG.aspx>

B

Bayefsky, Anne F., The UN Human Rights Treaty System: Universality at the Crossroads, New York: Transnational Publishers, 2001

Bowman, Michael, Towards a Unified Treaty Body for Monitoring Compliance with UN Human Rights Conventions – Legal Mechanisms for Treaty Reform, Human Rights Law Review 7:1 (2007), 225–249

Brazil, Questionnaire in Relation to General Assembly Resolution 68/268, Comments by Brazil, accessible: <https://www.ohchr.org/EN/HRBodies/HRTD/Pages/3rdBiennialReportbySG.aspx>

Broecker, Christen/Gaer, Felice D., The United Nations High Commissioner for Human Rights: Conscience for the World, Jacob Blaustein Institute for the Advancement of Human Rights, Brill Nijhoff 2013

Broecker, Christen/O'Flaherty, Michael, Policy Brief, The Outcome of the General Assembly's Treaty Body Strengthening Process: An Important Milestone on a Longer Journey, Universal Rights Group, June 2014, accessible:< https://www.universal-rights.org/urg-policy-reports/the-outcome-of-the-general-assemblys-treaty-body-strengthening-process-an-important-milestone-on-a-longer-journey/>

Broude, Tomer/Shany, Yuval (eds.), Multi-Sourced Equivalent Norms in International Law, Hart Publishing, Oxford 2011

Bulgaria, Contribution by the Government of Bulgaria to Questionnaire in Relation to General Assembly Resolution 68/268, February 2019, accessible: <https://www.ohchr.org/EN/HRBodies/HRTD/Pages/3rdBiennialReportbySG.aspx>

Bundesverfassungsgericht, Order of the Second Senate of 29 January 2019, 2 BvC 62/14 -, paras (1–142), ECLI:DE:BVerfG:2019:cs20190129.2bvc006214

Bundeswahlgesetz, 7 May 1956, Bundesgesetzblatt Nr. 21, Teil I, p. 383 ff. in the version promulgated on 23 July 1993 (BGBl. p. 1288, 1594), most recently amended by Art. 2 of the law of 10 July 2018 (BGBl. I p. 1116)

C

Canada, Canada's Response to the OHCHR questionnaire on implementation of GA resolution 68/268, April 2019, accessible: <https://www.ohchr.org/EN/HRBodies/HRTD/Pages/3rdBiennialReportbySG.aspx>

Center for Reproductive Rights, Submission from Center for Reproductive Rights to OHCHR Questionnaire in relation to General Assembly resolution 68/268: Comments on the state of the human rights treaty body system in view of the upcoming review by 9 April 2020, of the effectiveness of the measures taken in order to ensure the sustainability (of treaty bodies), and, on any further action to strengthen and enhance the effective functioning of the human rights treaty body system, accessible: <https://www.ohchr.org/EN/HRBodies/HRTD/Pages/3rdBiennialReportbySG.aspx>

Centre for Human Rights, Faculty of Law, University of Pretoria, Pretoria Statement on the Strengthening and Reform of the UN Human Rights Treaty Body System, 20–21 June 2011, accessible: <https://www.ohchr.org/EN/HRBodies/HRTD/Pages/Documents.aspx>

Centre of Human Rights Education (PHZ Lucerne), Lucerne Academic Consultation on Strengthening the United Nations Treaty Body System, 24–25 October 2011, accessible: <https://www.ohchr.org/EN/HRBodies/HRTD/Pages/Documents.aspx>

Chairs of the Human Rights Treaty Bodies, Implementation of human rights instruments, Report of the Chairs of the human rights treaty bodies on their thirty-first annual meeting, 30 July 2019, UN Doc. A/74/256

Committee against Torture, Committee against Torture, Rules of procedure, 1 September 2014, UN Doc. CAT/C/3/Rev.6.

Committee against Torture, Report of the Committee against Torture, 37th session 6–24 November 2006 and 38th session 30 April-18 May 2007, UN Doc. A/62/44

Committee of Experts of the European Charter for Regional or Minority Languages, Rules of Procedure of the Committee of Experts of the European Charter for Regional or Minority Languages, 2001 and modifications thereto on 24 March 2004 (17th meeting), on 25 September 2014 (48th meeting), on 17 June 2016 (54th meeting) and on 18 March 2019 (62nd meeting), MIN-LANG (2019) 7, accessible: <https://rm.coe.int/minlang-2019-07-comex-rules-of-procedure-final/1680954878>

Committee of Ministers of the Council of Europe, Decision of the Committee of Ministers, 10.4 European Charter for Regional or Minority Languages, e. Strengthening the monitoring mechanism of the European Charter for Regional or Minority Languages, 28 November 2018, CoE Doc. CM/Del/Dec(2018)1330/10.4e

Index of Authorities

Committee of Ministers of the Council of Europe, Decision of the Committee of Ministers, European Social Charter, Governmental Committee of the European Social Charter, New system for the presentation of reports on the application of the European Social Charter, Proposal of the Governmental Committee, adopted at the 923rd meeting on 3 May 2006, CoE Doc. CM/Del/Dec(2006)963/4.2

Committee of Ministers of the Council of Europe, Outline for Reports to be submitted pursuant to Article 25 Paragraph 1 of the Framework Convention for the Protection of National Minorities, 30 September 1998 at the 642nd meeting of the Ministers' Deputies, CoE Doc. ACFC/INF(98)1

Committee of Ministers of the Council of Europe, Outline for the State Reports to be submitted under the fourth monitoring Cycle, in conformity with Article 25 Paragraph 1 of the Framework Convention for the Protection of National Minorities, adopted at the 1169th meeting of the Ministers' Deputies on 30 April 2013, CoE Doc. ACFC/III(2013)001

Committee of Ministers of the Council of Europe, Outline for the State Reports to be submitted under the third monitoring Cycle, in conformity with Article 25 Paragraph 1 of the Framework Convention for the Protection of National Minorities, adopted at the 1029th meeting of the Ministers' Deputies on 11 June 2008, CoE Doc. ACFC/III(2008)001

Committee on Economic, Social and Cultural Rights, Rules of Procedure of the Committee, Provisional rules of procedure adopted by the Committee at its third session (1989), 1 September 1993, UN Doc. E/C.12/1990/4/Rev.1.

Committee on Economic, Social and Cultural Rights, General Comment No. 14: The Right to the Highest Attainable Standard of Health (Art. 12), adopted at the Twenty-second Session of the Committee on Economic, Social and Cultural Rights, on 11 August 2000 (Contained in Document E/C.12/2000/4)

Committee on Economic, Social and Cultural Rights, General Comment No. 1: Reporting by States Parties, 24 February 1989, UN Doc. E/1989/22, p. 87 f. (Annex III), reprinted in Compilation of General Comments and General Recommendations, adopted by Human Rights Treaty Bodies, 12 May 2003, UN Doc. HRI/GEN/1/Rev.6 at 8

Committee on the Elimination of Discrimination against Women, Homepage of the Committee on the Elimination of Discrimination against Women, <https://www.ohchr.org/EN/HRBodies/CEDAW/Pages/InquiryProcedure.aspx>

Committee on the Elimination of Racial Discrimination, Rules of Procedure of the Committee on the Elimination of Racial Discrimination, 1 January 1989, UN Doc. CERD/C/35/Rev.3

Committee on the Protection of the Rights of All Migrant Workers and members of Their Families, Committee on the Protection of the Rights of All Migrant Workers and members of Their Families, Rules of Procedure, 8 February 2019, UN Doc. CMW/C/2

Committee on the Right of Persons with Disabilities, Rules of Procedure, 10 October 2016, UN Doc. CRPD/C/1/rev.1

Committee on the Rights of Persons with Disabilities, General comment No. 1 (2014): Article 12: Equal recognition before the law, 19 May 2014, UN Doc. CRPD/C/GC/1

Committee on the Rights of the Child, Committee on the Rights of the Child, Rules of procedure, 1 March 2019, UN Doc. CRC/C/4/Rev.5

Constitution of the Food and Agriculture Organization, 16 October 1945, reprinted in Basic texts of the Food and Agriculture Organization of the United Nations, Volumes I and II, 2017 edition, p. 3 ff., accessible: <http://www.fao.org/3/a-mp046e.pdf>

Constitution of the International Labour Organisation, 1 April 1919, 15 UNTS 40

Convention against Torture and Other Cruel, Inhuman or Degrading Treatment or Punishment, 10 December 1984, 1465 UNTS 85

Convention Concerning the Protection of the World Cultural and Natural Heritage, 16 November 1972, 1037 UNTS 151

Convention for the Protection of Human Rights and Fundamental Freedoms, 4 November 1950, CETS No. 005

Convention for the Protection of Human Rights and Fundamental Freedoms (as amended by Protocols No. 11 and No. 14, 1 June 2010), 4 November 1950, CETS No. 005

Convention on the Elimination of All Forms of Discrimination against Persons with Disabilities, 8 June 1999, OAS Doc. A-65

Convention on the Elimination of All Forms of Discrimination against Women, 18 December 1979, 1249 UNTS 13

Convention on the International Trade in Endangered Species of Wild Fauna and Flora, 3 March 1973, 993 UNTS 243

Convention on the Rights of People with Disabilities, 13 December 2006, 2515 UNTS 3

Convention on the Rights of the Child, 20 November 1989, 1577 UNTS 3

Council of Europe Convention on preventing and combating violence against women and domestic violence, 11 May 2011, CETS No. 210

Council of Europe, Homepage Council of Europe, Details of Treaty No. 139, European Code of Social Security (Revised), <https://www.coe.int/en/web/conventions/full-list/-/conventions/treaty/139>

Council of Europe, Homepage Council of Europe, European Social Charter, Reporting procedure of the European Code of Social Security, <https://www.coe.int/en/web/european-social-charter/reporting-procedure>

Council of Europe, Homepage Council of Europe, European Social Charter, Reporting system of the European Social Charter, <https://www.coe.int/en/web/european-social-charter/national-reports>

Covenant of the League of Nations, 28 April 1919, reprinted 13 American Journal of International Law Supp. 128

Crawford, James, Brownlie's Principles of Public International Law, 9th ed. 2019

D

Dannemann, Gerhard (ed), German Law Archive, accessible: <https://germanlawarchive.iuscomp.org/?p=228>

d'Aspremont, Jean, 'The Systemic Integration of International Law by Domestic Courts: Domestic Judges as Architects of the Consistency of the International Legal Order' in Nollkaemper & Fauchald (eds), The Practice of International and National Courts and the (De-) Fragmentation of International Law (Hart Publishing 2012), 141–165.

de Schutter, Olivier, International Human Rights Law, 2nd edition, Cambridge University Press, Cambridge 2014

Devereux, Annemarie/Anderson, Catherine, Reporting under International Human Rights Treaties: Perspectives from Timor Leste's Experience of the Reformed Process, Human Rights Law Review, 8:1 (2008), 69–104

Dörr, Manfred/Schmalenbach, Kirsten, Vienna Convention on the Law of Treaties – A Commentary, 2nd edition, Heidelberg et. al. 2018

Dublin II Meeting, Strengthening the United Nations Human Rights Treaty Body System, Outcome Document, 10–11 November 2011, accessible: <https://www.ohchr.org/EN/HRBodies/HRTD/Pages/Documents.aspx>

E

Egan, Suzanne, Strengthening the United Nations Human Rights Treaty Body System, Human Rights Law Review 13:2 (2014), 209–243

Estonia, Estonia's comments on the implementation of the General Assembly resolution 68/268 'Strengthening and enhancing the effective functioning of the human rights treaty body system', accessible: <https://www.ohchr.org/EN/HRBodies/HRTD/Pages/3rdBiennialReportbySG.aspx>

European Charter for Regional or Minority Languages, 5 November 1998, CETS No. 148

European Code of Social Security, 16 April 1964, CETS No. 048

European Code of Social Security (revised), 6 November 1990, CETS No. 139

European Committee of Social Rights, Homepage of the European Committee of Social Rights, <https://www.coe.int/en/web/european-social-charter/european-committee-of-social-rights>

European Court of Human Rights, Case of Hirst v The United Kingdom (No.2), 6 October 2005, Application no. 74025/01, ECLI:CE:ECHR:2005:1006JUD007402501

European Social Charta, 18 October 1961, CETS No.035

European Social Charter (Revised), 3 May 1996, CETS No. 163

F

Framework Convention for the Protection of National Minorities, 1 February 1995, CETS No. 157

G

Gaer, Felice D., First Fruits: Reporting by States under the African Charter on Human and Peoples' Rights, Netherlands Quarterly of Human Rights 10(1) (1992), 29–42

Gaer, Felice D., The Institutional Future of the Covenants: A World Court for Human Rights? in: Daniel Moeckli/Helen Keller/Corina Heri, The Human Rights Covenants at 50: Their Past, Present and Future, Oxford University Press 2018, 334–356

Garner, Bryan A. (ed), Black's Law Dictionary, 9th edn, Thomson Reuters, St. Paul 2010

Geneva Academy of International Humanitarian Law and Human Rights, Optimizing the UN Treaty Body System, Academic Platform Report in the 2020 Review, 7 May 2018, accessible: <https://www.geneva-academy.ch/research/publications/detail/356-optimizing-the-un-treaty-body-system>

Index of Authorities

Geneva Academy of International Humanitarian Law and Human Rights, Submission by the Geneva Academy of International Humanitarian Law and Human Rights to the Questionnaire in Relation to General Assembly Resolution 68/268 circulated by OHCHR, academic input into the 2020 review, accessible: <https://www.ohchr.org/EN/HRBodies/HRTD/Pages/3rdBiennialReportbySG.aspx>

German Federal Foreign Office, Treaty Body reform, comments from Germany, May 2019, accessible: <https://www.ohchr.org/EN/HRBodies/HRTD/Pages/3rdBiennialReportbySG.aspx>

Government Offices of Sweden, Ministry for Foreign Affairs, Department for International Law, Human Rights and Treaty Law, Questionnaire re. General Assembly resolution 68/268 – Swedish response, 26 March 2019, accessible: <https://www.ohchr.org/EN/HRBodies/HRTD/Pages/3rdBiennialReportbySG.aspx>

Governmental Committee of the European Social Charter and the European Code of Social Security, Abridged report concerning Conclusions 2012 of the European Social Charter (revised), Appendix II, 13 December 2013, CM Documents CM(2013)168

Governmental Committee of the European Social Charter and the European Code of Social Security, Rules of procedure, adopted by the Committee at its 134th meeting (2016), GC(2016)16

Governmental Committee, Report Concerning Conclusions 2017 of the European Social Charter (revised), 31 January 2019, GC(2018)24

Governmental Committee, Report Concerning Conclusions XXI-2 (2017) of the 1961 European Social Charter, 31 January 2019, GC(2018)23

Group of Experts on Action against Violence against Women and Domestic Violence (GREVIO), Rules of Procedure, adopted by GREVIO at its 1st meeting (Strasbourg, 21–23 September 2015), amended by GREVIO at its 9th meeting (Strasbourg, 14–17 February 2017), amended by GREVIO at its 12th meeting (Strasbourg, 9–13 October 2017), amended by GREVIO at its 13th meeting on 20–23 February 2018, GREVIO/Inf(2015)RoP-amdt3

Group of Experts on Action against Violence against Women and Domestic Violence (GREVIO), Questionnaire on legislative and other measures giving effect to the provisions of the Council of Europe Convention on Preventing and Combating Violence against Women and Domestic Violence (Istanbul Convention), adopted by GREVIO on 11 March 2016, GREVIO/Inf(2016)1, accessible: <https://rm.coe.int/CoERMPublicCommonSearchServices/DisplayDCTMContent?documentId=09000016805c95b0>

H

Hampson, Francoise J., Overview of the Reform of the UN Human Rights Machinery, Human Rights Law Review 7:1 (2007), 7–27

Hathaway, Oona A., Do human rights treaties make a difference?, The Yale Law Journal, Vol. 111 (2002), 1935–1959

Heyns, Christof, The African Regional Human Rights System: The African Charter, Penn State Law Review, Vol. 108:3 (2003), 679–702

Heyns, Christof/Killander, Magnus, Africa, in: Daniel Moeckli et al, International Human Rights Law, 2nd edition, Oxford University Press 2014, 441–457

Heyns, Christof/Viljoen, Frans, The Impact of the United Nations Human Rights Treaties on the Domestic Level, Human Rights Quarterly 23(3), 2001, 483–535

Holy See, Questionnaire in Relation to General Assembly Resolution 68/267, Replies by the Holy See, accessible: <https://www.ohchr.org/EN/HRBodies/HRTD/Pages/3rdBiennialReportbySG.aspx>

Human Rights Committee, CCPR General Comment No. 25: The right to participate in public affairs, voting rights and the right of equal access to public service, adopted at the fifty-seventh session of the Human Rights Committee, 12. July 1996, UN Doc. CCPR/C/21/Rev. 1/Add. 7

Human Rights Committee, CCPR General Comment No. 26: Continuity of Obligations, adopted at the sixty-first Session of the Human Rights Committee, 8 December 1997, UN Doc. CCPR/C/21/Rev.1/Add.8/Rev.1

Human Rights Committee, CCPR General Comment No. 30: Reporting Obligations of States Parties under Article 40 of the Covenant, adopted at the seventy-fifth Session of the Human Rights Committee, 18 September 2002, CCPR/C/21/Rev.2/Add.12

Human Rights Committee, Consolidated guidelines for State reports under the International Covenant on Civil and Political Rights, 26 February 2001, UN Doc. CCPR/C/66/GUI/rev.2

Human Rights Committee, Decision on additional measures to simplify the reporting procedure and increase predictability, 126th session, 1–26 July 2019 (will be reflected in the Committee's annual report (UN Doc. A/75/40, to be issued in 2020), accessible: <https://www.ohchr.org/EN/HRBodies/CCPR/Pages/PredictableReviewCycle.aspx>

Human Rights Committee, Focused reports based on replies to lists of issues prior to reporting (LOIPR): Implementation of the new optional reporting procedure (LOIPR procedure), 29 September 2010, UN Doc. CCPR/C/99/4

Human Rights Committee, Rules of Procedure of the Human Rights Committee, 22 September 2005, UN Doc. CCPR/C/3/Rev.8.

Human Rights Committee, Simplified reporting procedure, Report of the Working Group, 6 December 2018, UN Doc. CCPR/C/123/3

Human Rights Law Centre of the University of Nottingham, The Dublin Statement on the Process of Strengthening of the United Nations Human Rights Treaty Body System, 29 November 2009, accessible: <https://www.ohchr.org/en/hrbodies/hrtd/pages/documents.aspx>

I

Inter-American Commission on Human Rights, Guidelines for Preparation of Progress Indicators in the Area of Economic, Social and Cultural Rights, 19 July 2008, OAS Doc. OEA/Ser.L/V/II.132, Doc. 14

Inter-American Commission of Women, Homepage of the Inter-American Commission of Women, CIM Mission and Mandate: <https://www.oas.org/en/cim/about.asp>

Inter-American Convention against Racism, Racial Discrimination and related forms of Intolerance, 5 June 2013, OAS Treaty No. A-68

Inter-American Convention on Protecting the Human Rights of Older Persons, 15 June 2015, OAS Treaty No. A-70

Inter-American Convention on the Prevention, Punishment and Eradication of Violence against Women ('Convention of Belem do Para'), 9 June 1994, OAS Treaty No. A-61, 33 International Legal Materials 1534 (1994)

Inter-Committee Technical Working Group, Harmonized guidelines on reporting under the international human rights treaties, including guidelines on a common core document and treaty-specific documents, Report of the Inter-Committee Technical Working Group, 10 May 2006, UN Doc. HRI/MC/2006/3

Inter-Committee Technical Working Group, Harmonized Guidelines on reporting under the International human Rights Treaties, Including Guidelines on a Common Core Document and Treaty-Specific Documents, Report of the Inter-Committee Technical Working Group, Corrigendum, 11 July 2006, UN Doc. HRI/MC/2006/3/Corr. 1

Index of Authorities

International Commission of Jurists, The ASEAN Human Rights Declaration: Questions and Answers, 30 July 2013 accessible: <https://www.icj.org/all-what-you-need-to-know-about-the-asean-human-rights-declaration/>

International Convention for the Protection of All Persons from Enforced Disappearance, 20 December 2006, 2716 UNTS 3

International Convention on the Elimination of All Forms of Racial Discrimination, 21 December 1965, 660 UNTS 195

International Convention on the Protection of the Rights of All Migrant Workers and Members of their Families, 18 December 1990, 2220 UNTS 3

International Court of Justice, Reparation for Injuries Suffered in the Service of the United Nations, Advisory Opinion of 11 April 1949, ICJ Reports 1949, p. 174

International Court of Justice, ICJ Arbitral Award of 31 July 1989, Judgment, ICJ Reports 1991, p. 53

International Court of Justice, International Court of Justice Kasikili/Sedudu Island (Botswana/Namibia), Judgment, ICJ Reports 1999, p. 1045

International Court of Justice, International Court of Justice, Certain Iranian Assets (Islamic Republic of Iran v. United States of America), Preliminary Objections, Judgement, 13 February 2019, General List No. 164

International Covenant on Civil and Political Rights, 16 December 1966, 999 UNTS 171

International Covenant on Economic, Social and Cultural Rights, 16 December 1966, 993 UNTS 3

International Integrated Reporting Council, Homepage, Integrated Reporting, accessible: <https://integratedreporting.org/>

International Integrated Reporting Council, Homepage of the International Integrated Reporting Council, <https://integratedreporting.org/>

International Law Commission, Draft articles on Responsibility of States for Internationally Wrongful Acts, with commentaries, 2001, adopted by the International Law Commission at its fifty-third session, in 2001, and submitted to the General Assembly as a part of the Commission's report covering the work of that session (UN Doc. A/56/10)

International Law Commission, Draft Articles on Responsibility of States for Internationally Wrongful Acts, Yearbook of the International Law Commission: 2001, vol. II(2), also available as Report on the work of the fifty-third session (2001), UN Doc. A/56/10 + Corr. 1, IV. E., p. 32 ff.

International Seminar of Experts on the Reforms of the United Nations Human Rights Treaty Body System, The Poznan Statement on the Reforms of the United Nations Human Rights Treaty Body System, 28–29 September 2010, accessible: <https://www.ohchr.org/en/hrbodies/hrtd/pages/documents.aspx>

International Service for Human Rights, ISHR submission to OHCHR Questionnaire in relation to General Assembly resolution 68/268, May 2019, accessible: <https://www.ohchr.org/EN/HRBodies/HRTD/Pages/3rdBiennialReportbySG.aspx>

J

Jacob Blaustein Institute for the Advancement of Human Rights, Recommendations for the Third Biennial Report of the UN Secretary-General on the Status of the Human Rights Treaty Body System, 24 April 2019, accessible: <https://www.ohchr.org/EN/HRBodies/HRTD/Pages/3rdBiennialReportbySG.aspx>

Japan, Japan's comments on the Questionnaire in relation to General Assembly resolution 68/268, accessible: <https://www.ohchr.org/EN/HRBodies/HRTD/Pages/3rdBiennialReportbySG.aspx>

Johnstone, Rachael Lorna, Cynical Savings or Reasonable Reform – Reflections on a Single Unified UN Human Rights Treaty Body, Human Rights Law Review 7:1 (2007), 173–200

K

Kadelbach, Stefan, International Law and the Incorporation of Treaties into Domestic Law, German Yearbook of International Law 42 (1999), 67–83

Kälin, Walter, Examination of state reports, in: Keller/Ulfstein (eds), UN human rights treaty bodies: law and legitimacy, Cambridge University Press 2012, 16–72

Keller, Helen/Ulfstein, Geir, Introduction, in: Keller/Ulfstein (eds), UN human rights treaty bodies: law and legitimacy, Cambridge University Press 2012, 1–15

Keller, Helen/Ulfstein, Geir, UN Human Rights Treaty Bodies: Law and Legitimacy, Cambridge University Press 2012

Kingdom of the Netherlands, Kingdom of the Netherlands' response to OHCHR's questionnaire on the UN Treaty Body System review Introduction, accessible: <https://www.ohchr.org/EN/HRBodies/HRTD/Pages/3rdBiennialReportbySG.aspx>

Kirkpatrick, Jesse, A Modest Proposal: A Global Court of Human Rights, Journal of Human Rights, Vol. 13(2) 2014, 230–248

Kjaerum, Morten, State Reports, in: Gudmundur Alfredsson et al. (eds.), International Monitoring Mechanisms: Essays in Honour of Jacob Th. Möller, 2nd rev. edn, Brill 2009, 17–24

Kornblum, Elisabeth, A comparison of self-evaluating state reporting systems, International Review of the Red Cross, 35(304) (1995), 39–68

Krommendijk, Jasper, The domestic effectiveness of international human rights monitoring in established democracies. The case of the UN human rights treaty bodies, The Review of International Organizations, Volume 10, Issue 4 (2015), 489–512

Kyoto Protocol to the United Nations Framework Convention on Climate Change (United Nations Framework Convention on Climate Change), 11 December 1997, 2303 UNTS 162

L

Lauer, Sabrina, Die Implementierung menschenrechtlicher Verträge in Afrika, Saarbrücker Studien zum Internationalen Recht, Volume 60, Nomos 2018.

League of Arab States, Arab Charter on Human Rights, 22 May 2004, reprinted in 12 International Human Rights Report 893 (2005)

League of Arab States, Homepage of the League of Arab States, accessible: <http://www.lasportal.org/ar/humanrights/Committee/Pages/Reports.aspx>

Lhotský, Jan, Human Rights Treaty Body Review 2020. Towards and Integrated Treaty Body System, European Inter-University Centre for Human Rights and Democratisation, EMA Awarded Theses 2016/2016, https://doi.org/20.500.11825/675

Linderfalk, Ulf, Who Are 'the Parties'? Article 31 Paragraph 3(c) of the 1969 Vienna Convention, and the 'Principle of Systemic Integration' Revisited, Netherlands International Law Review, Vol. 55(3) (2008), 343–364

M

Maastricht Centre for Human Rights, The Universal Periodic Review Process and the Treaty Bodies: Constructive Cooperation or Deepening Divisions? Recommendations arising from the seminar held on 25 November 2011, Maastricht, The Netherlands, accessible: <https://www.ohchr.org/EN/HRBodies/HRTD/Pages/Documents.aspx>

McLachlan, Campbell, The Principle of Systemic Integration and Article 31(3)(c) of the Vienna Convention, The International and Comparative Law Quarterly, Vol. 54, No. 2 (2005), 279–319

Index of Authorities

Merkouris, Panos, Article 31(3)(c) VCLT and the Principle of Systemic Integration, Normative Shadows in Plato's Cave, Queen Mary Studies in International Law, Volume 17, Brill Nijhoff 2015

Ministry of Foreign Affairs and International Cooperation, Inter-ministerial Committee for Human Rights, Italy's Contribution, In Light of Questionnaire on UN General Assembly Resolution 68/268, 30 April 2019, accessible: <https://www.ohchr.org/EN/HRBodies/HRTD/Pages/3rdBiennialReportbySG.aspx>

Ministry of Foreign Affairs of Finland, Questionnaire in relation to the General Assembly resolution 68/268, Response by the Government of Finland, 30 April 2019, accessible: <https://www.ohchr.org/EN/HRBodies/HRTD/Pages/3rdBiennialReportbySG.aspx>

Moeckli, Daniel/Keller, Helen/Heri, Corina, The Human Rights Covenants at 50: Their Past, Present and Future, Oxford University Press 2018

Moeckli, Daniel/Shah, Sangeeta/Sivakumaran, Sandesh/Harri, David (eds), International Human Rights Law, 2nd edition, Oxford University Press 2014

Montreal Protocol on Substances that Deplete the Ozone Layer (with annex), 16 September 1987, 1522 UNTS 3

Morijn, John, Reforming United Nations Human Rights Treaty Monitoring Reform, Netherlands International Law Review 58(3) (2011), 295–333

N

National Human Rights Commission of Korea and the Korea Foundation, Seoul Statement on Strengthening the UN Human Rights Treaty Body System, 19–20 April 2011, accessible: <https://www.ohchr.org/EN/HRBodies/HRTD/Pages/Documents.aspx>

Nollkaemper, André/Fauchald, Ole Kristian (eds), The Practice of International and National Courts and the (De-) Fragmentation of International Law, Hart Publishing 2012

Norwegian Centre for Human Rights, Response by the Norwegian Centre for Human Rights (NCHR), Faculty of Law, University of Oslo, to the Questionnaire on the implementation of General Assembly resolution 68/268 on 'Strengthening and enhancing the effective functioning of the human rights treaty body system', University of Oslo, 18 March 2019, accessible: <https://www.ohchr.org/EN/HRBodies/HRTD/Pages/3rdBiennialReportbySG.aspx>

Nowak, Manfred, The Need for a World Court of Human Rights, Human Rights Law Review 7:1 (2007), 251–259

O

Oberleitner, Gerd, International Human Rights Institutions, Tribunals and Courts, Springer 2018

Oette, Lutz, The UN Human Rights Treaty Bodies: Impact and Future, in: Oberleitner (ed), International Human Rights Institutions, Tribunals and Courts, Springer 2018, 95–115

Office for Foreign Affairs, Principality of Liechtenstein, Questionnaire in relation to General Assembly resolution 68/268, Submission by Liechtenstein, 28 March 2019, accessible: <https://www.ohchr.org/EN/HRBodies/HRTD/Pages/3rdBiennialReportbySG.aspx>

Office of the High Commissioner for Human Rights, Consultation for States on Treaty Body Strengthening, Geneva, 7 and 8 February 2012, accessible: <https://www.ohchr.org/EN/HRBodies/HRTD/Pages/Documents.aspx>

Office of the High Commissioner for Human Rights, Consultation on treaty body strengthening with UN entities and specialized agencies, 28 November 2011, accessible: <https://www.ohchr.org/EN/HRBodies/HRTD/Pages/Documents.aspx>

Office of the High Commissioner for Human Rights, Homepage of the Office of the High Commissioner for Human Rights on Treaty Body Strengthening: <https://www.ohchr.org/EN/HRBodies/HRTD/Pages/TBStrengthening.aspx>

Office of the High Commissioner for Human Rights, Homepage Office of the High Commissioner for Human Rights, Treaty Body Strengthening – Outcome documents, reports and statements, <https://www.ohchr.org/EN/HRBodies/HRTD/Pages/Documents.aspx>

Office of the High Commissioner for Human Rights, Homepage Office of the High Commissioner for Human Rights, Third biennial report by the Secretary-General, <https://www.ohchr.org/EN/HRBodies/HRTD/Pages/3rdBiennialReportbySG.aspx>

Office of the High Commissioner for Human Rights, Report of the Informal Technical Consultation with States parties in Sion, Informal Technical Consultation for States parties on Treaty Body Strengthening, Sion, Switzerland, 12–13 May 2011, accessible: <https://www.ohchr.org/EN/HRBodies/HRTD/Pages/Documents.aspx>

Office of the High Commissioner for Human Rights, Report on the Third Consultation for States parties, New York, 2 and 3 April 2012, accessible: <https://www.ohchr.org/EN/HRBodies/HRTD/Pages/Documents.aspx>

Office of the High Commissioner for Human Rights, Homepage of the Office of the High Commissioner for Human Rights, Treaty Body Database, Core Documents, accessible: <https://tbinternet.ohchr.org/_layouts/15/TreatyBodyExternal/CoreDocuments.aspx>

Office of the High Commissioner for Human Rights, Questionnaire in relation to General Assembly resolution 68/268, 31 January 2019, accessible: <https://www.ohchr.org/EN/HRBodies/HRTD/Pages/3rdBiennialReportbySG.aspx>

Office of the High Commissioner for Human Rights, Homepage, About Us, Navanethem Pillay, <https://www.ohchr.org/EN/AboutUs/Pages/NaviPillay.aspx>

Office of the High Commissioner, Homepage of the Office of the High Commissioner for Human Rights, UN Treaty Body Database, Late Reporting accessible: <https://tbinternet.ohchr.org/_layouts/15/TreatyBodyExternal/LateReporting.aspx>

Office of the United Nations High Commissioner for Human Rights, Effective Functioning of Human Rights Mechanisms, Treaty Bodies, Note by the Office of the United Nations High Commissioner for Human Rights, 26 February 2003, UN Doc. E/CN.4/2003/126

O'Flaherty, Michael, The Concluding Observations of United Nations Human Rights Treaty Bodies, Human Rights Law Review 6:1 (2006), 27–52.

O'Flaherty, Michael/O'Brien, Claire, Reform of UN Human Rights Treaty Monitoring Bodies: A Critique of the Concept Paper on the High Commissioner's Proposal for a Unified Standing Treaty Body, Human Rights Law Review 7:1 (2007), 141–172.

O'Flaherty, Michael, Reform of the UN Human Rights Treaty Body System: Locating the Dublin Statement, Human Rights Law Review 10:2 (2010), 319–335

O'Flaherty, Michael, The High Commissioner and the Treaty Bodies, in: Broecker et al, The United Nations High Commissioner for Human Rights: Conscience for the World Account, Brill/Nijhoff 2013, 101–119

Olowu, Dejo, An integrative rights-based approach to human development in Africa, Pretoria University Law Press 2009

Open-ended intergovernmental working group on transnational corporations and other business enterprises with respect to human rights, Revised draft legally Binding Instrument to regulate, in International Human Rights Law, the Activities of Transnational Corporations and other Business Enterprises, 16 July 2019, accessible: <ohchr.org/en/hrbodies/hrc/wgtranscorp/pages/igwgontnc.aspx>

Index of Authorities

Optional Protocol to the Convention on the Rights of Persons with Disabilities, 13 December 2006, 2518 UNTS 283

Optional Protocol to the Convention on the Rights of the Child on the involvement of children in armed conflict, 25 May 2000, 2173 UNTS 222

Optional Protocol to the Convention on the Rights of the Child on the sale of children, child prostitution and child pornography, 25 May 2000, 2171 UNTS 227

Organization of American States, Homepage of the OAS, Committee of Experts, <http://www.oas.org/en/mesecvi/experts.asp>

Organization of American States, Homepage of the OAS, MESECVI Secretariat, <http://www.oas.org/en/mesecvi/secretariat.asp>

Organization of American States, Mechanism to Follow Up on Implementation of the Inter-American Convention on the Prevention, Punishment, and Eradication of Violence Against Women, 'Convention of Belém do Pará', adopted June 6 2006, AG/Res. 2162 (XXXVI-O/06)

Organization of American States, Mechanism to Follow Up on the Implementation of the Inter-American Convention on the Prevention, Punishment and Eradication of Violence against Women 'Convention of Belém do Pará'-MESECVI (First Hemispheric Report), First Multilateral Evaluation Round: Second Conference of States Parties, Caracas, Venezuela 9–10 July 2008, accessible: <http://www.oas.org/en/mesecvi/hemisphericreports.asp>

Organization of American States General Assembly, Standards for the Preparation of the Periodic Reports Pursuant to Article 19 of the Protocol of San Salvador, adopted 7 June 2005, approved by OAS Doc. AG/RES. 2074 (XXXV-O/05)

Organization of American States General Assembly, Protocol of San Salvador: Composition and Functioning of the Working Group to examine the Periodic Reports of States Parties, adopted 5 June 2007, AG/RES. 2262 (XXXVII-O/07)

Organization of American States General Assembly, Protocol of San Salvador: Composition and Functioning of the Working Group to examine the Periodic Reports of the States Parties, adopted 4 June 2009, AG/Res. 2506, (XXXIX-O/09)

P

Pakistan, Pakistan's inputs in relation to UNGA Resolution 68/268 Strengthening and enhancing the effective functioning of the human rights treaty body system, accessible: <https://www.ohchr.org/EN/HRBodies/HRTD/Pages/3rdBiennialReportbySG.aspx>

Permanent Mission of Israel to the United Nations in Geneva, Reply, 30 April 2019, accessible: <https://www.ohchr.org/EN/HRBodies/HRTD/Pages/3rdBiennialReportbySG.aspx>

Permanent Representative of Liechtenstein to the United Nations, Annex to the letter dated 13 June 2003 from the Permanent Representative of Liechtenstein to the United Nations addressed to the Secretary-General, Report of a meeting on reform of the human rights treaty body system, Malbun, Liechtenstein, 4–7 May 2003, UN Doc. A/58/123

Permanent Representative of Liechtenstein to the United Nations, Letter dated 14 September 2006 from the Permanent Representative of Liechtenstein to the United Nations addressed to the Secretary General, Annex (Chairperson's summary of a brainstorming meeting on reform of the human rights treaty body system ('Malbun II'), 18 September 2006, UN Doc. A/61/351

Peters, Anne, Realizing Utopia as a Scholarly Endeavour, The European Journal of International Law, Volume 24, Issue 2, May 2013, 533–552

Peters, Anne, The refinement of international law: From fragmentation to regime interaction and politicization, I–CON (2017), Vol. 15 No. 3, 671–704, DOI: 10.2139/ssrn.2823512.

Poland, Questionnaire on the implementation of the GA resolution 68/268 "Strengthening and enhancing the effective functioning of the human rights body system", Comments on the implementation of the GA resolution 68/268, accessible: <https://www.ohchr.org/EN/HRBodies/HRTD/Pages/3rdBiennialReportbySG.aspx>

Portugal, Strengthening and enhancing the effective functioning of the human rights treaty body system (implementation of General Assembly Resolution 68/268, of 2014), 1 March 2019, accessible: <https://www.ohchr.org/EN/HRBodies/HRTD/Pages/3rdBiennialReportbySG.aspx>

Protocol to the African Charter on Human and Peoples' Rights on the Rights of older Persons in Africa, 31 January 2016, reprinted in African Yearbook of International Law Online, Vol. 22 (2017), 269–280

Index of Authorities

Protocol to the African Charter on Human and Peoples' Rights on the Rights of Persons with Disabilities in Africa, 29 January 2018, accessible: <https://au.int/en/treaties/protocol-african-charter-human-and-peoples-rights-rights-persons-disabilities-africa>

Protocol to the African Charter on Human and Peoples' Rights on the Rights of Women in Africa, 13 September 2000, CAB/LEG/66.6; reprinted in African Human Rights Law Journal, Vol. 1 (20019, 40–64

Protocol 1 to the Convention for the Protection of Human Rights and Fundamental Freedoms, 20 March 1952, CETS No. 009

Protocol to the European Code of Social Security, 16 April 1964, CETS No. 48A

R

Rachovitsa, Adamantia, The Principle of Systemic Integration in Human Rights Law, International and Comparative Law Quarterly, Vol. 66(3) (2017), 557–588

Republic of Korea, ROK's input to the OHCHR questionnaire on implementation of GA resolution 68/268, accessible: <https://www.ohchr.org/EN/HRBodies/HRTD/Pages/3rdBiennialReportbySG.aspx>

Republic of Slovenia, Ministry of Foreign Affairs, Reply of the Republic of Slovenia to the Questionnaire concerning the General Assembly Resolution 68/269, 25 February 2019, accessible: <https://www.ohchr.org/EN/HRBodies/HRTD/Pages/3rdBiennialReportbySG.aspx>

Republic of the Philippines, Comments and inputs to A/RES/68/268 and A/RES/73/162, accessible: <https://www.ohchr.org/EN/HRBodies/HRTD/Pages/3rdBiennialReportbySG.aspx>

Royal Norwegian Ministry of Foreign Affairs, Section for Human Rights, Democracy and Gender Equality, Reply to Questionnaire in relation to General Assembly Resolution 68/268 on Strengthening the Human Rights Treaty Body System, accessible: <https://www.ohchr.org/EN/HRBodies/HRTD/Pages/3rdBiennialReportbySG.aspx>

S

Scheinin, Martin, Human Rights Treaties and the Vienna Convention on the Law of Treaties – Conflict or Harmony, Report, 8 September 2005, European Commission for Democracy through Law (Venice Commission), CDL-UD(2005)014rep

Scheinin, Martin, The Proposed Optional Protocol to the Covenant on Economic, Social and Cultural Rights: A Blueprint for UN Human Rights Treaty Body Reform without Amending the Existing Treaties, Human Rights Law Review 6:1 (2006), 131–142

Scheinin, Martin, Towards a World Court of Human Rights, 2009 Swiss Initiative to Commemorate the 60th Anniversary of the Universal Declaration of Human Rights, accessible <https://www.eui.eu/Documents/DepartmentsCentres/AcademyofEuropeanLaw/CourseMaterialsHR/HR2009/Scheinin/ScheininClassReading1.pdf>

Schimmelfennig, Frank, Strategic calculation and international socialization: Membership incentives, Party constellations, and Sustained Compliance in Central and Eastern Europe, International Organization, Vol. 59(4) (2005), 827–860

Schöpp-Schilling, Hanna Beate, Treaty Body Reform: The Case of the Committee on the Elimination of Discrimination against Women, Human Rights Law Review 7:1 (2007), 201–224

Shaw, Malcom N., International Law, 8th edition, Cambridge University Press 2017

Shelton, Dinah L., Regional Protection of Human Rights, Oxford University Press 2008

Šimonović, Dubravka, Convention on the Elimination of all Forms of Discrimination Against Women, United Nations Audiovisual Library of International Law 2009, accessible: http://legal.un.org/avl/ha/cedaw/cedaw.html

Smith, Rhona K. M., Textbook on International Human Rights, Oxford University Press 2003

Spenlé, Christian A., Die Staatenberichtsverfahren der UNO-Menschenrechtsverträge, Schultheiss, Zürich et al. 2011

State of Palestine, Ministry of Foreign Affairs and Expatriates, Multilateral Affairs, Questionnaire in relation to the General Assembly Res.68/268, accessible: <https://www.ohchr.org/EN/HRBodies/HRTD/Pages/3rdBiennialReportbySG.aspx>

Statute of the International Court of Justice, 26 June 1945, 15 UNCIO 355, Blackstone's International Law Documents, 14th edition, Oxford University Press, Oxford 2019, 30 ff.

Steiner, Henry J./Alston, Philip/Goodman, Ryan, International Human Rights in Context, 3rd edition, Oxford University Press 2007

Study Group of the International Law Commission, Report of the Study Group of the International Law Commission, Finalized by Martti Koskenniemi, Fragmentation of International Law: Difficulties Arising from the Diversification and Expansion of International Law, 13 April 2006, UN Doc. A/CN.4/L.682

Index of Authorities

Switzerland, Response of Switzerland to the OHCHR questionnaire on General Assembly resolution A/Res/68/268, 28 February 2019, accessible: <https://www.ohchr.org/EN/HRBodies/HRTD/Pages/3rdBiennialReportbySG.aspx>

T

Thailand, Thailand's submission for the questionnaire in relation to General Assembly resolution 68/268, accessible: <https://www.ohchr.org/EN/HRBodies/HRTD/Pages/3rdBiennialReportbySG.aspx>

The Merriam-Webster.com Dictionary, Merriam-Webster Inc., accessible: <https://www.merriam-webster.com/dictionary/obligee>

Tomuschat, Christian, Human Rights, – Between Idealism and Realism, 3rd edition, Oxford University Press 2014

Trechsel, Stefan, A World Court for Human Rights?, Northwestern Journal of International Human Rights, Vol. 1:1 (2004), Article 3

Turkey, Comments of the Government of Turkey in Response to the Questionnaire Sent by the Office of the High Commissioner for Human Rights in Relation to General Assembly Resolution 68/268, accessible: <https://www.ohchr.org/EN/HRBodies/HRTD/Pages/3rdBiennialReportbySG.aspx>

U

United Nations, Homepage, United Nations Treaty Body Database, <https://tbinternet.ohchr.org/_layouts/TreatyBodyExternal/LateReporting.aspx>

United Nations, Homepage, United Nations Treaty Collection, Vienna Convention on the Law of Treaties, <https://treaties.un.org/Pages/ViewDetailsIII.aspx?src=TREATY&mtdsg_no=XXIII-1&chapter=23&Temp=mtdsg3&clang=_en>

United Nations Convention on the Prohibition of the Development, Production, Stockpiling and Use of Chemical Weapons and on Their Destruction, Annex on Implementation and Verification ('Verification Annex'), 13 January 1993, 1974 UNTS 361.

United Nations Educational, Scientific and Cultural Organization, Homepage of the United Nations Educational, Scientific and Cultural Organization, accessible: <https://whc.unesco.org/en/periodicreporting/>

United Nations Educational, Scientific and Cultural Organization, Intergovernmental Committee for the Protection of the World Cultural and Natural Heritage, Operational Guidelines for the Implementation of the World Heritage Convention, 12 July 2017, WHC.17/01

Index of Authorities

United Nations General Assembly, Draft International Covenants on Human Rights, Annotation by the Secretary-General, 1 July 1955, UN Doc. A/2929

United Nations General Assembly, Reporting obligations of States parties to international instruments on human rights and effective functioning of bodies established pursuant to such instruments, 8 December 1988, UN Doc. A/RES/43/115

United Nations General Assembly, 64th Session, Report of the Committee against Torture, 41st-42nd Sessions, 3–21 November 2008 and 27 April – 15 May 2008, 28 September 2009, UN Doc. A/64/44, Supp. (No. 44)

United Nations General Assembly, Strengthening and enhancing the effective functioning of the human rights treaty body system, 21 April 2014, UN Doc. A/RES/68/268

United Nations General Assembly, Resolution adopted by the General Assembly on 17 December 2018, Human rights treaty body system, 8 January 2019, UN Doc. A/RES/73/162

United Nations General Assembly, Implementation of human rights instruments, Report of the Chairs of the human rights treaty bodies on their thirty-first annual meeting, 30 July 2019, UN Doc. A/74/256

United Nations Secretariat, Status of Preparation of Publications, Studies and Documents for the World Conference, Note by the Secretariat, Addendum, Interim report on updated study by Mr. Philip Alston, 22 April 1993, UN Doc. A/CONF.157/PC/62/Add.11/Rev.1

United Nations Secretariat, Methods of Work relating to the State Reporting Process, Background document prepared by the Secretariat, 11 April 2003, UN Doc. HRI/ICM/2003/3

United Nations Secretariat, Compilation of General Comments and General Recommendations Adopted by Human Rights Treaty Bodies, 12 May 2003, UN Doc. HRI/GEN/1/Rev.6.

United Nations Secretariat, Guidelines on an expanded core document and treaty-specific targeted reports and harmonized guidelines on reporting under the international human rights treaties, Report of the Secretariat, 9 June 2004, UN Doc. HRI/MC/2004/3

United Nations Secretariat, Concept Paper on the High Commissioner's Proposal for a Unified Standing Treaty Body, Report by the Secretariat, 22 March 2006, UN Doc. HRI/MC/2006/2

United Nations Secretariat, International Human Rights Documents, Compilation of Rules of Procedure adopted by Human Rights Treaty Bodies, Note by the Secretariat, 28 May 2008, UN Doc. HRI/GEN/3/Rev.3

United Nations Secretariat, Preliminary non-paper on legal options for a unified standing treaty body, accessible <https://www.ohchr.org/EN/HRBodies/HRTD/Pages/FirstBiennialReportbySG.aspx#SingleReport>

United Nations Secretary-General, Reporting obligations of States parties to the International Covenants on Human Rights and the International Convention on the Elimination of All Forms of Racial Discrimination, 20 September 1984, UN Doc. A/39/484

United Nations Secretary-General, Effective Implementation of International Instruments on Human Rights, Including Reporting Obligations under International Instruments on Human Rights, Note by the Secretary-General, 8 November 1989, UN Doc. A/44/668

United Nations Secretary-General, Effective Functioning of Bodies Established Pursuant to United Nations Human Rights Instruments, Note by the Secretary-General, 27 March 1997, UN Doc. E/CN.4/1997/74

United Nations Secretary-General, Strengthening of the United Nations: an agenda for further change, Report of the Secretary-General, 9 September 2002, UN Doc. A/57/387

United Nations Secretary-General, Status of implementation of actions described in the report of the Secretary-General entitled 'Strengthening of the United Nations: an agenda for further change', 5 September 2003, UN Doc. A/58/351

United Nations Secretary-General, In larger freedom: towards development, security and human rights for all, Report of the Secretary-General, 21 March 2005, UN Doc. A/59/2005

United Nations Secretary-General, In larger freedom: towards development, security and human rights for all, Report of the Secretary-General, Addendum, 26 May 2005, UN Doc. A/59/2005/Add. 3

United Nations Secretary-General, Compilation of Guidelines on the Form and Content of Reports to be submitted by States Parties to the International Human Rights Treaties, Report of the Secretary-General, 3 June 2009, UN Doc. HRI/GEN/2/Rev. 6

United Nations Secretary-General, Report of the Secretary-General, Compilation on the form and content of reports to be submitted by States parties to the international human rights treaties, 3 June 2009, UN Doc. HRI/GEN/2/Rev.6

United Nations Secretary-General, Report of the Secretary-General, Measures to improve further the effectiveness, harmonization and reform of the treaty body system, 7 September 2011, UN Doc. A/66/344

United Nations Secretary-General, United Nations reform: measures and proposals, Note by the Secretary-General, 26 June 2012, UN Doc. A/66/860

United Nations Secretary-General, United Nations reform: measures and proposals, Note by the Secretary-General, 26 June 2012, UN Doc. A/66/869

United Nations Secretary-General, Status of the human rights treaty body system, Report of the Secretary-General, 18 July 2016, UN Doc. A/71/118

United Nations Secretary-General, Report of the Secretary-General, Status of the human rights treaty body system, 6 August 2018, UN Doc. A/73/309

United Nations Secretary-General, Status of the human rights treaty body system, Report of the Secretary-General, Supplementary information: 24 statistical annexes, 6 August 2019, UN Doc. A/73/309 (Annexes)

United Nations Secretary-General, Report of the Secretary-General, Status of the human rights treaty body system, 10 January 2020, UN Doc. A/74/643

United Nations Secretary-General, Homepage United Nations, United Nations Secretary-General, Former Secretaries-General, <https://www.un.org/sg/en/content/former-secretaries-general>

United Nations Secretary-General, Homepage United Nations, United Nations Secretary-General, Biography, <https://www.un.org/sg/en/content/sg/biography>

University of Nottingham, Report of the Expert Workshop on Reform of United Nations Human Rights, Treaty Monitoring Bodies, Human Rights Law Centre, University of Nottingham, 11–12 February 2006, accessible: <https://www.nottingham.ac.uk/hrlc/documents/publications/treatymonitoringbodies2006workshopreport.pdf>

V

van der Burg, Wibren, The Merits of Law: An Argumentative Framework for Evaluative Judgements and Normative Recommendations in Legal Research (February 22, 2018). Archiv für Rechts- und Sozialphilosophie, Forthcoming; Erasmus Working Paper Series on Jurisprudence and Socio-Legal Studies, No. 17–01, February 22, 2018. Available at SSRN: https://ssrn.com/abstract=3020624 or http://dx.doi.org/10.2139/ssrn.3020624

Vienna Convention on the law of Treaties, 22 May 1969, UNTS, vol. 115, 331

Viljoen, Frans, International Human Rights Law in Africa, 2nd edition, Oxford University Press 2012

W

World Health Assembly, Implementation of the International Health Regulations (2005), Resolution A61/7, Sixty-First World Health Assembly, 3 April 2008, accessible <http://apps.who.int/gb/archive/e/e_wha61.html>

World Health Organization, Homepage of the World Health Organization, Strengthening health security by implementing the International Health Regulations (2005), accessible <https://www.who.int/ihr/procedures/annual-reporting/en/>

World Health Organization, International Health Regulations (2005), 2nd ed., World Health Organization 2008, accessible <http://www.who.int/ihr/publications/9789241596664/en/>

Franziska-Carolin Kring

Responsibility to protect (R2P) revisited

Towards climate change-related obligations of states?

Humanitarian catastrophes as a consequence of progressive climate change are one of the greatest challenges of the 21st century. Franziska Kring underlines the important role of the international community of states in combating and mitigating climate change.

In her innovative approach, the author applies the concept of Responsibility to Protect (R2P), which was originally intended to prevent human rights violations, to climate change-related humanitarian catastrophes. To this effect, she argues that state responses to such events correspond perfectly with the R2P framework. In particular, the understanding of state sovereignty as responsibility can be used as a theoretical basis for such commitments.

The author concludes: Although a general obligation of states to take measures to mitigate climate change cannot be based on R2P, its application in the case of climate change-related humanitarian catastrophes is politically and morally justified.

2020, 312 S., kart., engl.,
52,– €, 978-3-8305-5031-0
eBook PDF 978-3-8305-4196-7
(Bochumer Schriften zur Friedenssicherung und zum Humanitären Völkerrecht)

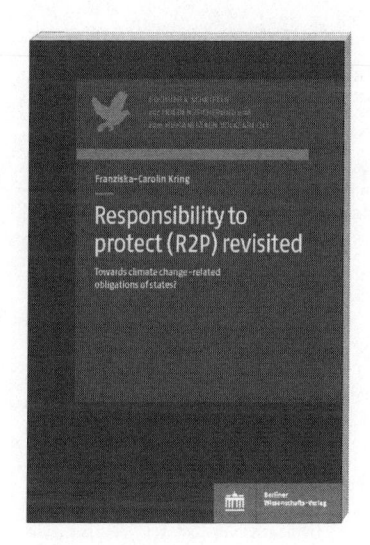

DIE AUTORIN

Dr. Franziska Kring, geb. 1990, Studium der Rechtswissenschaft an der Ruhr-Universität Bochum, 2019 Promotion an der Ruhr-Universität Bochum, seit November 2018 Rechtsreferendarin im Oberlandesgerichtsbezirk Düsseldorf.

AUS DEM INHALT

Introduction | Human rights dimension of climate change | The responsibility to protect | The impacts of climate change as potential crimes under R2P | Extension of the R2P | General Conclusion and Outlook

Berliner Wissenschafts-Verlag | Behaimstr. 25 | 10585 Berlin
Tel. 030 84 17 70-0 | Fax 030 84 17 70-21
www.bwv-verlag.de | bwv@bwv-verlag.de

Berliner Wissenschafts-Verlag

Hans-Joachim Heintze

Legal Opinion on the 1993 Resolutions of the UN Security Council

Concerning the Conflict between Armenia and Azerbaijan and the Following Legally Relevant Documents of International Bodies

– The Humanitarian Dimension –

Soviet nationality policy has led to numerous conflicts in and between the successor states of the Soviet Union, some of them violent. The military occupation of large parts of Azerbaijan by Armenia in 1993 is a particularly drastic example of the consequences of this nationality policy. The UN Security Council reacted to the armed conflict between the two states with four resolutions. It called for an end to the occupation, the withdrawal of the occupying forces and the return of displaced persons. These demands have not yet been met, but they are nonetheless legally binding and form the basis for the necessary peace settlement.

2020, 45 S., kart.,
17,– €, 978-3-8305-5026-6
eBook PDF 978-3-8305-4191-2

DER AUTOR

Prof. Dr. Hans-Joachim Heintze, born in 1949, studied law at the University of Leipzig. Dissertation in 1977 and habilitation in 1983 at the same University. Since 1991 at the Institute for International Law of Peace and Armed Conflict at the Ruhr University Bochum. Research interests: minority rights and the right of self-determination of peoples, international humanitarian law.

AUS DEM INHALT

History of the relevant Resolutions of the Security Council | Resolution 822 (1993) of 30 April 1993 | Resolution 853 (1993) of 29 July 1993 | Resolution 874 (1993) of 14 October 1993 | Resolution 884 (1993) of 12 November 1993 | Overall assessment of the four Security Council resolutions | Developments relating the Security Council Resolutions | The issue of ethnic cleansing and the IDP's | The durable solution

Berliner Wissenschafts-Verlag | Behaimstr. 25 | 10585 Berlin
Tel. 030 84 17 70-0 | Fax 030 84 17 70-21
www.bwv-verlag.de | bwv@bwv-verlag.de

Berliner Wissenschafts-Verlag